Published in hardcopy by:
Booksurge Publishing
5341 Dorchester Road, Suite 16
North Charleston, SC 29418

First published in part as *The British Butler's Bible* by Mansion Publishing, 2001

First Edition, April 2002
Second Edition, June 2002
Third Edition, July 2003
Fourth Edition, February 2004
Fifth Edition, February 2005

Ferry, Steven M.
      Butlers and Household Managers, 21st Century Professionals
ISBN 1-59109-306-6

BookSurge, LLC North Charleston, SC
Library of Congress Control Number: P0000074257.1

Books are available at discount for schools and libraries or when used to promote products or services. Please contact the publisher, or author services at:

411 Cleveland Street, #234, Clearwater, FL 33755, USA
or via *www.modernbutlers.com*
or by telephone: (USA) 1 813 354 2734

Cover design and photograph by *Words & Images*

BUTLERS

& HOUSEHOLD MANAGERS

21ST CENTURY PROFESSIONALS

By Steven M. Ferry

Butlers & Household Managers
21st Century Professionals

By **Steven M. Ferry**

Foreword

*B*utlers *&* Household Managers, 21st Century Professionals is designed to assist those seeking a new and rewarding career as a butler or the American equivalent, the household manager, as well as those seeking to employ them, whether in stately home, hotel, corporate setting or elsewhere. In the increasingly competitive and mechanistic world in which we live, service is often the only differentiator between one provider and another. Having a competent butler is one way to develop that much-needed edge.

Butlers & Household Managers, 21st Century Professionals is also useful for any man or woman who would like to use some of the butler's know-how to enhance his or her own life style.

The many checklists in *Butlers & Household Managers, 21st Century Professionals* cover every kind of situation a butler deals with and are designed, in conjunction with the chapter they supplement, to walk a person successfully through those situations and so increase his or her confidence. No amount of copying actions mechanically will make a butler, however. It is necessary to understand the point of view of the butler to then handle any given situation as a butler would. That is why chapters are provided to explain the butler rationale.

I wrote this book because I perceived a need for a text in a profession that had gone years without one. Having worked in personal service in England many years ago, I decided to train as a butler in one of the schools offering such an education and then worked in the United States as a butler. It was during these years that my path crossed with many other British butlers around the country and so I founded the Guild of Traditional Butlers to pool our knowledge and experience and offer assistance to each other. I was able to compile the information that you find in this book by drawing on my own training and experience, as well as that of my peers, and ransacking research libraries and old bookstores on the Strand in London.

The book has been used as a text at a number of butler schools and training venues and been refined continually to reflect the realities of butling today in private homes, hotels and other premium locations. You will find within these pages the basics of butling and running a household successfully—or if an employer, everything you need to know about what your butler or household manager could and should be doing, and how to manage him or her.

Who Likes to Read?

A glossary is provided at the back of the book to clarify industry words that may be unfamiliar and which will generally not be found in a regular dictionary. Unless the word is defined in the text at the time it is first mentioned, it will be written in italics to signal its inclusion in the glossary.

May I recommend to you a fine procedure for studying successfully, as covered in *http://www.appliedscholastics.org/learning.htm*? We have all attended schools of one kind or another and some of us are pretty sure we know how to study, while others have not enjoyed too much success at it. If you consider your own studies for a moment, you may have to look long and hard for any instructions on *how* to study. Plenty of times you were told to study, no doubt, but how many times how to go about it successfully?

There is a right way to do most things, and plenty of wrong ways. One usually finds the right way by studying or being told. Did anyone ever tell you *how* to study, or give you a manual on how to study? Did anyone ever tell you that study has certain liabilities connected with it? Maybe you went to school in the last twenty years in the United States and were told to guess what a word means from the context.

Another habit readers can fall into is ignoring sections that do not make sense. The problem with this approach is that one inevitably ends up skipping whole chapters and then throwing away the book as "useless." I would hate for you to spend a bunch of money on this book, raise your hopes about a possible new career or mastering your current one, and then throw it all away just because nobody told you how to study. So do yourself a favor: check out the Web page above. It may be written for children, but the ideas are that much easier for everyone to grasp and *use*.

Finally, while the book is a useful reference, it does not supplant doing a properly certified course, such as the ones offered by the International Butler Academy in the Netherlands or several other butler schools around the world in order to seek employment as a butler, or the Starkey Institute in Denver, Colorado, for training as a household manager. Insist upon receiving the guidance, feedback, drills and certification you will need to join the profession and excel at it.

If you have any questions about *Butlers & Household Managers, 21st Century Professionals*, please feel free to contact me and I will be happy to respond.

Steven Ferry

1-813-354-2734
or via *www.modernbutlers.com*

Acknowledgements

I would like to thank the many people who have contributed to this work: my mentors, who passed on the basic knowledge, fellow butlers and household managers, past employers, staff, clients and students I have worked with, all of whom have provided the raw materials, and Mr. L. Ron Hubbard, for his insights into human nature. I also want to thank Mr. Donald Weedon and Mr. Ivor Spencer for their significant contribution concerning the traditional technology of butling, Ms. Patsy Paul for her contributions on the history of private service, and lastly, members of the profession such as Ms. Josephine Ives, Ms. Pam Spruce and Ms. Mary Louise Starkey, and Mssrs. Jeffrey Landesberg, Werner Leutert, John Robertson, Robert Watson and Robert Wennekes, who every day keep the profession alive and relevant in a world that continues to change at a frenetic pace.

BUTLERS
& HOUSEHOLD MANAGERS
21ST CENTURY PROFESSIONALS

TABLE OF CONTENTS

CHAPTER SIX
LOOKING AFTER GUESTS 64

CHAPTER SEVEN
VALET—THE GENTLEMAN'S GENTLEMAN 68

Preface

Butlers have been a rare breed, too thin on the ground to form a union or warrant a university degree with accompanying texts; so standards and definitions have assumed no identifiable form beyond capsules of dictionary thought that struggle to cram into one phrase, the entirety of an evolving and disparate profession. By nature, butlers themselves are low-key and unwilling to make possibly controversial statements; they have written few books.

There is, as well, a certain mystique to being a British butler, living in the shadows of the rich and famous, which may come into too sharp a focus through a down-to-earth analysis.

The screen, and books such as P.G. Wodehouse's series featuring Jeeves, create stereotype butlers whom we find amusing for their restraint and biting wit in the face of monumental stupidity; and endearing for their willingness to work behind the scenes while their employers blithely strut across the stage, playing out their own pre-ordained roles.

The handful of non-fiction books that have been written over the last two centuries hardly bring the butler image down to earth, detailing as they do only some of their duties and skills. None were so presumptuous as to claim such a thing as a butler psyche, or to trumpet its value in our society, where moral values slowly erode into a grand canyon that was once the solid ground of trust and dependability.

This book is therefore an attempt to detail the skills and scrutinize the persona of the traditional British butler—a breed that differs sufficiently in my view from its household management cousins, the European major domo and the American household manager, to warrant its own pedigree. Let's sublimate the cardboard, cutout character into a breathing reality that leaves moist on the mirror and recognition in the reader of seemingly ancient values and skills still worth striving for.

Whether answering the phone or dealing with difficult situations, there is something about the serenely aloof British butler that many find fascinating and possibly worth emulating. Hopefully, this book will provide the necessary insight. The good news is that this book is not alone, for we live in exciting times as our economy moves increasingly onto a service-based platform. More and more people are beginning to realize that they not only can, but should, employ butlers to manage their households or service their guests. More and more people are realizing that the butler represents the pinnacle in service.

Over the last two decades, household service has been moving out of the Dark Ages of hard-to-find knowledge and into a bright future as various schools bring standards and uniformity to the profession for the first time. Definitions now exist, techniques have been standardized and codes laid down that finally give household service professionals the same advantages as other professions—a body of accessible knowledge.

Butlers & Household Managers, 21st Century Professionals talks of the household management profession. For a profession it is, requiring a wide range of skills and know-how in order to provide the high-end service that employers are looking for in this fast-paced, high technology world. It's not a profession for everyone, but for those who like to serve and who have a desire to excel, life doesn't get any better.

If more butlers are hired by employers eager to turn over the running of their households to someone they can trust; if the hospitality industry adopts even some of the color of the butler or if do-it-yourself butling becomes a reality at home or in the workplace; if the profession becomes that much more accessible and standardized, then the time spent huddled over piles of papers, clutching a stubby pencil, will have been well spent.

Steven Ferry

Chapter One

Outside Hollywood, What is a Butler?

For most people today, butlers are amusing mannequins on the screen, sometimes starchy, sometimes scathingly sarcastic, but forever symbolizing the discrete pleasures available to those who have arrived.

For me, a butler is a frame of mind rather than a status or a series of duties. It is a mindset that anyone can adopt in any situation in life to very satisfying results, because it is founded on the truths that it is better to serve than be served, and that life can be rational and serene when one assumes responsibility for all things. In almost every person, there is a penguin-suited figure dying to get out and bring order and happiness to the lives of those around him or her. This book may focus on the traditional duties of the British butler, but between the lines and chapters you will discover a mindset that anyone can apply in life—much along the lines of the movie, *Being There*—to bring a surprising level of equanimity and happiness to those in their vicinity.

Officially, according to dictionary consensus, the butler is "a male servant and head of the household." The Oxford English Dictionary breathes some life into the word with the tidbit that "buticula" meant "bottle" to the Romans. Presumably, after enough bacchanalian orgies, the bottle became synonymous with the person bringing it around to the average reveler; and even though the word evolved from Latin, through French and into its current English form of "butler," the idea has remained essentially the same: a butler is a person who caters to the needs and pleasures of the wealthy.

Like the huge vats and dusty bottles of claret and malmsey that he so lovingly looked after in the cobwebbed cellar, the butler has matured over the centuries into a richer, rarer and more complex figure in the household. This maturing process is best illustrated by reviewing the development of domestic work as a whole in England.

Two thousand years ago, a steward cared for the master's animals. It took less than a thousand years for the master to realize that he could also use some attention himself. So by the Eleventh Century, the steward had been promoted to supervising the domestic affairs of his master's castle, such as the service at the table, directing the staff and managing the finances. At that time, the butler, under the steward's direction, was still only responsible for the wines.

During the Middle Ages in England, most domestic staff were men, usually themselves of "gentle" birth, working for the nobility as part of their training for court and other activities. The only women who worked were washerwomen, nurses and "gentlewomen" who waited on the ladies of the castle.

By the Seventeenth Century, a major shift had occurred in domestic work with the emergence of a middle class. These merchants, officials and professionals had enough wealth to employ domestics, but were obviously not appropriate employers for gentry on their way up in the world. This middle class thus drew their household staff from the "lower classes" that they treated poorly, affording them little of the respect shown their more educated and refined predecessors.

This new middle class also began to employ more women in their households because they were cheaper and easier to control. The taxing of male servants from 1777 onward reinforced this trend away from male domestic employment: to raise money for the war against the American colonies, even the powder men used prodigiously in their hair was taxed!

Although unusual, women were also employed as "butleresses." The first female butler on record appears to have been named "Bunch," and employed in the vicarage of a Reverend Sydney Smith, who said of her, "I...put a napkin in her hand and made her my butler. The girls taught her to read, Mrs. Sydney to wait and I undertook her morals. She became the best butler in the county."

According to E. S. Turner in *What the Butler Saw*, "In the Eighteenth Century, the duties of butler, *valet* and footman were not so sharply differentiated as they became in the Nineteenth Century. They also included some unusual responsibilities, such as in the story of "the eleventh Duke of Norfolk, known as 'the dirty duke,' who regularly drank himself insensible. This gave his servants their only chance to wash him, for he could not face soap and water when sober."

"A manservant, whatever his nominal title, had to be ready for all sorts of informal duties which could not well be defined in a handbook: guarding his master's clothes when he went swimming; bleeding his master; holding him down for the surgeon; dragging him from under the dinner table and putting him to bed; depriving him of the means of suicide during attacks of hypochondria; lifting gouty guests into, and out of, carriages; and so on. At election times, if filled full of liquor, he would be ready to bay (shout) at any candidate who held views in conflict with those of his master."

During the Industrial Revolution in the Nineteenth Century, the middle class expanded still further. Whereas wives had worked in the house alongside the maids, a new expectation grew amongst the middle class: that the wives should not soil their hands with work. These housewives sought to prove they were ladies by acquiring and running the largest staffs their husbands could or could not afford. At the same time, poorer women who had until then subsisted by cottage industries (e.g. making clothes at home), were undercut by the opening of factories and were thus forced to either work in those factories, or enter domestic service. The result was a burgeoning of the female domestic workforce, so that by the beginning of the Twentieth Century, fully one third (1.3 million) of all women were employed in households other than their own, where they out-numbered the men by 32 to 1.

By this time, the lower rung of the middle class had been redefined in London to include anyone who could afford only three servants. The butler had risen to prominence as the male servant, acting increasingly as the go-between for the employers and the rest of the staff. His phlegmatic approach to resolving the various crises generated by staff and employers alike earned him increasing value in the household.

Working as a domestic at this time varied from the huge households of the aristocracy, with three or four hundred staff, down to those able to afford only one domestic (who had to do everything from scrubbing the floors to cooking the meals).

On large estates, there existed an elaborate hierarchy amongst the servants and an opportunity to advance oneself up the ranks. An errand boy, over time, could become a butler or house steward. A scullery maid (dishwasher) could work her way up to cook. And a chambermaid could rise, in time, to the post of head housekeeper. Those at the bottom of the domestic servant hierarchy often served those at the top.

The butler was responsible for the hiring, firing and the organization of the rest of the household staff. His duties included organizing special functions like dinner parties or receptions. He would manage the household accounts and deal with contractors or any other outside personnel, supervising their work. And he would, of course, also be responsible for buying wine and organizing the wine cellar. The butler would deal with all vendors of goods to be delivered to and used by the household. These butlers acquired their expertise by apprenticeship and learning on the job.

The fixed ideas about classes of people, combined with the lack of real understanding of how to manage people or what made them tick, resulted in repressive and petty treatment of staff. Maids in some households, for instance, could be fired (resulting in no references and thus being forced into prostitution) for being seen after midday—the time by which all their cleaning should be done, and the family free to enjoy the house without hint of servants.

This state of affairs was frequently exacerbated in middle class households by the restricted lifestyles of the ladies of the house, who were able to find little worthwhile to do with their leisure time other than sitting on top of their servants. Having recently arrived, they maybe felt the need to assert their superiority over their servants. The very wealthy, who already *knew* they were superior, had different problems, developing the usual stable of peccadilloes and eccentricities that characterize those who do nothing worthwhile in life, even having their hair parted by others. The aristocracy and church had a tradition to draw on, and in the case of the gentry, sufficient wealth; so they were more likely to treat their servants with some small dignity and give them some measure of primitive comforts (providing a bed, for instance). Although humanitarian employers certainly existed, the net culture that arose was one of harsh and unrewarding drudgery and petty tyranny that was pleasant for neither the servants nor, ultimately, the employers.

When laborsaving devices were invented in the Nineteenth Century (mainly in the United States), the British middle-class employers retarded household modernization by between fifty and one hundred years with the attitude that these devices were not needed when servants existed to do all the drudgery. They were cheap, after all—a month's wages for a scullery maid in 1900 was little more than ten shillings, the cost of a good dinner at the best hotel. So, it's not surprising that many of the staff they retained were the ones who were willing to be drudges. When domestic robots (metal ones like the two made famous in the *Star Wars* movies) were envisioned in a space-age fantasy in the early Twentieth Century, they were seen as the solution to the lack of intelligent and reliable domestic help.

A number of factors acted to reduce household employment after the First World War, significant among which were the increase in the legal minimum wage for most domestic workers and social security and worker's compensation programs, all of which conspired to raise the cost of employing domestics. After the Second World War, households of forty or more staff—with butlers, valets, first, second and third footmen, steward's room boy, hall boys, chauffeurs, stable staff, gardeners and a full complement of housekeeper and kitchen staffs—all but disappeared in England, together with some of the families and fortunes they had served. Education had improved the employment prospects of men and women alike, and the war had forced them out of the household into other occupations. The end of the war saw few returning to a life of underpaid drudgery.

The many middle-class employers who had created the huge demand for a domestic workforce a century before were anyway no longer able to afford the higher wages and so finally resorted to doing the work themselves, using labor-saving devices. The wealthier employers, who had let their large staffs go to war, had been forced at the same time to curtail their life style by the rationing of such as fuel and food, thus reducing their need for so many staff. Buckingham Palace, with over three hundred and fifty staff, is one of the few surviving examples of what was once the status quo in wealthy Europe.

Within the last fifty years, the domestic scene has contracted further to the occasional housekeeper or cleaning lady, a driver or more often, gardener. Domestic staff still refers to those who perform the more menial tasks and who continue to be drawn from the poorer and (relatively) less well-educated segments of society. Their numbers have dropped as most wealthy people live in smaller mansions and their staff use modern, laborsaving appliances. Those who choose to afford a traditional butler or his modern American equivalent, the household manager, are generally employing well-educated and increasingly trained service experts.

More than economics, however, the major problems with household work around the world have been inadequate or no training and an incorrect frame of mind— both issues applying to employer and household staff alike.

From Slave to Servant to Staff—Changing Perceptions and Attitudes

Perceptions and expectations of the wealthy and staff alike have changed. No longer is it acceptable to work twenty-hour days, seven-day weeks, and all for $200 a year. The vestiges of feudalism have disappeared.

Additionally in the last fifty years, media attention on the rich and famous, together with increased education levels and exposure to more cultures, has deflated the mystique the common man held toward those with the power to employ him or her. The British royal family, once the bastion of the upper class and its philosophy of master/servant, has been secularized in the public eye by the media. Ever salivating for a story, which the royals are by definition, the media have barraged every drawing room with familial scandals and financial revelations that have shown the royals to suffer from problems quite the same in essence as any of their subjects, but on a grander scale.

The Christian ethic, that all men are born equal before God, has an important corollary: that some are born more equal than others before they get to meet God— and there is nothing new in this condition. What is new is the understanding that we are all mortals playing out different and transient games on a blob of rock somewhere in a vast universe. Where there is respect for the royal family by the British, it is not based on peasant-like awe at the family's innate superiority, but on their good deeds over the years toward the people they serve, as well as the continuity they provide to those things that the British consider to be their essence. For domestics in particular, wealth, power and status of employers may impress, but ultimately it's only because the wages are paid and they personally can get along with their employer, that they agree to serve.

Mention "domestic service" to most people today, and a negative response usually follows. As described earlier in this chapter, domestic work has developed a reputation for poorly remunerated drudgery and tyranny. The reasons are simple, as is the cure. There was a time when domestic work was an honored profession, and there is no reason it cannot again be so.

The rich and powerful have had others take care of their domestic chores for centuries. While the Romans used slaves for domestic work (their word for servant actually meant "slave" and the word "free" meant anyone in the household who was related to the head of the household), this perception of servants persisted among the less bright of employers in later centuries. They were plagued with staff problems, naturally, because no slave ever willingly volunteered anything, nor really cared for his or her owner's welfare, nor stayed longer than he had to.

Such slaves were purchased either on the open market, captured during battle, sold by their families or "bred" from existing stock. Slavery of Moorish and Asiatic boys still existed in the British Isles up until the end of the Seventeenth Century. During the Eighteenth Century, it became quite fashionable for the wealthy to be served by young, black boys or Blackamoors, dressed in fine silk costumes with turbans and plumes. They were often sent to school, instructed in the Christian religion and baptized. This was quite different from the treatment of black slaves in America. It was another 150 years before black slavery was discontinued in the United States.

Looking further at the roots of the culture of bondage in US households, one finds the system of indentured servants first appearing in Virginia during the Seventeenth Century. Penniless Europeans sold themselves to ships' captains in return for a sea passage to the New World. The captain would then sell them to settlers as indentured, all-purpose servants. These men and women were bound by strict indentures for a fixed term of years (depending upon the size of the debt to be repaid) and could be compelled to do any and every job indoors or outdoors. During their term of indentureship, they were forbidden to enter taverns, marry without permission, stay out at nights, traffic in goods or seek another place of work.

The system had most of the stigmata of slavery, and indeed many Negro slaves were treated more humanely than indentured whites. And not all indentured servants went into this service willingly. If a child's parents died on the voyage to the New World, he or she was indentured until the age of twenty-one. Some were unwary individuals in seaport towns who were either seduced, knocked senseless, drugged or kidnapped and then sold to ships' captains bound for the New World. But, if such a servant were tough and resolute, the system offered him a road to independence. By the 1870s, domestic servants became wage earners in the United States and in most European countries. Domestic service had finally evolved from slavery into paid household staff—albeit poorly paid—but still with the lowly status established by its heritage. It is no surprise, therefore, that the most common refrain to be heard among household employers was: "It's so hard to find good help these days."

Emily Post couldn't have said it better in 1922, in response to complaints about servants, when she wrote, "Perhaps a servant problem is more often an employer problem. I'm sure it is." [1]

In 1949, Dorothy Marshall researched the subject thoroughly and brought a sigh of relief to all maligned domestics with the following:

"Every generation considered itself badly served...each generation of employers was convinced that its particular griefs were peculiar to itself, and that the golden age, when servants were everything that they ought to be, was only just beyond its own memory.... It is a pure myth that the majority of servants in the past stayed for years in the same place; most of them were as fond of change as their Twentieth Century counterparts. In practice, also, good servants were rare and their employers terrified that they might leave...thus...the very dependence which most people have upon their servants gave them a bargaining power." [2]

Increasing democracy, free markets, legislation and education have given domestic staff even more opportunity to avoid oppressive employers. But in some undemocratic cultures, no such freedoms exist for some servants who are locked in, abused and even raped without recourse. This kind of employer can count on little staff loyalty while holding the lowest opinion of staff.

You reap what you sow, as the saying goes, and the few employers who treat their staff well are (and were) generally rewarded with loyalty and good service.

It is an interesting question, of course; what is the proper way to treat staff and keep them?

For the last several hundred years, employers have wanted to regiment and control their servants, while treating them with needless humiliations, giving them unnecessary tasks and capricious management, providing poor living and working conditions and low pay. Small wonder that their servant turnover has been high and that domestics developed a culture of unexpressed resentment, finding ways to covertly repay in kind unpleasant guests or employers for indignities and meanness. Employers have generally wanted robots as domestics because they failed to make the servants and their operating climate sufficiently intelligent to function sensibly. A Lady H., whom I was visiting to determine if we were suitable for each other, presented me one day with a mind-numbing list of actions to do at a precise time each day, such as when to draw which curtain. She had obviously compiled the list in an effort to counteract the omissions she had experienced with former employees. As she showed me round her estate, we came across examples of obvious negligence, such as her own bed unmade at 5.30 p.m. Only two bedrooms and beds needed to be serviced in the house, yet she had several maids scurrying around the house looking worried and busy. She spent the entire interview bemoaning the lack of quality staff and their inability to do the simple actions they were paid to execute.

When I spoke to Lord H, whose businesses employed 75,000 people, he felt I would be unlocking the secret of handling personnel if I could find out why they did not perform the duties they had been instructed to perform. The Lord and Lady in question were so convinced all servants were robots that they were unable to see their own attitude and approach to handling their staff had created that very robot culture. The tradition that the butler is haughty and aloof with inferiors is born of the same out-dated mindset that actually prevents a household from running efficiently and smoothly.

If staff members were properly instructed in the requirements of the house, given principles and rules that they could think with, as well as checklists of actions to undertake, they would undoubtedly fulfill their duties. They would be able to observe and evaluate different situations as they cropped up, and resolve them intelligently. If employers expected the staff to take pride in their work and left them free to do so without continual interruption and recriminations, then the staff would grow gradually into a happy, caring and efficient workforce. They would show initiative within the boundaries set by the employer, and provide the employer with real assistance.

It comes down to the difference between owning a slave, controlling a servant, and employing a staff member.

This attitude problem is not limited to the English; the Americans have their fair share of it, ably described by Desmond Atholl in his book, "At Your Service."

The Butler Today

In response to shifting demands in the marketplace, several different types of butler job-descriptions exist today, each one as valid as the other when the butler understands and adopts the "mindset" that is unique to the butler.

The very wealthy will always want a formal butler figure, if only for the status symbol he represents. But people of more modest means can also make excellent use of a "butler-combination" to enhance their lifestyles. Any professional family could afford one, as in the television series, "Who's the Boss?" and "Mr. Belvedere." He might be called a houseman, a butler or even a house manager, depending upon his duties. Whatever those duties, if he understood the purpose and ethic of the British butler and the standards required in the household, he would be a butler rather than a glorified cook or maid.

The classic concept of the butler is one who answers the phone and door, introducing or screening callers; he looks after the wine cellar, serves the drinks and sometimes lays the table and serves the food. This is a formal and limited role.

An expansion of duties can be found in the butler who acts as the manager of the house and the staff: supervising staff, including hiring and firing; purchasing, and supervising suppliers and contractors. He looks after the needs of the family, from serving morning tea in bed to organizing dinners and events, and acting as a valet.

"Major domo," literally "chief of the house," is the Sixteenth Century Spanish and Italian term for the equivalent of this butler administrator. The English used "major domo" to describe butlers or house stewards in wealthy homes abroad, and this term is the one often used in California, with its strong Spanish heritage. The house steward used to perform these same functions in larger estates in England, while the more-lowly butler was assigned them in smaller homes. As the number of large households declined, the steward disappeared and the butler-administrator gradually became the senior male servant. Mr. Hudson, as seen in the TV series, "Upstairs, Downstairs," approximates this kind of position. As the profession has developed in response to changing social and technological conditions, the term "butler administrator" is being replaced gradually by the term "household manager."

A butler might also take on the duties of a *valet* or *personal assistant*, organizing his employer's personal and social life, traveling with him or her, acting both as a business secretary and social secretary—in other words, the "gentleman's gentleman." In the Sixteenth Century in England, factotums (literally, "does everything") managed all personal and household matters for their masters, and were perhaps the precursor of the Twentieth Century personal assistant. The famous Jeeves would be such a character. In America, "personal assistant" is the term generally used for the female equivalent of the gentleman's gentleman, and certainly describes in more modern terms the functions of the job, no matter the gender of the holder of the title.

A houseman is a modern day synthesis of the factotum and the Victorian "single-handed manservant." A jack of all trades, he emerged in the 1930's as the answer to general domestic needs in private houses and hotels: he would cook, clean, drive, serve at table, look after the children and generally perform all the work that the staff of forty used to perform in England. Such a Man-Friday butler, or houseman, might have a housekeeper, chauffeur and contractors to share in some of the work.

All of the above functions can be mixed, according to the needs of the employer, but it would be impossible for one person to cover them all consistently. If one is busy all day cooking, it is hard to also handle the driving, or the arrangements for the champagne cocktail party for two hundred that weekend.

Some corporations employ butlers, mainly to manage conventions, banquets and meals, but also to run private hotels for their executives and clientele. Along the same line, some hotels have butlers who tend to be a cross between their waiters, the concierge and room service. Butlers are even appearing in catering services to add a touch of class to an otherwise pedestrian occasion. A critical element for butlers in "public service" is that they do not serve one or a few individuals, but a series of guests. The subject of tips is strong in their minds, therefore, because they are usually not well remunerated but are expected to make a good portion of their income from tips. Such butlers are therefore not able to enter entirely into the spirit of selfless service to an individual or family. Those who do their best, of course, understanding the true nature and value of a butler, will probably make the most tips for the very reason that they focus on providing stellar service, not collecting tips.

Another phenomenon that comes with such "commercial" versions of the butler is the degrading of the image and service by calling anything that offers superior service in some small area, "a butler." Some hotels have launched forth with "bath butlers," "fireplace butlers, "technology butlers," "baby butlers" (who provide rocking chairs and watch children), "dog butlers," "ski butlers," and "beach butlers."

At least when the term valet was extended to "dumb valet," that furniture item upon which one lays out clothing for the following day, there was no pretence that this was the real item. Fortunately for the profession, the public were not fooled or taken in by these "butlers" and the practice has faded relatively rapidly—before it could sour the public mind on the concept of butlers. Fortunately so for the many butlers working in top hotels around the world, who do justice to the profession.

There is another category of butler: the freelance butler, who hires himself out to families and corporations and provides any of the services listed above. Apart from the work performed, he also provides the cachet and mystique of a butler to help create a special occasion or event.

And lastly, there is the butler who works as a consultant to families who have recently acquired great wealth and need to be shown how to spend it in establishing themselves and their household, while avoiding both miserliness and ostentation. With ninety percent of the millionaires in America being "new money," there is quite a need for such a service. He or she also consults businesses and corporations on matters concerning quality of staff performance, such as at restaurants, hotels and cruise ships; the presentation of a corporate image; or the production of an event, such as a convention or conference.

The butler can take on additional duties, such as those of toastmaster at large functions, and more recently, as a bodyguard.

How can one claim these widely differing roles are all butlers? Formal butlers of the old school would probably have a discrete apoplectic fit at the idea, while asserting that they were, and are, the only true butlers!

There is a middle ground, however, which is very easy to walk as soon as one defines the essence of butling. Those old-style butlers will go the way of dinosaurs and troglodytes, and the cardboard butlers in the catering businesses will go the way of all cheap imitations, unless they grasp the essential points that make a butler, and apply those to today's (and tomorrow's) markets.

A butler exists essentially to smooth the lives of his or her employer and/or family by taking over many household and personal functions they would otherwise have to perform themselves, thus freeing them up for more worthwhile pursuits. But a butler is more than an extra pair of arms and legs. He commits himself to his employers and cares enough to exceed their expectations and create extra-special moments. Good service is only the starting point: it is the creativity in bringing about the moments of exquisite pleasure and happiness that is the butler's true mission.

A thousand years ago, butlers had to know how to make and care for alcoholic drinks. A hundred years ago, not only did they have to know how to serve the wine and food, but also how to care for the silver, how to valet if required, and even how to run the whole household.

The simple matters that we take for granted, such as packaged products, did not exist back then; they had to be made, grown or raised on site. Toothpaste didn't arrive in tubes, nor did other cleaning supplies. Wine did not arrive in bottles ready to serve. Refrigerators did not exist. Ice cream wasn't provided but took hours to churn. Clean-burning, self-cleaning ovens were something a cook could only dream about as she stoked the fire and sweated over the soufflés at the start of an eight-course meal for thirty guests. These large estates achieved the conveniences of modern day, pre-packaged luxuries that many people now enjoy, by employing large numbers of staff who made the products themselves and learnt their trades by apprenticeship and working their way up from the bottom.

In time, changing household needs resulted in the butler taking on more and more duties, so that he might be called upon to do what all the other staff used to do. Today, butlers are used according to the perceptions and needs of their employers. In every case, the idea is that they perform household and personal duties that free up the employer.

Today, living is a technological and bureaucratic tour de force that has resulted in heavy specialization. We hire someone to fix the TV, but he can't or won't clean the swimming pool nor do our taxes. One way to combat such a phenomenon is to hire and train technocrat butlers, who combine the character and personal service of the traditional butler with sufficient skills in the myriad systems we use in society. Such a flexible yet well-grounded individual could relieve employers of the burdens of the day-to-day running of the house. The tray-wielding butler, specialist in decanting fine wines and serving at table, is an anachronism—a figurehead of past glories who can find employment in but a few households today.

But he has a modern counterpart who can be a real asset, not just in the private home or mansion, but even in corporations. There is a market for the tradition and cachet that a butler represents, especially when combined with the technological butler who acts as the right-hand man or woman in the household. The ethic and rationale of a butler stand on their own and have value in modern society, quite apart from the traditions he keeps alive.

And to highlight the main theme of this book, there is nothing a butler does that anyone cannot pick out and do just as well, given the information contained in this book and the opportunity to practice. Whether a housewife or a bachelor, you can use these techniques for entertaining, or handling guests smoothly, or looking after the wardrobe or any number of things. For the husband, there are some pointers for improving the security of the family, or for making a smooth move to another state, or even as simple an idea as a ritual morning tea with the papers for your wife and yourself to start off the day smiling. Even if a person cannot afford a butler or domestic staff, they can always have a hint of the luxuries of the rich and famous if they will do that time-honored of American traditions: improvise and do it themselves!

For the several hundred thousand Americans and many others around the world who have invested in one or more large properties, the smart and only thing to do is hire a trained butler/household manager and let him or her take the weight off your shoulders. You wouldn't try to run your business on your own or take on unskilled employees, so maybe the same principles should apply to "Home, Inc."

As a side-note about the British royal family, it would be a mistake for anyone to think that a book on butling would ever malign the British royal family; maligning anyone, especially an employer, would be a most un-butler-ish thing to do. As a butler is not part of the family yet lives and works intimately with one, he sees members of the family with their hair down and social graces turned off. The attitudes and characteristics required to deal with this phenomenon successfully are in part what make the butler so unique and so prized, and are covered in the next chapter.

Chapter Two

Essence of a Butler

Gone are the Eighteenth and Nineteenth Century ideas of a butler as one who had worked his way through the ranks from hall boy and knew his position: as long as he could hear, see and above all, say nothing, he would probably do.

In the Victorian heyday, considerate employers were rewarded by a staff that was loyal and who stayed with them for decades. The majority of employers, however, did not know the first thing about managing people and so suffered from a regular turnover of staff, quite contrary to the popular image portrayed of the doddery manservant, loyal to the end.

Despite the many books written at the time, none were able to isolate the attributes that really mattered, so blinded were the authors and readers by social standing, the minutiae of "correct" procedures and a lack of people skills and understanding of the human mind. As a result, butlers had no clear role models and employers had no way of recognizing a butler worth his salt.

The social and economic changes that reduced household staff to mainly housekeepers over the last century could have been successfully countered, had the real values and uses of butlers and other household and personal staff been properly established and applied to the changing condition of the household.

There is an identifiable set of characteristics that allows an outsider to successfully interact intimately with another family. This, coupled with expertise on the mechanical actions of the profession, can re-create the household as a job-market for many, while providing many families with the kind of help that they need in the home.

Until recently, no real consideration, beyond supplying a few rules of conduct, has been given by existing books and courses to the mental and social skills needed by the household or domestic employee. And yet this is the very rock that household staff, employers and agencies keep floundering on. This is all the more true today, as a deteriorating school system turns out a large percentage of illiterate graduates who have not only been made unresponsive by street and psychiatric drugs, but have been carefully taught that morals are passé. Apart from the damage being done to society by the replacement of a real education with psychiatric programs of behavior control, it makes it harder to find employees who are capable of caring and acting responsibly. The conclusion is far from bleak, however. When one finds a person capable of freely and openly giving selfless service, and they definitely do exist, one should cherish them and train them.

A Good Butler's Basic Attributes

1. Trustworthiness is the most basic characteristic that makes a butler. An employer relies on honesty and reliability when he hands over his house, family, finances, and possessions to a butler. He doesn't want his possessions disappearing, chores left undone, family sickening from food poisoning or funds being diverted.

2. He does not want to be talked about behind his back or slandered to family and guests, nor to see his name in print via the butler—so loyalty is another key ingredient.

3. He does not wish to be upstaged by the butler, or big emergencies made out of small ones. So the butler is always in the background, smoothing things over and seeking to make his employer's life as pleasurable as possible. To "butle" successfully, one has to be willing to cause things quietly and let the boss take the credit; or conversely, take the blame in public for a boss's goof without becoming defensive. One is, in essence, an actor on the stage playing a part to perfection. As long as one keeps that in mind, the occasional indignities become part of the script and not a life-or-death matter.

4. The boss would like to feel that his butler really cares for his welfare and that of his family. He wants his butler to be helpful and willing—a "can-do" type who wants things to work out for the family and who helps them wherever possible.

5. The butler has to have some social graces—tactful when confronted with tricky situations so that family and guests are not made to feel uncomfortable. He knows and follows the accepted manners and customs; he keeps track of likes and dislikes of family and guests and obliges them accordingly; he treats each person individually and with equal dignity, no matter how bizarre they may appear.

6. Six hundred years ago, the "age of discretion," (the time when a person was able to discern that there were other players in life who needed to be included in any decisions made) was set at fourteen years old. This status meant a person was able to keep his or her own counsel and remain quiet about something until the right time and place to divulge the knowledge presented itself, rather than flying off the handle. Sir Winston Churchill's advice to diplomats has some applicability: "A diplomat is a man who thinks twice before saying nothing." Discretion is not something one sees in most teens or even adults today, but it

is a vital requirement for any butler to live successfully within the bosom of another family.

7. In time, he becomes almost as well loved as the rest of the family, but only when he conducts himself as if he isn't; because there is an invisible line that he cannot cross. The upstairs and downstairs (or "back" and "front," as it used to be known in country houses, in contrast to smaller, city dwellings) division reflects a familial boundary, more than a societal one. Caring toward the employer's family is therefore felt and shown, but always with a certain measure of decorum. Familiarity breeds contempt in the long run, so a butler maintains a professional demeanor at all times. It is a matter of actually caring, while maintaining a certain friendly formality in his actions. Being chummy and being impersonal are two extremes, neither of which work for a stranger allowed into the closeness of the nest.

8. By keeping track of his employer's penchants and moods, he can predict or anticipate and provide the item or the *environment* that his employer needs or will want before being asked for it. The butler's attitude is: "I am going to do whatever I can to make my employer comfortable and happy." It's a game he plays and the rewards are pleasing to both himself and the employer. In essence, the providing of service is a given for a butler. It is the starting point, not the finish line. What marks the real value of the butler is that extra perceptiveness, inventiveness and caring that allow him or her to create those extra special moments for the employer, family members, guests, and indeed, even other employees and vendors.

9. A fundamental distinction is that a good butler serves, but is not servile. He is there to provide a service that he enjoys. He is willing to accept criticism, and if not justified, to let it ride, or correct it where and when appropriate. But he no longer owes his continued existence to his employer and so can walk tall, if discreetly!

10. Whereas he is flexible about the amount of time he works, he is most punctilious about timing, never being late.

11. With regard to other staff in the household, he is also friendly without being too familiar. He is firm about the amount and quality of work done. He cares as well for the staff—that their lives are running well, remembering birthdays and the like.

12. He is a good organizer, who can manage many people and activities according to a schedule, while keeping up with all the paperwork.

13. He pays great attention to detail so as to achieve high standards and so essentially communicates an aesthetic message to his boss, the family and any guests. For instance, breakfast could be some greasy eggs served on a cracked,

cold plate by an unshaven, unkempt butler with a cigarette stub sticking from his lips and a body odor more in place at a zoo. Or it could be a plate of perfectly poached eggs, bacon, mushrooms and grilled tomatoes as the third course in a breakfast that is served on a sunlit balcony by a butler in morning coat and pinstripes. He offers more hot coffee and the morning's newspapers and all the while, music is playing softly in the background. That's the level of creativity the good butler deals in: the making of beautiful moments to put people at their ease and increase their pleasure.

14. At the same time, he has to deal with the raw emotions of upset staff, imperious family members, discourteous guests, indignant bosses, shifty contractors and the best-laid plans falling apart at the last moment—all the while maintaining his composure, his desire to provide the best possible service, and ensuring events turn out satisfactorily. He is much like the proverbial sergeant in the army—the one who organizes the men and actually meets the objectives, sometimes despite the commissioned officers.

15. And at the end of the day, the good butler still has the energy and humility to ask, "Was there anything I could have improved about my service today?"

There is a bit of the butler in everyone—the honesty, the creativity, the caring, the social graces, the phlegmatic; it is rare to find someone with all these qualities who is able to keep them turned on day in, day out, despite all the reasons not to. All of which reinforces the value of the butler in all his various manifestations.

These qualities are not the sole preserve of men—there are many women who could make excellent butlers, too. Unfortunately in such a heavily tradition-oriented occupation, butlers have almost exclusively been expected to be male by those who employed them over the last two thousand years. A valid job requirement, perhaps, in 50 AD, but not necessarily in the year 2,000. I know of only two butleresses, and they do a fine job. We could use many more in the profession.

It is worth pointing out that the butlers most people see on the silver screen do not usually demonstrate many of the qualities listed above. When Black Adder makes disparaging and scathing remarks to the Prince of Wales' face or behind his back, he may be funny, but he is not being an honest-to-goodness butler that any employer would keep for very long—possibly because employers are never quite as naively daffy as they are made out to be.

To be sure, a butler will meet many a situation that challenges his idea of what is sensible. Does it need to be said, however, that a sensible butler will be sensible in dealing with such incidents? The next chapter describes the kind of embarrassing moments anyone can run into on occasion, and the way a butler would deal with them smoothly for all concerned.

Chapter Three

Butler Etiquette and Sticky Wickets

A sticky wicket is a term derived from cricket, describing a ball that is hard to hit for the batter because the ground it bounces on is slick. It refers, by extension, to a situation that is tough to resolve. Butlers obviously are confronted with sticky wickets, and it is the smoothness with which he resolves them that is a hallmark of good butling. He is never confrontational, opinionated or judgmental, rather preferring to put all parties as much at ease as the situation will allow.

It may be that the employer is involved in something illegal as a way of living; in this case, it is best for the butler to hand in his resignation and keep his own counsel. If serious crimes are being committed, then he has to follow his own conscience. That would be a worst-case scenario, as few employers are like this.

If a butler is asked to do something illegal or immoral by the employer or a guest (such as procuring a prostitute or drugs), it would be better for him to keep his nose clean, and hopefully the guest's, by declining politely and gently. "I hope you don't mind me mentioning this, Sir, but I really cannot oblige you in this matter," would be one way of ending it right there.

In principle, the butler should be willing to take the blame publicly for any goof by an employer, so the employer does not lose face. But this should not extend to doing anything that is illegal and has to be played by ear according to the situation, the employer's situation and the relationship between butler and employer. If it's a matter, for instance, of the employer continuing in an unethical pattern, such as visiting with ladies of the night, then that's not something a butler should assist, and certainly not cover up for (or become involved with) when his wife finds out. Lying and doing anything illegal is odious to anyone, most especially a butler. But there are ways in which one can inventively make clever excuses and provide assistance to protect the employer in a situation where he (or she) finds himself genuinely and uncharacteristically embarrassed—on the basis that the better the employer does, the better the employee does.

While the butler is always honest and upright, there is room for a judgment call when the employer's vital interests are at stake, as long as this view is tempered by the butler's responsibilities to the rest of society. Taking the rap for a manslaughter charge is not the same as having some points added to a driving license. And if the employer would as soon feed the butler to the lions as play another round of golf, then no tacit understanding exists upon which the butler can safely draw in helping an employer out of a jam and then expecting assistance from him afterwards to resolve the matter.

Another possible area of friction is when a husband and wife are at loggerheads. In this case, it is vital to remain neutral, taking neither one side nor the other. A butler is quite likely to witness or know of an indiscretion by one party that is being withheld from the other. If the butler is then asked if any such indiscretion had taken place, he has to answer the question without really answering it: "I really couldn't say, Madam," "Not to my knowledge, Sir," or "If anything were to occur of a similar nature with yourself, I am sure you would expect me to respect your privacy, Sir," would most likely answer the question without answering it, or at least put an end to the questioning. If the person insists on confirmation, the butler would be better sticking to his guns with: "I would rather leave, Sir, than be asked to comment."

If any member of the family feels that you cannot be trusted, then the basis of your relationship as an outsider in the house is undermined. The idea is not to become involved, as such family problems generally exist to one degree or another and will not resolve by your taking sides.

This non-involvement refers only to the husband and wife or long-term common-law relationships, where both people act as employers. If the common-law relationship is only short term, and the employer asks the butler about the other, then the butler could suggest that there might have been some indiscretions (if there had been), but he would prefer to leave the matter at that. Then, if pressed, he could comply with his employer's demands for more information so that he or she might be appraised of the true character and risks of the other party.

In the event of indiscretions by children, it would be sensible to note the problem but make no mention of it. Only if the butler notices a pattern or habit forming might it be appropriate to confront the child or teenager in a way that apportions no blame, but which consults his understanding and increases his control over the peccadillo. In this way, the child will not regard the butler as an enemy who must be avoided, and may even seek out the butler for help when in trouble. However, if the behavior does continue, and it is of a serious nature such as the taking of drugs, it would be wise to ask the employer for a moment of his or her time, and make the facts known.

If a guest were doing something illegal that could compromise the employer, it would be better to alert the employer. If of a minor nature, or a matter of morals rather than law, then the butler would keep his own counsel.

There are quite a few tricky situations that can occur in caring for guests, the more so as they can often be prima donnas requiring kid-glove treatment.

Let us take the case of a guest who is pumping the butler for information that he or she dares not ask the employer for directly. Obviously, if a staff member is the perpetrator, he can be told firmly to mind his own business, but such an approach could upset a guest.

"How much did he pay for this vase?" might be answered with, "I believe it was the fair market price." And if the questioning continued, "Well, if you will excuse me, Sir, I have duties to attend to." The idea would be to give a non-committal no-answer and disengage as swiftly and graciously as possible, so that no more questions could be asked. If the person insisted on being told the answer, the butler could always counter with, "I will mention your interest to (employer), so that he can answer your question himself."

A more serious but far rarer occurrence would be theft of an item by a guest. In this case, it would be possible for the butler to tell the employer that "(Guest) accidentally/absent-mindedly put (item) into his/her pocket." The employer may let it ride, but if he/she would like the item retrieved, the guest could be approached as follows: "Excuse me, Sir, I understand you were going to have the (item) cleaned/repaired, but we have someone coming tomorrow to do it, so could I please take it off your hands?" Spades are not called such by butlers, as you can see; non-accusatory euphemisms and white lies are employed overtime to keep the social intercourse running smoothly for family and guests alike. While the butler would be more direct with the staff, he would still be courteous and skillful enough in his communications to keep the erring staff member on his side.

On one occasion, the host called his butler to the head of the table. The host asked him to remove a drunk and disagreeable guest from the dining room to avoid further embarrassment for all present. Rather than drawing attention to the host being the instigator of the guest's removal, the butler played at bringing the host an extra condiment from the sideboard. Once outside, the butler summoned and briefed an assistant of the same sex as the offending guest, returned to the dining room and told the offending guest: "Excuse me, Sir, a telephone call for you." When outside and out of earshot, the butler apologized for his ruse, explaining that there had been no phone call. The host had asked that the guest leave the house to avoid causing himself and the other guests any further embarrassment.

The guest was at first belligerent, so it was appropriate to have the extra staff member to hand, but as events turned out, the guest calmed down and became remorseful. The butler then asked for the guest's car keys, as there had been no valet service that evening, and asked if the guest wanted a coffee before leaving. The butler then sent the staff member to the kitchen to order a coffee to be brought to the side room, and to bring the guest's car around. When the staff member returned, and another had brought the coffee, the butler returned to the dining room and whispered in the ear of the guest's partner that the guest had been taken slightly ill, and would she like to stay or leave with him. She could drive their car back or be driven back. She was savvy enough to know what had happened and elected to be driven back. The butler then called a cab, fetched the coats of the departing guests and sent the guests home in the taxi, while a staff member followed in the guest's car. The staff member caught a ride back in the cab, which the butler then paid off. The butler, meanwhile, had cleared the two vacant covers and seats, and closed up the gaps left between the remaining guests.

An equally embarrassing event is the arrival of uninvited guests at a function, either trying to gate crash, or arriving coincidentally. A good way to resolve this situation in brief, would be as follows: The butler welcomes the uninvited guest(s), has the housekeeper take their coats and invites them into a separate room. If they have arrived without knowing there is an ongoing event, they can be told the situation and that their host is seeing his or her guests. The butler can offer them a drink before he lets the host know of their arrival. When he tells the host, he could suggest that, unless the host wants to see the uninvited visitor(s), he will relay his best wishes and apologies and fix an appointment for another visit. The butler relays the host's message, answers any questions, and asks if they would like a refill before he fetches their coats. After the refill, he brings their coats and sees them out of the door. If they try to stay longer, the butler can apologize, saying that he really must attend to the guests at the dinner, and unfortunately, the policy of the house does not allow guests to be left unattended.

If the unexpected guests think that they have been invited when they haven't, or feel that they should have been, the butler again invites them into a side room and says something along the lines of: "I am sorry, a mistake has been made; there's a dinner party tonight, and I don't appear to have you on the guest list. I am very sorry about this." He then asks if they would like a drink before fetching their coats and promises to let the host know of their brief visit. If they insist on the host knowing straight away, the butler sees the host and continues with the steps outlined in the preceding paragraph.

In the event that a guest who has been staying at the house is asked to leave by the host, for whatever reason, then equally tactful handling is required. Take the case of the guest who had been making advances toward the hostess, even during the meal. The butler was called by the host after the meal, and instructed to tell the offending guest that he was no longer welcome. The butler went to the guest's room and found him hangdog about his behavior, which he realized had upset the host. The butler apologized about making his announcement, but made it anyway. The guest wanted to know why he was being asked to leave, but the butler sidestepped the question, preferring not to argue the case, as the host had not asked him to explain the reason why.

The butler was genuinely sorry for the guest's predicament, and said whatever he could to make him accept the host's decision. He offered to make the flight arrangements, which the guest accepted. As the flight was not until later that evening, he provided the guest with dinner in the guest's room, and had a cab arrive to pick him up afterwards. He was taken out of the back door so that the other guests, dining with the host, would not be aware of his departure.

The above examples provide an idea of the type of situations a butler may run into from time to time, and the flavor of the responses.

Chapter Four covers in detail how a butler might resolve the problem of employers who, perhaps as a result of some problem in their own life, are taking it out on the staff. As this tends to be a long-term problem rather than an acute sticky situation, I've devoted a whole chapter to it.

Chapter Five includes some sticky situations a butler may encounter in the course of running staff—such as hiring and firing them—as well as the handling of crooked or goofy suppliers and service personnel. As always, the purpose of each suggested handling is to smooth over situations and handle them as much as possible to be benefit of everyone involved.

As an example, when a car detailer accidentally buffed the paint off a black, $200,000 car, the employer wanted nothing more to do with him. This detailer was a small-businessman who would go belly-up from the negative word-of-mouth that could be generated by this incident, as well as his lack of funds to pay for the damage caused. The butler involved had the insurance company cover the repainting costs; the detailer took care of the deductible, and the employer was given a discount on all future washes. That way everyone came out ahead. The detailer still had his business, his goodwill and his accounts; the employer had a new paint job, a detailer who would do anything to please him, and lower-priced washes; and the butler had a smoothed over situation while avoiding the need to locate a new vendor, with all the trials and tribulations that entails.

There can also be problems with staff who are resentful, or lazy, or completely contrarian. A butler's concerns are primarily that staff members are performing their jobs well and that they are working together as a team in doing so. Both of these goals can be achieved by instruction, example and good leadership. If a staff member remains defiantly negative or wholly shiftless despite the butler's best efforts, only then is it time to replace him or her.

Compassion and caring go a long way in developing loyalty from the staff; this can include taking an interest in their family life, as well as their problems on the job. Helping salvage a marriage is the kind of sticky situation that a butler may be required to address so that his housekeeper isn't in the doldrums when she should be working happily.

Another point that could be considered a bit of a sticky wicket is the subject of breakage by household staff. As a general rule, it is always better to let the employer know (preferably after the item has been repaired if a simple enough task, so that no problem is created for the employer). However, if the item is small and would not be missed (such as an inexpensive plate used by the staff) it is not worth informing the employer. But for bigger-ticket items, the employer would, after an initial upset, feel happier to have been told so that she is not wondering what else has been broken without her knowledge, and so she can express her wishes concerning the repair of the item. Note: Very expensive items are often covered by insurance, and smaller items are usually of little or no concern to the employer in the first place.

For example, an antique, crystal vase was delivered by the post office to a winter residence in many more pieces than it had left the summer residence, even though it had been packaged properly. Naturally, the butler had insured the item for its full worth; he made sure that all the papers were properly filed before telling the employers the unhappy news. Because everything had been taken care of, hard feelings were minimized.

When all is said and done, sticky situations add spice to life and are a learning experience as long as one has some measure of security in knowing how to deal with them.

There is one situation butlers may well encounter that goes beyond the sticky wicket into what can only be described as a quagmire—a circumstance butlers are best never entering in the first place, as the next chapter shows.

Chapter Four

A Fly in the Ointment

As stated earlier, a usual cause of friction between employer and household staff often comes from a spouse whose training and background has been essentially the same as that of the household manager. Suddenly, someone arrives on the scene and starts taking over their game. Oops! The game *can* continue happily if the family members want to employ a butler, but they need to delineate everyone's duties in order to permit the butler to perform his or hers without continual interference. For any employer having trouble adjusting to a (new) status as lord or lady of the house, the first thing they could or should realize for themselves is that they indeed *are* the lord or lady of the house, and not the cook, or the major domo, or whatever.

As also covered earlier, when most employers consider "household staff," they tend to pigeonhole them as domestics and feel tempted to perpetuate the servant stereotype. The relationship of service is like any other relationship—two adults coming to an agreement about a relationship that they enter because they have the freedom of choice and the dignity and skills needed to play the game. One chooses to serve, the other to be served, both understanding the relationship to be reciprocal and professional.

The power enjoyed by the wealthy can be used either in the understanding that real richness in life comes from friendship and positive accomplishment, or by someone who has nothing constructive to offer. Whether some wealthy people are unable to find anything worthwhile to do with their own lives, or they consider they hold an absolute power within their own households, I have noticed a tendency for these *idle* rich to be troublesome as bosses. As the saying goes, "The devil finds work for idle hands." It seems those who have nothing to contribute to society, and therefore lack self-esteem, turn to strange games to amuse themselves.

The likes of Bertie Wooster in the "Jeeves" stories and the Prince of Wales as depicted in the BBC television series "Black Adder" characterize just such idle rich, with nothing worthwhile to do, but they are the harmless types. Miss Daisy in "Driving Miss Daisy" provides a mild example of the type of employer for whom time sits heavily and staff suffers as a result.

Often, the games can be relatively harmless, such as a phobia about cleanliness. One employer suffered from this to the point where she would insist on personally cleaning the house from top to bottom, paying close attention to cleaning those places that had already been thoroughly cleaned by the maid. The result was an unhappy maid kept busy with useless motions while the furniture and fixtures gradually eroded. But such dysfunctional, idle rich are not the kind of mean-spirited bosses that cause the most grief and which I'd like to discuss now. These do exist, as many a still-sore butler will testify, yet dealing with them is not a subject that is covered in any butler textbook or course—employers are generally described as good-natured, if eccentric; and the butlers long-suffering, if tolerant, as in Jeeves and Wooster.

Only in the real world, "eccentric" is often a euphemism for being mean towards anyone unfortunate enough to be in that person's vicinity. Being "long-suffering" in the presence of such a person is not a solution but a ticket to unhappiness. Butlers, in fact, are encouraged to bite the bullet and endure all sorts of insults—it's almost a trademark of the profession. While this may be a workable procedure when faced with the occasional unpleasant moment, it is exactly the wrong approach when confronted with a meanie who revels in being able to lash out constantly at or undermine someone who can't fight back.

The time to spot these employers (or butlers) is ideally during the job interview, or certainly by their actions and speech during the trial period on the job, so one can disengage as rapidly as possible. Although I couch these experiences in terms of butlers plagued by employers, they apply equally well to employers plagued by butlers or by anyone else. One doesn't earn too many points for spotting Saddam Hussein as a meanie. Neither is it hard to spot an employer who is always flying off the handle, firing employees, causing untold upset and making life miserable for one and all.

But what about those meanies who hide their true character? How does one spot a Richard Dahmer before one ends up on his lunch plate? Employers do not usually froth at the mouth and hold dripping butcher knives during job interviews. In one case where I had failed to ask enough questions to draw out the employer's real character, several weeks elapsed before I realized a problem existed with my employ.

One day, I noticed that the housekeeper, who was in her sixties and had been with the family for a quarter of a century, was very ill: flushed, coughing, and weak. I told her to go home and rest, and alerted my employer to the fact. The employer responded by telling me that *I* was lucky to get sick pay, as they didn't normally allow it. Not being baited by this non-sequitur (illogical) response, I pointed out that the grandchildren would be arriving soon and that it might be risky for them to keep the ill housekeeper around. The employer would have none of it until the thought occurred, "It's bad for ME," at which point she rushed out to send the housekeeper home (while pointing out to her that she was not going to receive any sick pay).

The poor housekeeper returned two days later after visiting a local walk-in clinic. She had not recovered at all, but was unable to afford any more unpaid sick leave. She had pleurisy (walking pneumonia), a blood pressure of 190 and a temperature that had been measured at the clinic at 104-5 degrees. When the employer heard this, the only response was to assert that the housekeeper had only had the "sniffles" and "she always exaggerates her temperature."

I once provided a meal for a member of the family who lived nearby. The relative phoned the next day to thank my employer for a wonderful meal. Later that day, my employer made no mention of that message at all, instead complaining that the dessert was much too heavy, insisting it been made with whole wheat flour. Factually, the dessert had been made with white flour according to the recipe, and was light and delicious (even if I say so myself). Fortunately, the relative gave me the proper message when I saw her in person later in the week.

Another time, I was cautioned against taking an evening constitutional (walk) in the guarded community in which we lived, because "it was very dangerous," and "security is walking around with dogs." The person went on to say that a club member had been arrested and sent to jail the night before for walking around after dark. Being wise to the employer's games by this time, and knowing that my many earlier walks had been completed without mishap, I decided to take my intended walk, enjoying the fresh air and calm night, admiring the stars in the sky and generally letting my thoughts wander. I chatted with a security guard (without dog) a short while later and confirmed that there had been no arrest or jailing of anyone.

Once, the employer emerged from the basement to accuse the housekeeper and butler of raising the thermostat down there. The employer had been the only person down there all morning and also often complained of the house being too cold. So one didn't have to be a Sherlock Holmes to determine who had turned up the heat (not that turning up the heat is a crime to be making much of a fuss over).

Another time, a maid was accused of burning a silk tie with the iron. The maid vehemently denied the charge to no avail. Another staff member later consoled the maid by revealing to her that she had seen the employer earlier in the day, trying to iron that very same tie.

Looking at these examples, one might be inclined to shrug off these incidents as minor—they do not paint a picture of someone who goes ballistic at the slightest provocation and skins live cats for a hobby (the easy ones to spot).

But imagine day in, day out, living in this kind of environment. The joie-de-vivre soon disappears and one settles down to a life of recrimination and fear. Who needs it?

I therefore would like to recommend another Web page to you, *http://www.scientologyhandbook.org/sh11.htm,* where you can read about these mean-spirited people and how to spot them. As the saying goes, forewarned is forearmed. Don't be ambushed!

As a butler, one needs to know about the possibility of unpleasant employers, because one is intimately involved with people in settings where they let their hair down and display their real personality in all its glory. One does not have the advantage of a nine-to-five job, where one can at least disengage from an unpleasant personality every evening and weekend. If the employer is unpleasant, he or she will be unpleasant twenty-four hours a day, three-hundred-and-sixty-five days a year. I am sure some butlers in the past were virtual slaves for their whole lives, locked into a no-win situation, thinking themselves inadequate. For the Twenty-first Century butler, however, this state of affairs should not be part of the job description. There are enough employers around who do appreciate one's talents, so go ahead, and reject one if you see red flags flying. You owe yourself at least a game that is fun to play.

The butler-employer relationship can be a win-win proposition for all concerned, and hopefully the preceding chapters have provided enough tools to win even in the face of the direst circumstances. Most of the time, however, a butler's work is routine, without complication or high drama. The following chapter provides insight into the many mundane actions that go into running a household.

Chapter Five

The Butler Administrator, Managing the Household

The following chapter deals with the day-to-day running of the household. How you arrive at the point where you are running a smooth household is addressed at the end of Chapter 14.

Permanent Staff

A butler administrator or household manager is one because he or she runs a large household (or several), with anything from just a couple to tens of staff. Finding employees these days is difficult enough without then blowing them away with inconsiderate demands or poor management. Such a household has low morale, low standards of work and a reputation that drives away the more reputable staff and staffing agencies. Administrators or employers who have such problems can often be heard remarking on the difficulty in finding decent help, yet it never occurs to them that their problems are of their own making. Most people can be made into good staff with just a small amount of instruction and care. The butler administrator therefore can do much to set the tone of the household and ensure its smooth running for all concerned.

Perhaps the first question is, "How does one procure good quality staff?" The definition of good quality often refers to someone who has experience and decent references. This definition falls short, as "experience" frequently entails procedures learned in a former home that you do not want used in your home; and "good references" can be fabricated (e.g. by a former employer who was also the butler's lover, as happened once. The truth was only discovered after the butler in question had been fired after causing thousands of dollars worth of damage in separate incidents, and leaving with items belonging to his employers).

My definition of a good staff member is one who may or may not have some formal training and/or experience, but who, above all, is willing and able to learn and willing to work as a team member. Time spent training such a staff member is amply rewarded in terms of initiative, honest work and caring by that staff member. No amount of supervision or coercion and searching for "good staff" will produce the kind of calm efficiency that results from a household forged in this manner.

How does one go about staffing a household, then?

First, know where to look. You can certainly check the top staff agencies around the country, or even abroad. You can advertise in quality national and regional newspapers and magazines, using a blind ad (post office or newspaper box). These will give you the experienced and pricey staff prospects with good references. You just have to check then whether they have become soured and bitter, or prima donnas, which would make it hard for them to work with the rest of the staff.

There are many good cooking schools around the world one can contact for a personal chef. Less glamorous sources would be local employment agencies, local newspapers, and specific staff you may have seen in action with local catering firms. If you know any other butlers, or domestic staff, or employers of domestic staff, then they may be able to provide leads as well.

The next step would be to write a job description in the form of a proposed contract, which includes the following points:

1. duties;
2. wages paid weekly and reviewed annually; flexibility of schedule covering willingness and ability to work on their time off in exchange for time-off at a later date (time-off in-lieu or "TOIL"), as well as time and half pay (50% above normal);
3. chain of command, including whom they report to, and anyone they are responsible for supervising;
4. dress and hygiene codes;
5. possible body and room search in the event of a theft;
6. six weeks trial period (one week for a chef);
7. one month's notice required if leaving;
8. vacations, allowed holidays, sick leave time and starting pay;
9. procedure to follow if ill or injured;
10. team member emphasis;
11. any board and lodging provided;
12. any health insurance and worker's compensation;
13. disciplinary procedures and an idea of what is to be disciplined;
14. such a contract can possibly include a one-year commitment to work, if much training on the job is required;
15. confidentiality agreement.

Then ask the employer and his lawyer to approve the contract.

Weed out those resumes that are obviously incompatible, and telephone the remainder of the applicants to further narrow down the choice. During the phone call, describe the position in more detail and see if the applicant is interested in the job. Call in those still remaining on the list for an interview (which is best conducted on the day off of any person about to be let go).

If you are not paying the travel, room and board of the applicant upfront, tell him or her to keep receipts for any such expenses for reimbursement. A chauffeur or anyone needing to drive on the job would also need to bring a DMV printout of his or her driving record. In addition, you need to procure several Form I-9's (Employment Eligibility Verification) from the local INS office, to make sure that prospective staff are legally entitled to work in the United States, and have the applicant fill out his or her few lines on this form.

The procedure for the hiring of a personal chef can be more thorough, as your employer may want to check his expertise and cooking style first. In this case, tell the prospective chef that (s)he will need to make four different versions of four different courses of a particular cuisine or cuisines. Call him or her back to find out what ingredients he/she wants provided. You then purchase these ingredients the day before he/she arrives.

During the job interview, try to put the applicant at ease. These interviews can be intimidating, as you may recall from your own experience.

Have the applicant read the contract and answer any questions they may have. Meanwhile, take the time to observe the person's reactions to the contract and his or her surroundings. Is she negative and sour? Is he aggressive or angry? Does she ask loaded questions? These kind of people do not make good team mates. Does the applicant have social graces and some idea of manners? Does his questioning display any understanding of the job? Remember, willingness and an open heart are the signs you want to see. Experience and know-how would be excellent bonuses, but are not the primary criteria. You could ask the applicant to demonstrate some aspect of his/her skill as part of the interview, but remember that, except for senior staff who need quite extensive know-how (such as a chef, housekeeper, head gardener or nanny), the household functions are not so complex that they cannot be apprenticed on the job.

Allow the applicant to sign the contract once in agreement with it. If he or she will not, end the meeting there and then.

For a chef, assuming his attitude, qualifications and hygiene standards are adequate, the next step would be for him to cook the meals that evening. You sit down to sample the meals with the chef and your employers. In addition to assessing the quality of the cooking, note the chef's reactions to any comments made about the food. Is he flexible and concerned with pleasing the diners?

The employer may want any personnel handling food to be screened for communicable diseases. The employer would pay for the physical exam.

Tell the candidate you will phone him/her as soon as all the interviews are done— ensure you have his/her phone number. Collect any receipts, have them sign for the total, and reimburse any expenses. Then take him/her to any public transport for the return journey.

Phone the references, asking, "Would you employ him/her again?" This is a key question to check. If the answer is no, you might ask the reason why not. In this case, you should also consider checking a second or third reference by contacting employer(s) prior to the most recent one. Problems do arise between staff and employers from time to time, and it would not be fair to an otherwise acceptable applicant to summarily dismiss him or her based on one generalized report. You have to add up all the information you have on an applicant before deciding whether they are satisfactory or not. But if you do decide to take on someone who was not recommended by their prior employer, you have to make very sure that person really is a a good resource.

You should also use an investigative agency to run a credit and background check for criminal and driving histories.

If hiring a nanny or housekeeper, the lady of the house would probably want to interview personally those you found to be satisfactory (before they returned home).

Decide which is the best candidate, bearing in mind attitude, skill, appearance, hygiene, and references, as well as any liabilities, such as dependents or troublesome familial ties. Then present the best option(s) to your employer with your recommendation. Phone to confirm that the candidate concerned is still on the market and arrange to bring him or her to the house as soon as possible. Send a follow-up letter to the successful applicant, and also phone or write the unsuccessful applicants to let them know. It is wise, though, to maintain a file on any quality, rejected applicants in case of future need.

It is better to be over-staffed (whether with permanent or temporary staff) than under-staffed, in the interests of providing excellent service to employer and guests. They may not miss a few thousand dollars in extra wages, but they will certainly notice any missing or inadequate service.

It is also better to promote existing staff where feasible, as the staff will see a greater future for themselves and so remain with you, and your employer will enjoy a proven and loyal person in the higher position.

There may be matters of insurance to deal with, such as health insurance and auto insurance, which should be resolved before or as soon as the person starts. Driving his or her own car on household business, for instance, may well require additional insurance. It was over a year before I discovered that I had been driving $250,000 cars through the jungles of Los Angeles without any insurance at all, due to an oversight by my employer's accountants and my own failure to have checked into the matter more thoroughly. Of course, the butler expects to coordinate with the *Family Office* in such matters.

Supervising Staff

As the senior staff member, it is your responsibility to ensure all duties are carried out for the smooth running of the household. In a recently staffed household, this may even mean you do the work yourself, from making beds to cooking the dinner, while finding and instructing staff to take over the duties of the house. And having given a staff member a job to do and shown him how to do it, let him or her get on with it, ever mindful at first that you may have to jump in to complete the job properl.

But until then, refrain from issuing streams of instructions. It is the staff member's job to issue instructions to himself or herself, and the more you usurp this responsibility, the less willing and competent he or she becomes. In my experience, households run well where individual responsibility is exercised within the parameters of the person's skill and general staff duties.

Ideally, you would have enough competent and willing staff to accomplish all needed tasks. Your job would be the coordination of staff with each other, and the coordination of the staff's actions with the employer's wishes. Keep the staff briefed on daily requirements, special functions, guests, schedules, menus, and anything else that will help to make them into an intelligent, coordinated team. This can be accomplished by daily conferences with the heads of each department, and a weekly staff meeting to discuss progress, plans, suggestions and requests. Checklists should be made and marked off by each staff member, as they accomplish tasks assigned to them.

To avoid discord amongst the staff, discourage discussions of salaries and tips. Divide tips from departing guests between the staff according to an agreed upon apportionment.

Be consistent in praising and disciplining staff, thus avoiding favoritism: give the same scale of gifts at Christmas or birthdays. Avoid eating with staff too often so as to maintain your presence and avoid over-familiarity.

Do not allow staff to complain about conditions or employers unless their complaint is offered as part of a constructive suggestion to you alone.

Avoid allowing your own moods to color your demeanor while on the job—you want to appear accessible to the staff under your supervision.

In terms of address, it is normal to call the chef "Chef," the housekeeper, "Ms. (Family name)" and the staff by either their first or family names, depending upon the custom in the household. You yourself would be called "Mr./Ms. (family name)." Proper forms of address help keep relationships on a professional footing.

The employers are always called by the family name and any title by the staff, with the children referred to as "Master or Miss (family name)."

Obviously, if the employer demands otherwise, then one obliges. However, where that employer is new to household staff, it would be sensible to appraise him or her that familiarity generally breeds contempt, and it would be in their interests to maintain that demarcation between staff and family in forms of address. It is of interest to note that the introduction of a first name basis in professional circles came on the backs of salespeople trying to ingratiate themselves with their prospects. It may not seem comfortable, friendly or "democratic" to call employees "Mr. X" or "Ms. Y." But consider this: they *are* professionals. Drop the professionalism, and familiarity creeps in, and there goes the whole professional relationship a stranger needs in order to survive in the intimate surroundings of a family. The friendly thing to do is maintain that slight, invisible barrier.

Dismissing Staff

Once in a long while, it may be necessary for you to dismiss someone. How does one go about this in a society as vindictively litigious as today's?

Firstly, unless a security aspect is involved, try to keep the person on the job until a replacement can be found, even if a temporary help. Remember, your main responsibility is to keep the household running as smoothly as possible.

If the person is being let go because of overstaffing, this requires a completely different resolution. The person is called in and the situation explained to him or her. (S)he is given proper notice, with severance pay and any back vacation pay. If living in, ensure (s)he is allowed adequate time to find alternate accommodation. And (s)he is always given a good reference, as well as any leads for employment.

If, on the other hand, (s)he is being dismissed for continued incompetence, dishonesty or unwillingness to work, (s)he is treated to the same rights, but given no reference and no help in finding alternate employment. It would be wise to make a recording of the dismissing interview, and (s)he would be required to sign for any monies given. Collect any keys, uniform and household property in his or her possession, as well as a list of any incomplete projects.

The person being fired normally has no right to an individual audience with the employer, although if the staff member had been a member of the household for two years or longer, you would obtain the employer's approval before firing. In the event that (s)he was violent, or had stolen property and you had verified this to be the case, you might call in the police and press criminal charges. In such instances, you would need to have another staff member of the same sex as the employee in the interview room with you as a witness. He or she would also escort the person to his or her quarters and see that they packed and left straight away (in a taxi to the nearest public transportation if needed), without fuss, violence or further theft.

34

Disciplining Staff

One thing that can severely undermine staff morale and happiness, is the wrong-doing of one which is known about by another who keeps it to himself; either through fear of retaliation, or a disagreement with "snitching," or because they have similar misdeeds of their own to hide.

It is important to encourage a system that allows staff to keep a clean breast of things. If they break something accidentally, they should let you know, no matter the cost. They won't be fired for it, and if the item is very expensive, insurance should cover the loss anyway.

If they notice someone else doing something wrong, whether breakage, goofing off on the job or petty theft, or anything detrimental to the household, its staff or guests, then they should let you know about it if the person himself doesn't. You would act as a clearinghouse for this kind of information by keeping files.

These files would not be used against the person, but rather to help him or her; if something serious is reported, or you notice a pattern, you could interview him and show him the information you are operating on. If the information were incorrect, you would acknowledge it as such, make a note in the file and leave it at that.

If it were correct, you would help the person spot any pattern emerging and ask for his suggestions (or provide some) as to what he could do to correct it. Most people are blind to their own failings, so it helps to have someone draw their attention to them. Write up the interview and have the person sign it.

In the event that enough verified incidents accumulate, and the person just will not change, then it is time to start issuing ultimatums—shape up or ship out. If you do have to fire, you have the record of the signed interviews and reports of wrongdoings, should the person turn around and try to sue. I mention the worst-case scenario, but most people are only too willing to correct their failings and appreciate being given the chance to do so. This system, adopted by agreement by all staff, will help keep them working well together as well as, interestingly enough, preempt staff resignations.

Employee Records

For tax purposes, you should keep records for three years on each employee's hours worked, resultant pay including overtime, weekly sums expended for room and board, transport, etc, and the person's name, address and phone number. The local IRS office can supply copies and information on Forms 942 (to report Social Security taxes and wages paid), Form 926 (taxes for household employees) and Form W2 (annual wage and tax statement for each employee).

Hopefully, there is an accounting office the employer uses to deal with pay and tax matters. If not, the above gives you the basics, and you would be well advised to consult with some experts or burn the midnight oil pouring over the manuals, if you have been charged with these responsibilities yourself. The IRS isn't the animal it used to be, and will treat you right if you follow their rules (or honestly try to). The U.S. tax burden on each citizen is the lowest of all western democracies, so don't waste your breath bemoaning the system (although in my personal opinion, a national sales tax instead of an income tax has a lot to recommend it).

Temporary Staff

An early action when taking on a butler administrator or household manager position, is to locate reputable temporary domestic staff agencies. Use the yellow pages and word of mouth to contact the most reliable agencies and arrange an appointment to visit them. Points to look for are:

1.	Is the agency licensed and bonded?

2.	Is the agency in good standing with the Better Business Bureau?

3.	During your visit to the agency, observe
	- Are the offices and equipment in good order?
	- Are the staff members professional in dealing with you?

4.	Written terms of business and references from some of their clients.

5.	You will also want to know if:
	- the temporary staff are insured by the agency;
	- what uniforms, if any, the agency provides its staff;
	- what hours the staff are available, and their willingness to work beyond those hours, with or without overtime pay;
	- whether the agency checks references for its staff;
	- what qualifications their staff have.

6.	Normally the agency is the employer of the staff and is paid by you; verify this to be the case, and find out any arrangements for tips.

7.	Last, but not least, ask for their fee scale.

8.	If using them to locate permanent staff, do they guarantee a replacement free of charge in the event that an employee does not work out soon after arrival?

In this way, you will have a list of satisfactory and reliable agencies to contact, even at short notice, for temporary staff.

Your first requirement for temporary staff is that they know their jobs and can perform them professionally. Most temporary staff members are willing, and those who are willing and competent are definitely valuable. You will be busy enough telling them the peculiarities of the service required in your household, and where everything is, as well as the agenda for that day's functions. So you will not have time to show them the basic duties they should already know. In this regard, the emphasis for hiring temporary and full time staff is different.

Contractors, Suppliers and Services

The same sort of procedure can be used to build a yellow pages of reliable contractors, vendors and services. *Appendix 5A* provides a list of likely professions you may need to call on at one time or another. Aim for at least three sources in each profession, so that at short notice, you will not be confounded by one going out of business, being out of town, or being fully booked. Always select those that deliver the best quality, and only then, given a large choice, narrow the list down in terms of economy.

You may need to visit some of them, such as the fishmonger, but others you can ask to send samples of their work, such as printers. The idea is that you actually eyeball some of their products, to confirm that the standard and quality of their product is adequate for your employer.

As a note, while every reputable company can be trusted to act professionally, it is not always true of their employees. Unscrupulous job applicants can circumvent any screens established by an employer and arrive at *your* employer's house with the ostensible purpose of fixing a plumbing problem, but actually using every opportunity to "case the joint" or walk off with valuables. The best way to deal with this kind of situation is to limit access of vendors and contractors to areas "as needed," and where this might be a sensitive area, to have a staff member accompany them. Or at the very least, to make a very thorough check for any missing items on their imminent departure. This may seem like paranoid behavior, but it is better to err on the side of caution, given that a 10% criminal element in society makes life unpleasant for the majority of people who can play the game of a give-and-take, earn-your-own way society.

Another wrinkle on this problem is someone arriving at the residence to do some work. Whether they are expected or not, if you do not know them personally, you have no way of telling whether they actually have been sent by the vendor. The only way to find out is to have them wait outside or in a secure area until you have placed a quick confirmatory call with their dispatcher. It's worth pointing out that I have never run personally into any criminality, but the old umbrella principle I am sure had something to do with that—when I lived in England, as long as I carried an umbrella, it invariably rained somewhere else. If I set off without one, I usually returned with a stiff upper lip and soggy clothes.

The Housekeeper and Cleaning

Housekeepers perform much work in the house that often goes unnoticed. Sometimes they have to deal with thoughtless guests, or an employer who is overly concerned with cleanliness—requiring something that is already clean, be cleaned again. Their work, however, is very important, and it helps to acknowledge and thank the housekeeping staff for work well done on a regular basis.

You should spot check the housekeeper's rooms from time to time and bring to her attention, in a low-key manner, anything that might have been missed. The housekeeper used to just clean the upstairs rooms in days gone by, while the butler and his footmen primarily took care of the downstairs rooms. But times they are a-changing, and these days the housekeeping staff are responsible for cleaning the whole house. Cleaning and maintenance checklists make their job much easier.

The housekeeper can still help the butler at functions, serving at the table for a small party, or taking and minding coats at large functions. In the absence of an under-butler, the housekeeper really functions as the butler's deputy.

In many homes, the furniture and household items are often of very fine quality, sometimes fragile antiques of great value. The housekeeper in this case needs to know proper care and cleaning procedures, and these are listed below, in brief (some suggestions being summarized from *The National Trust Manual of Housekeeping* by Sandwith and Stainton, Penguin Books).

Anything of extreme value, or in very bad shape, should be cleaned (and restored) by experts.

Furniture

Examine the item for any weakness before moving it and be sure to grasp it by its strongest point. Avoid spreading dust by flicking the duster; instead, gather the dust in the duster and then discard it. If using a hog's hairbrush to remove dust from crevices, though, flick the dust away rather than trying to scrub it off. Do not rub or wash gilded items or gesso (chalky base for paint); instead, use a pony tail hairbrush. Once a year, polish the furniture lightly with a soft brush (unless you notice the veneer is lifting). Place nylon screening on upholstery before vacuuming, so that the fibers are not pulled out. Use a piece of stiff card to protect fringes and mirror frames when cleaning around them.

The sun can fade furniture over time, so cover windows with an ultra-violet absorbing film or have sunscreens installed, which can be pulled half way down on a dull day, and fully down on a sunny day, or all the time in a little-used room that is full of antiques.

Floors

Protect floors from workmen by using coverings, providing plastic or cloth socks or booties, or at a minimum, by placing metal or coconut mats outside to clean mud off boots. If possible, ask that shoes be taken off on entry, as is the custom in many houses. Quickly remove any liquid or mud to prevent it spreading.

Limit cleaning to dusting with a vacuum cleaner (slowly float the head, don't scrub with it). Use nylon screening for fragile carpets. Always vacuum underneath a rush mat. Clean a polished wooden floor infrequently (using very little water or a cloth soaked in paraffin or vinegar, making sure to dry it immediately afterwards), and polish it using brushes that are kept clean and supple. Lift curtains and hangings clear of the cleaning. Marble floors should be dry-buffed. Put special padding under rugs that are placed on such highly polished floors, to prevent slipping.

Ceramics

In general, when cleaning items that are located high up, use a stepladder so as to avoid cleaning above shoulder height, which is tiring and increases the risk of damage occurring.

Examine items for any weaknesses, and use both hands to pick up one piece or section at a time. Dust flat areas with a duster and crannies with a hog's hairbrush. Wash with a very mild detergent only when necessary, and without immersing.

Metalwork

Use plastic gloves when cleaning with a solvent, otherwise handle with cotton gloves on. Use a separate brush and cloth to clean each type of metal. Then wax (copper, steel and brass) a small area at a time.

Gold

Clean only with water and buff with an impregnated cloth. Clean separately, and do not polish or dry with the same cloth as is used for silver items, or the gold may become silver plated.

Books

Remove old books from shelves by gripping their sides firmly and pulling them out gently; where possible, push them out from behind first. Support large books underneath and carry them vertically. Clear and dust one shelf and its contents at a time, starting at the top. Stack books only a few on top of each other, and carry them a few at a time between thumb and fingers. Vacuum heavy dust from them with a brush-ended vacuum attachment. Dust edges with a shaving brush. Only then open and dust inside the covers with the shaving brush. Keep and label any pieces that come off, for fixing by experts; also note and report any recent damage by pests. Replace books exactly as you found them.

As with furniture in general, keep the temperature constant and mild, and the humidity at RH (relative humidity) 50-65%. High humidity and heat, as well as wild temperature fluctuations, are the main enemies to avoid.

Hair and Clothes Brushes

Poke the hair out with a thin rod between the lines of bristles. Using cold water, rub hand soap and then shampoo into the bristle, then rinse. Place bristle down on a towel to dry. If the bristles wear down or fall out, a valuable brush can be re-bristled (try Clements in the Burlington Arcade, London, if you happen to live nearby).

Cleaning Cloths

I heartily recommend cloths by Terga that collect dirt electrostatically. They only require water, meaning harsh, smelly and toxic household chemicals can be dispensed with. The cloths come in sets of three, one designed for glass and similar surfaces, one for most other surfaces, and the third for floors and heavy stains. They cost about $10 each but last two years if properly used. Cheap imitations of Targa cloth can be bought for a third of the price and work reasonably well, but not as well. For instance, they still leave lint on glassware and windows, which Targa cloths do not. As a final note, I do not own stock in Targa.

The Kitchen under the Chef

If you have ever worked with or under a chef, you will know how prima donna-ish they often can be. And if you have ever chef'd in a large kitchen for many people, you might understand why many chefs are like that. The chef is lord of his domain and usually works under great pressure to produce the right amount of food that is just right, at just the right time. As such, he deserves respect and the freedom to go about his business without interference. It would be a common courtesy for anyone entering the kitchen to knock first, and on entering, address the chef as "chef."

As a butler, you are administratively the senior, but the chef is boss in the kitchen when it is operating. Whether the chef or the butler purchases the food, the butler is overall responsible and should have the final say in matters of suppliers, checking quantity, quality and price.

Where the food presented falls short of expectations, or when hygiene or kitchen staff actions leave something to be desired, it is up to the butler to alert the chef so that he can correct as indicated. If the chef does not or will not correct, then you can correct it yourself if urgent, and sort it out with the chef afterwards. If he won't respond, look for a new chef, but only after consulting with your employer.

The employer may well provide requests for specific meals and menus. After you have checked your records to ensure any expected guests have not been given the same menu items recently, review the menu with the chef. Look for any potential problems with the proposed menu from the chef's point of view, as the expert in the field as well as the one who is being expected to provide the product. Explain any such problems to the employer at your next meeting, with recommended solutions. On the morning of the meal, you can confirm the day's menu with the employer after breakfast, and liaise again with the chef on any last minute changes.

If there is a large function planned for execution by household staff rather than caterers, you could hold a "working breakfast'" with the chef and housekeeper for coordination purposes.

Running an Efficient Kitchen

Safety is a primary consideration, as one has sharp, hot, cold, electrical and gas sources peppered throughout the environment, which in conjunction with stress and the rush to produce a meal on time can result in injuries. Apart from knowing their specific trade, an obvious concern, which is almost never mentioned, is that employees have to be reasonably happy with their own lives in order to be able to focus their attention fully on the job at hand.

The kitchen has to be free of encumbrances and piles of junk; everything should be stored in its rightful place. It should be spotless, including the areas that cannot be readily seen, such as extractor fan screens. Ideally, there would be two one-way doors—in and out, or at least a glass panel in a single door to prevent collisions. Glass should be kept out of the kitchen, except for any hors d'oeuvres dishes, etc. that are about to be used. Otherwise, glass and glasses are cleaned in the washing up area.

Glasses and knives are not left under water, out of sight, where someone might cut himself. Knives are kept very sharp, as the extra force needed to cut with a blunt knife often results in slips and cut fingers. Fully stocked first-aid boxes should be placed strategically, and two staff on each shift trained on first aid (so that one can tend to the other if needed). A good trick is to sprinkle some flour on hot items as a warning to others. Fire blankets and extinguishers should be placed strategically and operational. All the staff should be instructed on how to use them, and what to do in the event of a fire. There should be no running in the kitchen. All spills should be mopped dry immediately to prevent slipping.

Another matter of primary concern is hygiene. Flesh products should be cut on their own boards and the boards then disinfected. Contrary to established opinion, wooden boards are far more hygienic than the modern plastic versions, which harbor bacteria while the wooden ones are less hospitable to the wee beasties. Zappers can be installed for flies and a pest control company called in to spray and lay traps if needed. I once saw a rat scurrying up the wall of the food preparation area in an English pub. My shock turned to disbelief when the chef just shrugged his shoulders and did nothing to handle (he didn't have his job for long).

These kind of precautions are vital to avoid food poisoning. To this end, pets and animals (and children, for hygienic and safety reasons) should not be allowed in the kitchen. A hand basin should be positioned by the kitchen doors, with paper towels and a trash can, and used to wash hands by anyone newly entering the kitchen area.

If staff become ill with a communicable disease (from AIDS to the common cold), they should not be allowed to work in the kitchen. Quite apart from the fact that their own recovery is hastened by rest and recuperation, the all-too-common expectation that staff work through illnesses often results in diseases being passed on instead of contained. Staff should be eligible for sick pay, and temporary staff can always be brought in. The only requirements for returning to duty are that these ill employees bring papers from a health practitioner confirming the existence of the illness and that it is no longer contagious; and that they sign an Illness/Injury Book on their return. This book is kept in the kitchen and details what times have been taken off and for what reason. The chef, housekeeper or butler countersigns the book for their recovered staff. The purpose of the book is to prevent false claims, keep track of sick leave and isolate chronically ill staff, for possible further assistance.

The refrigerator should be kept clean inside, outside and behind; each section should be labeled so that different users always return food to the right place. Older food should be moved to the front of its shelf; raw meats kept at the bottom in case of dripping fluids; smelly items wrapped; raw meat covered, but allowed an air hole at each end to prevent sweating. An opened box of bicarbonate of soda can be kept in the fridge to neutralize any smells. It is a good idea to keep a list on the fridge door, that everyone can add to when they use the last of an item, or when it is running low. Refrigerator temperatures should be kept close to freezing, so always shut the door as soon as possible.

As for the freezer, the same rules apply in general; one should label and date, and properly wrap everything before placing it in the freezer. Nothing should ever be refrozen once thawed out, most especially raw meats, as bacterial growth will occur.

Have all kitchen appliances, including the freezer and refrigerator, serviced at least once a year.

Lastly, there is the matter of cleaning up after a meal. Larger kitchens usually employ a dishwasher and (s)he should know how to handle the finer items such as crystal and china, as well as the proper tools needed for cleaning different types of pots and pans. Teflon, for example, doesn't respond well to a wire scourer, just as a heavily encrusted and burnt pot will not respond to a sponge. The sink taps in the dishwashing area should be fitted with rubber protective nozzles to prevent the most common form of glass breakage—hitting the rims on the taps while rinsing.

Glasses should be washed by hand in hot water and mild detergent. Place them upright on a towel and dry with a dry cloth. For wineglasses, hold the bowl with the cloth on the outside, bunch the other end of the cloth and turn it in the bowl. Hold the foot to dry the foot and stem. This will prevent undue stress separating the bowl of the glass from the stem, by holding the one while drying the other. Polish glasses with another, lint-free cloth. Glasses should be stored upright in a dust proof cupboard. Decanters can be hard to access, so the best way to dry them is by turning them upside down and pouring hot water over the outside.

Silver should be treated to the same washing regimen. When dried, silver is best stored in acid free tissue paper to prevent tarnishing (see later in this chapter for more information).

Crystal is similar to glass: clean by hand with warm (not hot) water with a mild soap added if needed. Vases and decanters can be cleaned on the inside with Sterodent, or by swirling with a solution of raw rice added to warm, soapy water; or bleach can be left inside for two hours. Lime deposits inside vases, bottles (and kettles) can be removed by rinsing them with vinegar-and-water solutions or fresh-squeezed lemon or lime.

Bone-handled cutlery should be wiped, not washed, to prevent hot water from shrinking the bone and neutralizing the glue that fastens the bone to the metal.

Suppliers

Purchasing can be a large part of the butler's duties, whether it is the stocking of dry goods, selection of the best produce, the acquisition of appliances or the purchase of gifts for family members and guests.

When ordering goods to be delivered, it is wise to insist on known and kept delivery dates, as well as a guarantee of immediate replacement for spoiled or broken deliveries. As covered earlier, have at least three suppliers short-listed, and ensure they know about the others on the list, to encourage competition. Especially in the purchase of foods, take quality, then price, and then quantity as your signals to buy. After these three, you can go into bazaar mode and go for bulk discount if applicable, or a reduction in price: "That seems rather high."

On the quantity, it's always a good idea to order twenty-five percent more than numbers indicate, to cover any errors in delivery, mistakes in preparing the food, and extra guests turning up, or the guests liking the dish enough to want their plates freshened.

Even when the best supplier has been found, continue to check for changes in other suppliers, or the arrival of new ones. Also, continue to check for new products, but try them yourself or on the staff before introducing them to your employers. When shopping, always consult the specialists for tips on their finest quality items and recommendations for the day.

If you are taking over purchases from the chef, it would be advisable to take him with you until you know the places to go, the people to talk to, and the things to look for. If the chef continues to purchase the food under your supervision, then you will need to purchase the flowers, chocolates, beverages, wines, teas, coffees, fruits and toiletries.

Delivery

When produce or some item is delivered, review the packaging slip and then merchandise, cross-checking condition and quality, then weight, then price against the record of what was ordered according to the order-and-delivery-of-merchandise form (see *Appendix 5C*). Give the driver a drink while you check the delivery; handle any shortfall or poor quality with him/his office straight away; otherwise, give him a tip if appropriate and send him on his way. Warn suppliers (and the chef if needed) when you encounter inefficiency or dishonesty (shortfalls, loaded bills or poor quality) and if they continue, find an alternate source and switch supplier.

On the subject of tips and gifts, deliverymen are sometimes tipped for large or long-distance deliveries that have involved quite some work on the driver's part. All deliverers and suppliers are given small presents at the end of the year for Christmas.

If suppliers give you gifts, accept them on behalf of your employer and give them to him. If you accept them for yourself, you will be obligated to the supplier and lose purchasing power as a result. The gifts, anyway, are a return for your employer's purchases, not yours, so they rightfully belong to him (although he is just as likely to tell you to keep them).

Safety in the House

It falls upon the butler to organize matters relating to the safety of those in the house, as well as the integrity of the house itself. Chapter Twelve deals with the butler as a bodyguard; while this section below is a good deal less dramatic, it is far more likely to be needed to save lives and property.

It is wise to bring in experts on security and fire to recommend the best equipment and systems. When your employer has been appraised of any weaknesses in existing systems or their complete lack, as well as your recommendations with full costing, he should be willing to correct the matter without reservation. You can then supervise their installation at a time when the employers are away, as both may require quite some work to install. Set up and keep a log for the maintenance of these systems, as well as the drills done by staff in their use of them.

These automatic systems are valuable, but they alone will not accomplish the full job of security and protection; for that, you will need the co-operation of the staff and family, which is best accomplished by instruction and then drilling. A roster could be drawn up, showing each person's name and what their specific duties are in the event of a fire or, to take a leaf out of navy manuals, should they have to help repel boarders. The roster would need to be structured so that all functions were covered even though some staff might be away on their day off.

For the fire drills, some would be assigned to fire fighting, some to evacuation, and some to salvage work. Someone spotting a fire would yell "Fire" repeatedly, stating its location. He would hit the alarm button, if not already going, and do what he could to extinguish the fire; as the first minute or two are crucial in bringing a fire under control. The first person to hear the cry would phone the fire brigade and then go about his assigned fire duties.

The evacuation people would ensure everyone was directed out of the building, and the fire fighters would help with extinguishing the fire (until the fire trucks arrived, or until it became too dangerous to continue). The salvage people would remove pre-determined valuables from areas they could still access without risk (as a note: during the first fire-fighting drill, use the real items gingerly, just to make sure there are no problems with removing them; in subsequent drilling, use substitute items).

Everyone else would muster away from the building for a roll call, and the evacuation people would be sent back to bring out anyone still in the building as long as this were still feasible (being careful not to try to rescue someone who was actually not there at all, but in town or somewhere similar).

The staff billed as fire fighters would have to be instructed on how to put out different types of fires; those billed as evacuators would have to be instructed on carrying unconscious or injured people, and on first aid.

The fire drills would be done for real (you could light a fire in a bucket in an area where no smoke damage would be done), and the alarms would be hit (with word to the fire brigade beforehand that a drill was about to take place). You would want as much commotion and panic element generated as possible, to simulate a real situation. Smoke canisters could be purchased and set off. This may run contrary to fire drills recommended by others, but why run a drill that is completely unreal? In a real fire, people won't act as if they are walking into a church service. To be sure, panic is not the desired effect, but swift and effective action in the midst of great confusion (a burning house and endangered people and possessions are not an orderly affair by numbers) is what will win the day.

Windows and doors should be shut. The drill would be called at a set time at first and timed with a stopwatch to measure how long it takes to evacuate the building and bring the fire under control. The idea would be to have all the functions done as swiftly and calmly as possible. When the staff had the routine down, you would involve your employers once, so that they know what to do. And then you would spring a surprise drill (yelling: "Fire in the east wing - this is a drill"), preferably in the dark, to see how staff handle that!

These drills can be great fun, as well as marvelous team-builders, quite apart from their life-saving potential. Over time, it would be sensible to train each person in the household to perform each function, so that they can be of further use once they have accomplished their pre-assigned tasks. Instruction could include awareness by staff of what can cause a fire, so they can prevent them occurring in the first place. Lastly, ensure notices are posted in staff and guest areas, indicating where to go and what to do in the event of a fire.

A similar drill could be worked out for "repelling boarders," to borrow on old sea-faring concept. It would simply involve calling the police and getting away if possible to a pre-selected safe point. Or to cooperate with attackers in an effort to keep them calm until the police arrive. This drill could be extended for any staff interested and can include basic self-defense lessons, or possibly martial arts and small-arms training, should there ever be a need for such preparedness.

Ensure several people on staff are first-aid trained and work out some incentive to have them do the training if none volunteer (bonus, pay rise, time off).

Ensure there is an emergency generator for the house and that it is serviced and operational. Earthquakes, hurricanes, tornadoes, snowstorms or problems at the power company can all cause inconvenience through lack of power for basic activities.

Paperwork

Butlers are not exempt from paper shuffling, but these days, most of it can be done with a computer and printer. The centerpiece of a butler's paperwork is the "pantry book," so called because the butler's office used to be called the pantry and he would keep a book there with all his notes and information important to the position. Today, this book is more commonly referred to as the *"Butler's Book,"* or when used by a household manager, the *"Household Manager's Book."*

A good butler keeps a record of the likes and dislikes of his employers and their families, as well as guests; he records all his suppliers and the people he calls on for services at the house; he notes anything of interest and importance in running the house, not just for his own benefit, but so that his successor can step into his shoes and continue the work without interruption for the employers.

Appendix 5B provides a self-explanatory list of the type of information kept in this book. As it needs to be kept updated and changed over the years, a computer really proves its worth to the modern butler.

Several computer programs could be utilized, including a calendar program, a data base program for filing lists of things, an accounting program for keeping track of expenses, and a word-processing program for writing letters and memos.

Some hard-copy files still have to be kept, including contracts, statements, letters and receipts received, warranties and instructions for the running of appliances. Also, a press book could be kept of the employer's mentions in the media. A working file for each major function or event put on is also very useful.

Keeping Household Accounts

This subject is really very easy, as long as the system set up simply shows money in and out, and you keep the records up-to-date on a daily or every-other-day basis. If you leave it much longer, that receipt you mislaid without realizing it will result in your books not balancing later in the week or month, and you will have no hope of remembering what expense could account for the missing money. Keep all invoices, dockets, petty cash vouchers, check book stubs, charge card receipts, etc. in date order, filed by week and month, and use these to cross check accounts. Then update, summarize and print out the account monthly.

When an invoice is received, check it against the order book and ensure the delivery was made, and the amounts and prices align with those of the bill as well as the original order. Phone the supplier immediately if there be any discrepancy. Never pay an invoice, etc., no matter how small, without cross checking records and knowing what you are paying for. If an invoice is received for something not in the order book, check with the boss to see if he or another family member placed the order, what the order was for exactly, and whether it was delivered. In the case of a service rendered, cross check for earlier such statements to ensure the bill is in the right ballpark.

If you pay the staff wages from the household account, the employer's office normally takes care of all the paperwork and tax considerations.

Compile an annual report for the employer on expenditures, comparing them to earlier years, summarizing where the money went, giving the reason for any rise or fall, and making predictions of funds required in the year ahead. If the allowance is limited and not sufficient, then ask for an increase. One good statistic to keep track of on a daily basis, and include in the report, is the amount of money saved by reason of astute purchasing or management.

Appendix 5C suggests a simple but comprehensive form for keeping track of the ordering and taking delivery of merchandise; as well as a format for the bills paid ledger. Books can be used, but computers definitely have the edge now: with an accounting program, all financial records entered in are automatically added up, subtracted, divided and so on, as required. The work expended to set up the program is amply rewarded in time saved thereafter, while lessening the likelihood of errors in the accounting.

Appendix 5D provides a format for taking notes of phone calls. Several times I have been able to correct an erring contractor or delinquent supplier by reminding them of the exact original request.

Making an Inventory

This action of making an inventory of the employer's valuable possessions can be quite extensive when being done for the first time, but the subsequent entering of new purchases makes the annual update an easy proposition. The purpose of making and maintaining such an inventory is mainly for insurance, in case of theft, fire or breakage.

The inventory is best carried out with an assistant at a time when the family is away. The assistant adds an extra pair of eyes to spot what you might miss. If an inventory already exists, print a copy to work off; otherwise use a pad and pencil. Map out the house, assigning each room a number, including staff rooms. You simply walk into a room and note the details of all items of value. Once that room is complete, move to the next. Use a digital camera to photograph important items, noting on the back of the picture the room number and the date. Items commonly overlooked on inventories are clothes, carpets, clocks, the contents of garages and of ancillary buildings.

The following format includes the kind of information that you should record:

- Description of item (name; serial number, size, color, condition, pair or set)
- Place and date of purchase
- Original cost
- Replacement cost

Call in professional appraisers to value antiques and works of art. Once the inventory has been input into the computer, send copies with insurance update requests to the insurance company. Guest and staff property of value should also be covered in the policy. An "All Risks" insurance policy would cover possessions when removed from the house.

Once insured, send copies of the inventory to the bank manager and accountant, as well as keeping a copy in your safe (in which a copy of the insurance policy is also kept, and all receipts showing the purchase information for all the valuables).

Taking Care of Various Articles

Silver—Cleaning, Storage and Purchase

Silver should be rinsed quickly of salt and other food residues to prevent tarnishing. It may then be washed in hot, soapy water, rinsed and quickly dried (with a motion, when handling cutlery, that goes from handle to tip) using a soft dry cloth. Once a year, use a bleach solution on the inside of silver coffeepots, rinsing and drying after the solution bubbles up.

If the silver has become slightly tarnished, you can immerse the item in silver dip while wearing plastic, rather than rubber, gloves. Use cotton buds to access recesses in elaborate pieces. Note: Do not use this dip on silver-plated items, or if you do, dip very quickly and infrequently to avoid eroding the plate. Then rinse thoroughly in cold running water, dry with a soft cloth, and leave in an airing cupboard to dry any recesses.

If the silver has become heavily tarnished, use a long-term polish, which comes in two forms. If a liquid, apply it with a cloth and brush it off with a "plate brush" when it has dried. If a paste, apply it with a moist sponge and then wash off with cold, running water. Repeat this process until no more black tarnish comes off on the cloth. However, you should avoid rubbing over hallmarks too much, as they can be erased. Then polish the silver with an impregnated cloth.

Silver that has been waxed or lacquered should of course not be polished. If salt corrosion has blemished the silver, immerse the article in a solution of one tablespoon of salt to a pint of water for five minutes; then wash in hot soapy water and polish with long-term silver polish or foaming silver polish. If no improvement after this treatment, take the item to a jeweler for repair.

Once you have the silver well cleaned and polished, it is easy to maintain the shine and preserve the silver items by dipping them from time to time in "Superonic-N" or a similar product, then drying and polishing them.

Silver is best stored in a couple of layers of acid-free tissue paper (available from artist-supply and other shops at reasonable cost) so as to shield it from the air, without being airtight. Most other materials, including the time-honored felt or baize, contain acids and sulfur, which eat into the silver. They can also smell horribly when damp and thus impregnate the silver. Keep the silver in a dry, well-ventilated, safe area, using silicon gel sachets to help combat damp. Cutlery should be wrapped individually and placed side by side, rather than piled up. Silver (as with all other) jewelry should be stored according to type of material, so as to prevent scratching or other interactions.

If you are buying silver or gold, it helps to know the difference between the various types available. For gold, the higher the carat, the higher the gold content of the metal. Twenty-two to twenty-four carat gold is the highest quality, working well for wedding rings, but otherwise being too soft for most uses.

Gold leaf is a very thin sheet of gold placed over some other material, such as silver gilt, which is silver with a thin layer of gold over it.

Parcel gilt is silver with a thin layer of gold over some of it.

Britannia silver is pure silver alloyed with 4% copper.

Sterling silver is pure silver alloyed with 7% copper.

Sheffield plate is copper with a thin silver cover.

Electric plate is similar, but with less silver.

German silver and Britannia Metal contain no silver at all.

Sterling silver usually has a hallmark stamped on it, giving information about its authenticity. These small square shapes usually follow a sequence denoting a) the sponsor's mark, b) sterling silver mark, c) the assay office and d) a letter in a certain script indicating the date the article was made.

Cigars

Quality cigars are still somewhat of a luxury item, and something that one should know how to deal with properly for the occasion a guest wishes to indulge. Often, high-end hotels will have cigar rooms and humidor banks for their guests.

In England, we have no restrictions on Cuban cigars and so have no problem enjoying their superior smoke. Dominican cigars are available in the United States, however, and are the next best in quality. Many Cubans these days, it seems, however, are not Cuban at all, and can result in a rough smoke. Only those matured (up to fifteen years), are recommended. They become milder with age, and are only put on the market after five years. Authentic Havanas must have the leaf and seal, "Vulta Abajo," on the box. Cigars in good condition will feel firm to the touch while yielding to slight pressure.

There are various brands, with differing strengths, as follows:

- Rafael Gonzalez - very mild
- Canary Island - mild
- Romeo - mild
- Upman - medium mild
- Punto/Punch - medium mild
- Rey del Mundo - medium mild

- Dunhill - medium
- Partagas - medium strong
- Ramon Allongs - medium strong
- Monte Cristo - strong
- Hoyo de Monterrey - spicy
- Bolivar - strong
- Cohiba - very strong, rich (and expensive)

The darkness of the cigar is also a rough guide to its strength and spiciness. Ascuro (the term for the darkest) is not generally available. The strongest and darkest available is Maduro. Colorado is medium in color and strength. Claro is the lightest. Green cigars have an immature leaf and are rather tasteless.

It is better to buy cigars in bundles for better retention of flavor; the individual tin- or cellophane-wrapped cigars available are really only bought for traveling.

The different sizes of cigar include length and diameter, which is measured in ring gauges. They range from the Margarita, a four-inch, 26-gauge cigar for the ladies, to the giant Havana, at nine and a quarter inches and 47-gauge (some shorter cigars can be as thick as 54-gauge).

So much for the Cubans. The size of cigars available in the United States is indicated by their name as follows, although these sizes have not been standardized and so vary between manufacturers.

- Petit Corona, 5-inches long, 42 ring gauge
- Robusto, 5-inches long, 50 ring gauge
- Corona, 5.5-inches long, 42 ring gauge
- Corona Gorda, 5.5-inches long 46 ring gauge
- Lonsdale, 6.5-inches long 42 ring gauge
- Pantalela, 7-inches long, 38 ring gauge
- Churchill, 7-inches long, 47 ring gauge
- Double Corona, 7.6-inches long 49 ring gauge

The proper storage of cigars is an important duty for a butler, who should have humidors (cedar-lined wooden humidifier boxes) available that keep the relative humidity and temperature at 70 degrees. The sponges in these boxes should be kept moistened with purified water once every one-to-two months, so that the cigars neither dry out nor gain mould spots. If green or white spots do appear, reduce the amount of water in the sponges and brush the spots off to avoid a bitter smoke.

When stored in a dry environment, cigars will dry and crack. If stored in an overly moist environment, the tobacco releases tobacco mites, which occur naturally in the tobacco and create pin-sized holes in the cigar. Both conditions render the cigar unsmokable, so do not offer such to guests. When stored correctly as above, cigars will last indefinitely. If no humidors are available, then keep the cigars wrapped in cedros (a thin cedar lining) to sweeten and moisten the leaf. Or at the very least, use a plastic bag with a moist towel inside, making sure not to allow the cigar and towel to touch.

Offering and Lighting a Cigar

Yes, there is as much ritual and technique to this as the peace-pipe ceremony, and about as much enjoyment, too. The first requirement is that you know the cigar types and strengths being offered. Women have smoked pipes and cigars decades and centuries before women's lib, so do not feel timid about offering ladies a cigar. You might want to discourage the use of holders, as they deny the taste of the leaf on the lips.

Offer the person the humidor to select the desired cigar—a process the guest will most likely savor as he turns the cigars, feeling and smelling them before deciding. If not already present on the table, offer a cigar cutter and butane lighter (or a cedros or other spill the guest can light with a match and then use to light the cigar). Only if no other resource is available (hard to imagine, as a butane lighter should be one of a butler's standard possessions), should one use a match to light a cigar, and only once the initial flare has subsided and the chemicals, such as sulphur, have dissipated.

Off with his Head

The goal in cutting a cigar is to create an ample opening through which to smoke, without damaging the cigar's construction. The best type of cutter for the job is the guillotine cutter.

When using a *single-bladed guillotine*, the blade should be placed gently against the edge of the cigar, and then the blade moved through the cigar swiftly, otherwise the cigar will be pinched, damaging and often ruining the wrapper. Ensure the compartment sheathing the blade is kept free of loose tobacco to avoid jamming and compromising its effectiveness.

Double-bladed guillotines are the better option, as the cigar is cut simultaneously on both sides, giving a smooth, clean cut without the risk of pinching the cigar. Again, the best method is to bring the blades into contact gently with both sides of the cigar, and then cut with a swift motion.

On most cigars, cut about one-sixteenth of an inch from the cigar's head (end). Or look for the cigar's shoulder—where the cap of the cigar straightens out—and cut there.

Lighting the Cigar

The cigar should be rolled just above the yellow portion of the flame until there is a glowing ring around its circumference. Only then should the smoker inhale with a long, slow, even draw. If the cigar starts to burn down one side, put it down with the burning side underneath, until the end starts to burn evenly. Properly smoked, the end of the cigar will be ash, not a red-burning ember. Only if an inexperienced guest seems to be struggling might one quietly offer advice on how to enjoy the smoke—following the above procedures and taking long, slow draws, not puffing on the cigar furiously for fear it may go out.

Once the cigar has warmed enough to melt the glue, remove the brand name label if preferred. As a note, the paper rings on cigars were left on while smoking only to prevent the staining of the white gloves that smokers used to wear in days gone by.

If the cigar goes out, re-ignite and blow out before inhaling so as to avoid a charcoal flavor. If the cigar is to be finished later (that day), guillotine the head and blow any remaining smoke through the cigar, again to avoid the charcoal flavor that comes with re-lighting an extinguished cigar.

Flowers

You may have gardeners to look after the garden, and florists to bring arrangements every week, but you may also be called upon to re-arrange an existing arrangement, create some bouquets or vases from the flowers in the garden, or order appropriate arrangements for different rooms. In this case, you really should have some understanding of the basics of flower arranging. It would also help to know how to care for cut flowers, so that the arrangements in the house look fresher longer.

Arrangements are not restricted to flowers in a crystal vase. They can include flowers, wood, stones, fruit, vegetables, water, figurines, pottery, and so on.

Arrangements should fit the character of the table, room, furniture, or a meal being presented, in terms of texture, size, color, theme and purpose. Formal dinners, for instance, would probably have precious or fine flowers to match the china, silver and crystal in use. For the dining table, arrangements should be positioned in such a way, and be of such a size to allow guests to see each other easily without having to peer over or through the flowers.

There is a certain sequence to putting together an arrangement. The first step is to decide on the character of the piece, whether it is to be simple, such as a single rose in a small vase, or a resplendent and regal display. The size should be decided next, as well as the coloring and the outline (i.e., all around or to one side of the base). Availability of flowers and bases or containers may offer some constraints that you have to work within. Having an idea in mind, you can then start the arrangement.

Unless you're using a vase with a neck that holds the flowers in place, you will need to use either a green foam base that the flowers can be stuck into, or construct such a base out of wire meshing that is twice the height and width of the container (and which you crumple into the container so that some strands protrude slightly over the rim).

Establish the desired outline, using tall, fine pointed material on the outside or center of the design. Then place the dominant flowers with larger, heavier, textured blooms or dominant colors to provide visual weight and create the focal point of interest. Fillers are then placed, such as spray material or green or gray leaves, to bind the whole arrangement together visually.

Step back and see if the tall, outline flowers lead the eye down to the dominant pieces at the base of the main stems where they converge. Is the arrangement well balanced? This can be corrected by either drawing a line down the middle, with the materials on both sides being symmetrical; or by giving both sides visual weight with a long, light colored item on one side, balanced by a shorter, darker item on the other side.

Is the scale of the arrangement correct in relation to the table or the rest of the room; are the flowers scaled to the vase or base, and to each other? Does the piece have rhythm, a feeling of motion obtained by curving lines, graduating sizes, shapes and colors, especially those leading to or from the center? Do the colors complement each other, and are textures used to advantage? Have the lighter or brighter colors been used at the focal point of interest? Warm colors (red, yellow, orange) give gay, striking effects. Blues-pinks, mauves, blue, purple and gray give soothing and delicate effects.

This is a thumbnail sketch on putting together pleasing arrangements. You will improve the more you work on them and study the arrangements of others in magazines or real life. There will always be arrangements by the professionals that break all the tenets I have given and which look absolutely stunning.

If picking your own flowers, it is best done before they are fully mature. Pick them during the night or early morning, placing them in a container with water in it. When back in the house, strip off the lower leaves, re-cut the stem ends while still under water and leave them in deep water in a dark room until you are ready to arrange them.

If they are woody-stemmed, split the stem ends before putting them in water. Leaves and sprays of greenery (though not hairy leaves) should be submerged in water for several hours. If a flower bleeds much sap, hold the stem to a flame to cauterize it.

When picking wild flowers, place them in plastic or wet newspaper for transport home. If you receive hard-stemmed flowers by mail or courier, cut their stems and place them in warm water. Even cut roses, out of water and thoroughly wilted, can be revived by being submerged in warm water for one or more hours. In working with flowers, it is best to lay them on a damp cloth while working, and handle them as little as possible.

The best way to keep flowers once they are on display, is to top them up with warm water to which you have added two teaspoons of sugar per pint. A charcoal tablet placed in the container will prevent rotting of the stems.

The Bar and Cellar

The bar is obviously the butler's domain, and has to be kept fully stocked with every conceivable drink to cater for the tastes of guests. At least the butler no longer has to brew the beer for the staff (the most plentiful, cheapest and pure drink available in earlier centuries)! *Appendix 5E* gives a sample list of what to stock in the bar, as well as quantities required for a party of a hundred guests. Ice would have to be brought in for such a large party, but for average demand, an ice machine would suffice, preferably one that allowed the ice at the bottom to melt and drain away, and which was fed purified water.

Various books exist that detail the different types of glasses used for different types of alcoholic drinks, as well as the composition of various cocktails; these books are best purchased and kept in the bar for reference purposes.

When someone wants a refill or another of the same at the bar, provide it in a clean glass. Transport the drink on a salver and present it to the right (or left, if left-handed) of the person.

As for the wine cellar, it needs to be kept at a constant temperature of around 13° centigrade or 55° Fahrenheit, away from sunlight and motion or vibrations in order for the wine to stay well and mature. Temperatures can be as low as 45°F or as high as 70°F, but the important factor is that the temperature remains constant. I have drunk a superb thirty-five year old Lafitte Rothschild that was properly kept, and also a three-year old Pinot Noir that had been subjected to much temperature change and was only good for the sink. Bottles are laid on their sides so the corks stay moist, thereby maintaining their shape and keeping out the air.

As the butler, it is often up to you to choose or suggest the wines that will best match the food being presented at a meal. The old working maxims such as fish taking white wines and meat requiring red wines are too simplistic. It is best to know the various characteristics any wine has, and to practice combining these tastes with a meal in the same way that one plans any other part of the menu to form a pleasing whole.

For instance, it is better to match the degree of sweetness of the wine to the sweetness of the food. The same applies to the acidity of the food and wine. Flavor is another consideration: a strong, full-tasting wine is best matched with a tangy or rich tasting food, while a delicate wine works best with a mildly-flavored food. Mismatching on any of these points will result in the taste of either the food or the wine being lost.

Wine can be used, on the other hand, to offset some aspect of the food. A fatty dish can appear less so when served with a tangy, acidic wine, while a fizzy wine will work well in lightening a dish that is essentially heavy (such as a pudding). Sweet wines contrast well with salty or smoked foods.

Many books exist that describe the different types of wines available, and often the labels on the bottles give enough information for you to judge for yourself. In the end, though, you need to be able to confirm whether a wine is right for the meal or course before it is served.

Acidity is important, because too much will make the drinker pucker, and too little will make a flat wine that has no pizzazz. Sweet wines sometimes have this problem, so look for ones with higher acidic ratings.

Tannin in full-bodied red wines that are being drunk before they have properly matured also creates a puckering effect and leaves a furry feeling in the mouth. It is best to drink reds at the times indicated by various guides, but one can deliberately use a wine that is high in tannin to counteract fatty foods.

The amount of alcohol in wine (varies from 7% to 15%) will give a wine a heavy or light character, called its "body." Heavy wine is matched with strongly flavored foods and lighter, lower alcohol wines are preferred with delicately flavored foods.

Wines also have flavors of their own, often of different types of fruit. Young wines tend to be the fruitiest, and are best drunk alone. If combined with lightly flavored foods, they may well overpower them.

Drinks before meals, called aperitifs, are best when dry, sparkling, or tangy (champagnes, wines, or fortified wines) because they stimulate the appetite. Avoid cocktails which, being full of alcohol, will prevent proper appreciation of lighter wines during the meal.

If serving more than one wine at a meal, it is best to move from lighter, younger, drier or white wines to heavier, older, sweeter or red ones.

To best appreciate the flavors of each wine, full-bodied reds should be served at room temperature, newer reds slightly cooler; Beaujolais, roses and dry whites should be served cool; sweet whites slightly chilled; sparkling wines and champagnes well chilled. Of course, if the boss wants the red served chilled, then that's obviously the best way to serve it in that house. Red wines benefit from being exposed to the air before being served (for several hours or even a whole day if young, an hour or less if more mature) as oxygen helps develop the bouquet and taste. For this reason, decanting wines and serving them from decanters can be a smart custom. The best way to quickly cool a bottle is to place it in iced water for twenty minutes or more, and turn it upside down if not fully submerged.

There are various bottle openers on the market that are easy enough to master. The only bottles that require care in uncorking are old ones with corks that have decomposed, and champagne bottles. Cork extractors can be used to fish out cork in the bottle if a quick flick of the bottle fails to dislodge the cork together with a small amount of wine. The best opener for old corks that won't budge but just crumble used to be the pneumatic type; a needle is inserted through the cork and air pumped into the bottle that forces the cork up and out. Reports exist, however, that the pump can also explode the bottle, so a better approach is to use a regular cork screw and aim the tip at an angle against the inside of the bottle's neck.

For champagne, the trick is not to shake the bottle before or while opening; to hold the bottle at a slight angle; and to place a cloth over the cork to hold it still while slowly turning the bottle. Done properly, there will only be a slight "sigh" as the cork is released, and no wastage of champagne.

Some wines may need to be decanted, especially if they are old and sediment has accumulated, or if the cork falls into the bottle on opening and cannot otherwise be extracted. In this case, you "decant" using a candle or other light source to illuminate the contents of the bottle as you gingerly pour the wine through muslin or a coffee filter into a decanter, and stop before any of the sediment migrates into the neck of the bottle. It is wise if, in removing bottles from the cellar, they are kept horizontal and moved delicately, so that the sediment is not stirred. The best tool for this job is a wine basket that holds the bottle steady at an angle close to 45°. In this way, the sediment is encouraged to settle and remain at the bottom.

Having opened a bottle of wine, it is the unhappy duty of the butler to sample it and confirm it is still in good condition. If the wine itself smells of cork, then toss it. If it tastes overly acidic or unpleasant, toss it. If it is fizzing (secondary fermentation), toss it. If it is opaque, toss it. Otherwise, savor the taste!

Incidentally, after looking at the color and clarity of the wine and swirling it around in the glass to release its bouquet, the best way to determine the quality of the wine is to inhale the bouquet through mouth and nose at the same time; and then taking a sip, move it around in the mouth while identifying its taste and strength. Look for strength of tannin (in red wines), acidity, sweetness, body, how long the taste lingers in the mouth and with what levels of complexity (different flavors that manifest), and the overall balance of the taste. It should then be possible to sensibly match wines to menu.

In pouring the wine, half fill the glasses so the diners can savor the bouquet. You may want to show them the label and state the wine they are drinking, if doing so does not interrupt their conversations.

A way to prevent drips after pouring, is to bring the bottle to a horizontal position and give it a quick twist while raising the neck above the horizontal.

As a side note about purchasing crystal wine decanters: to ensure a decanter is of good quality, check that the stopper is airtight and has the same number etched on it as on the decanter itself.

Driving and Cars

Sometimes the butler is called upon to drive or care for dream cars, whether Bentleys and Rolls Royces or Ferraris and Lamborghini's. Maybe much chauffeuring is required, or perhaps just the occasional trip. Maybe taking the cars to the garage for routine maintenance is as close as you'll get to testing the car's strengths. The temptation is to go cruising, to pop wheelies and do zero to sixty in three seconds. If you want to keep your job, then a better operating basis would be to treat that car as you would your own. Not as an object of extreme veneration, but an object to be driven responsibly. An advanced driving course, including skid control, as well as a basic book on how cars work, will do wonders to improve competence behind the wheel. Then when you do inevitably put the car through its paces, you'll do it sensibly.

The essence of good chauffeuring is a smooth and safe ride. That means gradual application of accelerator and brake, and slow, long cornering. Perhaps they still do the full-wine-glass test in London, in which drivers only pass when none of the wine spills while driving through the city. If you can do this, you'll have arrived as a chauffeur.

Looking after cars usually means supervising the chauffeurs, or checking for obvious points oneself (such as tire pressure, fluid levels etc.); making sure the cars are kept cleaned, and are serviced on schedule or when needed. The key really is regular visual inspection of the cars, and maintaining easily consulted records.

Chauffeuring often requires picking up unknown guests and visitors from an airport, railway station or other public place. If you have time, have a picture e-mailed or faxed to you by the person's secretary so you can recognize them. Ask for a description of their luggage and the number of any cell phone they may be carrying. If you cannot obtain a picture, then you may resort to holding up a neatly printed card showing the person's name, or some other key word they will recognize if security is an issue. Have a porter to hand if luggage is more than you can comfortably manage. As soon as you have made contact, arrange for the luggage to be secured and escort the person, plus luggage, to the vehicle, which should be at the closest possible location to the meeting point. In some heavily trafficked locations, parking an unattended vehicle is not permitted. This would be the time to have an assistant standing in the wings with the vehicle, and call him or her in as soon as you make contact with the person being picked up. Even better is escorting the guest to the vehicle immediately, while another employee secures the luggage and returns in a second vehicle. The object of the exercise, of course, is a positive, speedy and secure pick-up and delivery to the intended destination.

Butler's Etiquette

For butlers, there are several time-honored procedures that still have their place in today's world.

Answering the Door

The butler customarily answers the door and phone, and there are certain points to keep in mind when doing so.

In answering the door, it is advisable to check your appearance in the mirror first. For security purposes, it is also better to verify who the caller is before opening the door. If the person is expected, then they are let in.

If the person is not expected, but is a friend or family and usually welcome to the house, then they are also let in.

If they are unexpected trades people, then you might keep them outside, as covered earlier, while confirming with their office that a delivery person fitting the description of the person outside, should be at your house at that time. If the office cannot confirm this, then call the police while keeping the person outside and under surveillance. This applies equally well to utility or phone companies demanding access for emergency work. At times like this, it is a good idea to have a mobile phone, in case wires are cut.

If the policy of the house is that uninvited guests are not allowed in, then your task becomes trickier, especially if family or friends are outside. You could say something along the lines of, "Just a moment, Sir/Madam, let me see if Mr./s.____ is in." If the employer *does* want to see the visitor, you only have a guest possibly miffed at being left outside while you checked.

If the employer does *not* wish to see that person, you have to persuade the visitor to leave without upsetting him or her. Try something like, "I am afraid Mr./s.____ is not available, but I will certainly tell him you called; may I relay a message to him, Sir/Madam?" If the person still insists, you would have to be firm, perhaps saying, "The rules of the house require an appointment, otherwise I am unable to allow anyone in—I am very sorry indeed. Might I suggest that an appointment be made?"

Is this just paranoia on the butler's or employer's part? It may be, but there is a good case for the rich or famous to be alert to the ploys of the criminal or fanatical elements in society—as they sometimes are targets. A person in the public eye or very busy at work also tires of intrusions and so resorts to strict policies on people dropping in, to protect his or her privacy. Someone living in New York City can appreciate these precautions. Someone living in San Luis Obispo, where the crime rate is low, might not go to such lengths.

Anyway, depending upon the rules of the house, let us assume that the visitor is welcome in the house. In this case, you open the door with a smile that says "Welcome" and usher them into the house. Ask if they have any baggage, and bring it in as soon as possible. If they came by public transportation, such as a taxicab, signal the cabby to wait, while noting the fleet and cab number. He will wait because he knows there's a tip at the end, and it allows you to check the trunk and the cab for any forgotten luggage. If he drives away, you can still contact the cab company for the return of any missing item.

If the guest is staying overnight, take him/her straight to their room, letting them know when the host will be free, when dinner will be served, and the dress code. Ask for any desired refreshments and bring it up straight away. Before leaving, go over the dinner menu for any preferences and ensure everything is to their satisfaction in the room.

If visitors are not staying overnight, ask to take their coats, and whether they would like to freshen up before seeing your employer.

Show them the rest room if required, and then the sitting room. Tell them when the host will be available, and ask if they would like a drink. If the employer is ready to see the visitors straight away, escort them to the employer, knock on the door, enter and announce the guests' arrival, standing by the door in anticipation of some refreshment being offered by the host.

These actions differ little from any considerate welcome for a visitor, but they include the attention to detail that make for a smooth stay.

Answering the Telephone

Answering the phone is simpler, though it follows much the same lines. Depending upon your employer's position, he may also want caution used for security purposes. A neutral, "Hello, who is speaking, please?" answer to the phone, repeated politely if required, allows you to know who is calling; it does not tip off a would-be criminal or a reporter about the owner of an unlisted number.

In a more open household, a cheery and forthright, "Good morning, this is the _____ residence, Jeeves the butler speaking, may I help you?" can be followed up with, "Let me see if ____ is available." And if not, "May I take a message? I will certainly tell him you called." Record the caller's phone number and any message. Never give out information on your employer's or staff's whereabouts, or any phone numbers or addresses over the phone, unless you are certain that the person at the other end is who he says he is, and your employer or staff member would want him/her to know.

As a courtesy, if you deal regularly with a person over the phone but never see him/her, an exchange of photographs would improve communications and rapport.

Daily Duties/Graces

There are some duties that are regular as clockwork when performed. In the morning, the house must be opened, daily papers rounded up, pets fed—the list can be quite varied, depending upon the needs of the employer.

The same goes for the end of the day. Curtains have to be drawn at dusk, lights turned on, and later turned off.

After dinner has been cleared away, the breakfast buffet has to be set up, as well as the morning (tea) trays, with the papers and flowers ordered as needed.

If not done in the morning, the employer may need a choice of two sets of clothes laid out for the following day.

Electrical appliances may need switching off, fires and cigarettes extinguished, any security alarm set.

There may be some guests staying up very late. It is best to offer to fetch anything else they might need before you retire, and having done so, ask that they properly extinguish any cigarettes in the clean ashtrays you have just provided. Ask that you be contacted should they wish to go outside, because the alarm has been set. On the other hand, if the employer is staying up late, the butler would stay with him, as long as there was an assistant who could take care of the morning duties.

Some butlers move with their employers between different houses, which requires a series of actions to close down or open up the houses. A checklist of likely actions is given in *Appendix 5F*.

The Greening of Butlers

Traditionally, butlers have been thrifty: they personally came from poorer families and, on the employer's estate, wished to properly utilize scarce resources and painstakingly homemade products. There is no reason this prudent attitude should not extend to the greater environment of which we are all a part. Butlers are in an unique position to steer a large household, and by influence, other households, into activities like reduction of waste, recycling, alternatives to heavy use of pesticides, energy conservation and so on.

This is something a butler would do behind the scenes and without bothering the employers beyond authorization for major changes or expenditures. Where employers are amenable, then the job becomes easier. Just the mention of recycling would send one particular employer into a tirade about "environmentalists" having all the attributes that the employer was herself dramatizing at that very moment. The butler found his efforts to be a responsible inhabitant and steward of planet earth constantly undermined. Chapter 4 provides some insight into the mindset of this type of person. Most employers, however, appreciate their home being "greened" as long as it is done gradually and without any drop in living standards.

The drive to be environmentally frugal should not be confused with enforcing low standards of living on the employer or staff. This is particularly true where a butler comes from poorer circumstances. Where the butler may have thought Greyhound, he must now think private jet. Where he thought Motel 6, he must now think George Cinque or The Four Seasons. "Only the best will do," and "Money is not an object," is the approach he should now take to managing the employer's household (unless the boss has stipulated Motel 6 and Greyhound as his preferred choices, of course). This expectation of the best is entirely consistent with environmental responsibility in most situations.

Some General Pointers Concerning Personal Etiquette and Professionalism

Always consult and use experts where you lack the know-how or skill.

As a butler in a stately home, carry items around the house on a small silver tray or platter, preferably with white gloves on, and walk at a sedate or stately pace. On the other hand, a fast-moving employer won't appreciate his right-hand man in the house moving with solemn dignity while executing his duties at a pace that would appeal to a turtle. Each house and employer will be different in its needs.

There are various rules concerning deportment and bearing that apply in any situation, however; such as one doesn't slouch, sit around smoking all day or carry on conversations as if one were negotiating at a fish market. But if one grasps the essence of a butler, one will have no trouble in moving around in the appropriate manner. Whatever "motion model" one decides upon, it will probably include varying degrees of dignity and decorum, smooth and well placed motions that efficiently achieve the results desired in the household without attracting undue attention.

A note of caution: one's attention needs to be on servicing one's family and guests and supervising staff, not on how one's own body is and should be moving, so the time to get all this sorted out is during training and then fine-tuning during the first day on the job.

Naturally, a butler is always impeccably dressed as suits the occasion, and in a low-key manner. Personal hygiene is a given, with hair and nails trimmed and clean, teeth brushed, body washed and neutral in smell—meaning no odors at one end of the scale, or strong after-shaves or perfumes at the other end of the scale. The purpose is to be there without attracting attention.

While one's behavior is expected to be highly professional when at work, there may be a temptation to let one's (well-groomed) hair down unduly while off duty. Nobody expects to see a butler walking stiffly through a shopping mall in full regalia, bowing to passers by and doffing his hat to the ladies as he does some window-shopping. Nobody expects to see him downing a pint at a local bar and taking the bar tender to task for failing to clean under his fingernails. But just as off-color is a butler who dons cut-off jeans and a dirty T-shirt, and walks around the grounds scratching his belly while ash falls from the ciggie butt hanging from the corner of his mouth. If a butler really feels compelled during his time off to do wheelies through town in the boss' car, irritating local law enforcement officials, or other actions designed to bring disrepute upon himself and by extension, the boss, then he should consider another career. If being yourself on your time off is a middle-of-the-road affair, then you will be fine.

With a clearer idea of ground zero for a butler and of his general duties, let's review how he would deal with one of the more important functions of his position: looking after guests. These are often close to the heart of the employer. He or she wants to welcome them into the home (and perhaps show off a little, too), and the butler is the point man for the job.

Chapter Six

Looking After Guests

This part of running a household deserves a special chapter of its own, as employers are usually most concerned with their guests' welfare. The rule is simple: treat guests as the most important people in the world. That attitude will see you through any difficulty.

A guest is anyone who has come to see your employer briefly, for a meal such as dinner (see Chapter 9) or who is staying for one or more nights.

For the casual visitor, the procedure is simple once you have assured yourself that they are who they say they are, and you have let them into the house. You will already have established with the employer what the general house rules are for such guests, what is off-limits and what they can be offered.

Take their coat and show them the rest room to freshen up. Then offer them refreshments, including food. Offer them anything they would like, and make suggestions if they don't know what to ask for. Show them to the room set aside for such guests, and make sure they know there are magazines and newspapers available there. If they have a long wait, provide them with television, even a video or the pool, according to the employer's rules.

Return briefly every now and then to ensure everything is to their satisfaction.

When your employer is ready to receive the visitor, show the person into the room, "Mr./s. _____, Sir," and stand by the door, waiting for any drinks or other requests.

Should the employer and guest meet before you can introduce them, ask the employer, at a moment where you will not interrupt any ongoing conversation, if you can fetch any drinks for him and/or his guests.

There is the question of bowing, a formality that has existed for centuries as a way of showing respect and recognition. It's a handy way for the butler to demonstrate that he recognizes the guest (or employer) and is at their service. It is not a servile action but a statement of intent, in a way. A neck bow often suffices, but one can bend at and to the waist—in the same way that a conductor often acknowledges his audience's applause—on more formal occasions, or when confronted with important personages. It is expected, certainly, when meeting with royalty.

Overnight Guests

Your employer will usually let you know in advance when overnight guests are expected. The first thing to do is find out from your employer how many guests are coming, their names, the rooms they are to stay in, their arrival and departure dates, and whether the Visitor's Book is to be presented. If the employer has any other instructions, such as menus, dinner parties, activities to be arranged, take notes during the briefing and action afterwards.

If at all possible, contact the guests, or their butlers, ahead of time to find out about their arrival and departure times, transport arrangements, and any requirements for transport to the house. If they are coming by car, you may need their car and license details for security purposes. Ask for special food requirements, favorite newspapers and magazines; any pet needs; any security requirements; and any communication needs (fax, modem, telephone).

List out anything needing attention from your employer or the guests. Contact your own staff or an agency and arrange for any back-up staff to provide enough valets and ladies' maids to service the guests. They may need instruction on their duties, if unfamiliar with them (see Chapter 7 on the valet), and can work under your supervision to start with. Wherever possible, provide a returning guest with the same maid or valet.

Obtain uniforms for all new staff and ensure there are spare dinner suits available in all sizes.

Use the Room Checklist (*Appendix 6*) to ensure the housekeeper has prepared the guest rooms. The information recently obtained from the guests, and your own Butler's Book, will provide useful information for the proper preparation of each guestroom.

Establish menus, ensure all supplies are ordered and arrive on time. Work out the schedule of events as well as alternative events should foul weather confound plans. Make any needed reservations at clubs or restaurants.

It might also be worthwhile to send each guest a checklist of items to bring, as well as information on the times they are expected to arrive and leave, directions for finding the house if needed, a schedule of events, and a list of the other guests invited. It would be considerate to assure them that their particular wants have been prepared for.

Unless the guests arrive in their own chauffeur-driven cars, have your staff gas, clean and service the guests' cars, and then have them garaged if space is available. If they arrive without cars, then have some hired for them if needed.

Have the guests' bags unpacked by the valets and ladies' maids.

Tips

The subject of tips can be awkward unless guests know what is expected. Tips were given as early as the Sixteenth Century in England. After two hundred years, the system had become so abused by staff expecting "vails" for the slightest action on their part (such as opening the door) that just going to dinner at a friend's house was liable to set a guest back by the equivalent of several hundred dollars at today's rates.

A society was even formed by the gentry to counter-attack, and although it had little direct impact, the Victorian era that followed put a damper on the excessive demands for tips. Maybe waiters, bellhops and skycaps are paid a low basic wage in the expectation that they will receive many tips, but this is not the case with butlers today. The butler's main concern is the comfort of the guest, which a concern on his part for remuneration does little to enhance. A low-key tradition of tipping discretely on departure has therefore evolved.

Tips do not have to be given by guests in a private house during their stay. It is really their temporary home, and they are told so if they try to tip. If guests would like to leave a tip, they place it in an envelope in their room when they leave, addressed to the butler (who shares it with the relevant staff) or they give it to him on leaving. Either way, it is a nice gesture and always accepted gracefully when it is offered.

For the person who tips ostentatiously, he is refused politely unless in so doing an upset begins to brew. Butlers, of course, would always like more money, but not at the expense of the equanimity of the guest or the discreet ambience that butlers like to create.

Visitors' Book

The employer may have a Visitors' Book. It is normally signed by the guest on the evening prior to departure, at the end of dinner, on the morning of their departure after breakfast, or just as they are on their way out. They can add any comments on their stay. The butler usually presents it with a: "At Mr. and Mrs. _____ request, would you care to sign the Visitors' Book?" The book can be viewed on a fine table in the hallway and is best bound in leather with vellum sheets and a top quality ballpoint beside it.

If a special event has brought the guests together, a separate page could be titled and dated. If any guests miss signing, pencil in their name and ask them to sign it next time they come to the house. Unless the guest is very important to the employer, guests for informal meals are not asked to sign the book.

In the event that your employer needs to travel as someone else's guest, you may be called upon to valet (or lady's maid), in which case the next chapter may be of interest.

Chapter Seven

Valet - The Gentleman's Gentleman

When Beau Brummel spoke of the gentleman's gentleman, he referred to the male servant who looked after the personal affairs of an employer. The valet usually took care of his master's clothing; helped with his personal appearance, including matters of hygiene and dressing; he sometimes even cooked and served the meals. The difference between a butler and a valet is that the valet principally looks after one male employer—traveling with him and seeing to all the organizing that traveling involves. The character Jeeves is really a valet for Wooster. As already mentioned, the modern term for the female equivalent is "personal assistant."

Valets have their origins in the middle ages, when they groomed the master's horses. By the Sixteenth Century, the idea of grooming the master himself had become de rigueur and the gentleman usher, responsible for the goings-on upstairs, came into being. After the English Civil War, ushers were no longer drawn from the ranks of the young gentry and were replaced by the sons of artisans and shopkeepers. So the valet (and lady's maid) emerged. Valets became too specialized a position as households were rationalized in the Nineteenth Century and so had their functions covered by the more versatile (and thus cheaper-to-hire) butler, and became a rarity. Where these men catered to wealthy bachelors, they found their duties expanded into factotums: men hired to do almost anything.

The valet has to have the same kind of personality as the butler, and, being that much closer to his employer, doubly discrete, as valets were warned:

"As the valet is much about his master's person, and has the opportunity of hearing his off-at-hand opinions on many subjects, he should endeavor to have as short a memory as possible, and, above all, keep his master's council." [3]

There are a few areas of expertise peculiar to a valet and valuable to any traveler that are worth detailing.

Packing a Suitcase

We used to have large trunks to travel to and from boarding school, as I thought it, so that we could throw clothes in and still have enough room for the illicit things that schoolboys seem to enjoy. It was not until I started to fly commercially that space became a premium, and I was obliged to master the finer art of folding clothes neatly.

But did you know it is possible to fold shirts and suits into suitcases, travel half way round the world, and unpack those same clothes without need for a single stroke of an iron to make them presentable? The secret lies principally in the use of acid-free tissue paper to pad shoulders, sleeves, and also place in the fold of clothing where it has to be folded to comply with the contours of the suitcase. You, of course, have to refrain from stuffing the suitcase so full that the whole family has to be brought in to stand on the lid while you attempt to ratchet the locks into place.

First of all, I would recommend using the large, hard, Samsonite-type suitcase with two separate compartments. If not lined, then line the suitcase with a layer of tissue paper. Then lay trousers (pants) in the bottom of the case, with the trouser legs protruding over the edge.

Do up the middle jacket button, fold the arms parallel with the jacket seams; stuff crumpled tissue paper into each shoulder. Place the jacket in the suitcase with the bottom sticking out of the suitcase. Fold the sleeves of each shirt to the back of the shirt, initially parallel with the shoulders, and then fold again down toward the bottom of the shirt, so that the sleeves lie parallel with the shirt seams. Then fold up the bottom of the shirt and sleeves just above the cuffs; fold once more so as to bring the cuffs to the back of the collar, and place in suitcase. Use tissue paper to separate different materials.

Once jacket and shirts have been placed in the suitcase, fold the trouser bottoms and bottom of the jackets back into the case, over the shirts. Close that compartment and pack everything else into the other compartment of the case.

For someone who is regularly on the go at a moment's notice, it is worth having a suitcase packed permanently with enough clothing for one or two days away. The items would have to be aired and allowed to hang free once a week.

On arrival, if there be any wrinkles, they can be erased with the use of a steamer. Another possibility is to turn the hot water on in the shower or bath so as to heavily steam up the bathroom, and then hang the clothes up for a maximum of two minutes.

If you are unpacking for another person, then leave embarrassing items, such as prophylactics and false teeth, in the sponge bag, while laying out the other items in the bathroom.

In packing, checklists are a must. I once hiked fourteen miles up a mountain in California; by midday, I was salivating at the prospect of the packed lunch I had in my rucksack. I finally reached the targeted lunch spot, an old cowboy's camp that had all sorts of curios to stimulate the imagination, including a pile of rusty (baked bean?) cans. Everything pointed toward lunch, so I found a log to sit on, opened my rucksack, and rummaged around. It seemed like I had poked around in every corner of the rucksack at least four times without encountering that lunch box. Alarm started to set in—where was my lunch? I up-ended the rucksack: snake bite kit, rainwear gear, extra sweater, gloves, water bottle...the list was long, but nowhere did it include the lunch pack. And then I remembered with startling clarity, it was still in the refrigerator at home. It takes a lot of calories to climb 7,000 feet from the desert floor to alpine meadows, and by the time I made it home, I had a federal-sized deficit. The one lesson I learnt from that experience was to use checklists in everything I do, not just at work.

Which illustrates the value of a checklist made up of the clothes you normally need in a suitcase for a couple of days away. Not just for use when packing in a hurry, but also for insurance purposes should the suitcase become lost in transit; as well as your return home, because you can be assured that everything you left with followed you back. This may seem like a chore, but the time spent compiling the list initially is made up the first time the case needs to be packed. The "Um, let's see, what else do we need now...(scratches head)," routine becomes a relic of past packings. In the event that something of value is missing, you can contact the hotel, airline, limousine service, etc. straight away and, if not located, submit a timely insurance claim if warranted.

A sample list of items to pack can be found in *Appendix 7A*, to which you can add or subtract items as fits your needs. There is one item on the list that may need clarification: the suggestion that you should take two matching sets of cufflinks. The reason is that the loss of one cuff link (not that unlikely) will still leave you with a workable set—even if you lose one from each pair!

Preparing for the Following Day

Whether staying at home or in a hotel, there are standard actions you can take to ensure the following morning goes smoothly.

Discover from your employer the next day's schedule as nearly as you can, starting with what time he would like to wake up and have his bath drawn. Arrange for the wake-up drink and paper to be delivered, and for the required breakfast to be delivered at the right time.

Lay out two choices of clothing for the next day. If your employer has a separate dressing room, this can be done after bringing up the morning-tea tray, or while the employer is taking his bath.

The most convenient way to lay out the clothes is as follows: place the suit jacket on the back of a chair (or use a dumb valet if available) with the trousers laid out over the chair seat with belts/braces attached. Place the shirt on top of the trousers, folded, with cufflinks and any collar studs already in place. Place the shoes to the side and front of the chair, with a shoehorn on top, and socks folded on top (in the royal fold, which is to say with the shin part folded down over the foot part). Place a choice of three ties and any pin, on a table in front of a mirror. Place undergarments on the chair seat, in front of the shirt.

Obviously, a lady may well have different items of clothing, and it might work better to let her make the choice of what to wear in the morning, unless she specifies her wishes beforehand.

Lastly, lay the breakfast table.

In the Morning

The following is the classic way of raising the boss from bed. There are variations, but in each case, the purpose is to make the experience as smooth and pleasant as possible.

While making the tea (or other drink) for the morning tray and ironing the creases out of the newspaper, find out the weather forecast by listening to the TV/radio or making a phone call (and eyeballing, too!). Evaluate the weather against the employer's intended activities for the day. Sunbathing, sailing, flying, golf, all require different conditions which it would be well for him or her to be appraised of first thing in the morning.

Why does one iron the newspaper? The real reason is that it prevents the ink from coming off on the fingers. Some newspapers now use ink that does not rub off, but for those others, an ironing of the front and back pages that are normally held, will provide a service to your employer, which they may only notice when you omit to perform it.

Take up the morning tray and newspaper, knock on the door twice, softly; if no answer is discernable, knock again twice but louder and let yourself in. If your boss tells you to go away, do so. If he has an important meeting he should not miss, telephone and remind him of that fact, and then take the tray up again. Put the tray down on a table and open the curtains. By this time your employer should be awake.

Let him or her know the weather for the day and place the tray on his or her lap (or if just a cup of tea, hand it to him and place the newspaper on the bed). Ask your employer when he would like the bath drawn, if breakfast will be at the usual time, and for any instructions for the day. Acknowledge whatever he says with a "Very good, Sir." And you can give a neck bow (slight nod of the neck). Then run the bath, ensuring the bathroom is properly stocked with towels, soap, bath mat, etc., and after the bath has run to the required depth, turn it off. Leave, picking up any dirty clothes as you go and taking them to the laundry or dry cleaners.

In taking up the morning tray, there is one circumstance that requires tactful handling, and that is the presence of a strange and unexpected bedfellow, in which case you should leave immediately you realize this to be the state of affairs. Return with another morning tray. Knock again as above, and if on entering some hanky-panky is in progress, leave the room, shutting the door with a slight bang (or coughing slightly before leaving), knock again and wait for word to enter. This is assuming that the boss needs to be up for some appointment. Otherwise, one could equally let him or her be and wait for a call when he or she is ready for breakfast. Place the tray down by the stranger, and if it is a lady in a state of dishabille, maintain eye contact until you reach her, and then place the tray on her lap while facing the same way as the visitor. Then, as you do not want the employer embarrassed by all the staff seeing his (or her) amour, you ask, "Breakfast in your room as usual, Sir/Ma'am?" even if breakfast is usually served downstairs. This gives the employer the option of keeping his or her rendezvous quiet.

Deliver the breakfast and leave. The idea is to be formal, not directly acknowledging the presence of the other person, and being minimally present. On leaving, you can retrieve the employer's clothes, but leave the visitor's.

You will have gently woken your employer and provided for his ease in washing and dressing. While he or she is rising, you can clean the shoes from the prior day, press the suit (if not being dry-cleaned) and attend to any instructions for the day. If the breakfast is a light one, you can prepare it, or if a heavier one, the chef would do so while you see to the stocking of the sideboard with condiments and the food when it is ready.

If your employer is to engage in some sport, ensure those clothes are prepared; or if going to the office, ensure his briefcase, money, coat, umbrella, and transport are ready. Or if he/she is traveling, ensure passport, tickets, visa etc. are ready.

If you will both be gone all day, then it would be well to also prepare any wear for the evening, such as a dinner suit.

Clothes

Whether you have a large wardrobe of your own, or an employer with an extensive wardrobe, proper organization is important. Here is a suggested format.

First of all, separate the winter and summer clothes. Then subdivide by business, casual, evening and sports wear. Subdivide again by type of clothes (i.e. jackets, trousers). Then categorize by color. An alternative is to group a jacket with two or three trousers and ties that match it, for ease of selection.

Ensure all the shirts and jackets face the same way. Then you can inspect all the clothes and any in need of cleaning or mending can be turned the other way. Keep a logbook of these as they are sent out for repair or cleaning. Mark them off when they are returned and you have verified that the needed work was completed satisfactorily.

It is a good idea, for insurance purposes, to inventory all the clothes, photographing any very costly articles.

Place lavender, potpourri or bay leaves to guard against moths, but without creating such a strong smell that the clothes then start to pick up an odor. When not in regular use, keep clothes in plastic bags and shake or brush them every couple of weeks to ensure no problem with bugs.

Wooden hangers are the best, and for the ladies, shaped and padded ones. Racks or shelves should be used for storing shoes.

If living in a hot climate, have perspiration pockets made for the jackets and clean the clothes more often. The wardrobe or closet would, of course, have to be kept clean, and an air-conditioner used to keep the room temperature and humidity low.

Special belt and tie racks exist, some of which are even motorized so that the press of a button allows the ties to be individually presented for consideration. Otherwise, ties can be rolled around four fingers, starting at the narrow end of the tie, and stored in drawers.

Care of Clothes after They Have Been Worn

Once the wardrobe has been organized, then the major part of your work becomes caring for the clothing after it has been worn. To this end, here are some tips, some of which may seem obvious, but they bear detailing.

First of all, keep cleaning to a minimum. When a garment is beginning to show dirt or smell is the time to clean it, not when it has been worn briefly. Too much cleaning wears out clothing.

Trousers (pants)

Empty all pockets, brush thoroughly, check for and fix any missing buttons, broken zippers or general wear and tear. Check for and erase any stains with a dry-cleaning solution if possible, or send to the cleaners. Let the trousers air and hang overnight, and if needed, place in a trouser press or iron them.

Jackets/Coats

Empty all pockets, check for and fix any missing buttons or wear and tear (i.e., rip in vent/pockets, lining gone, collar riding high). Brush thoroughly, including pocket linings. Check for stains and remove, or send to cleaners. Check for odors and air longer, or send to cleaners. Use a steamer on minor wrinkles that hanging does not remove. Polish the brass buttons on a blazer (unless they are lacquered).

In the case of Barbours (quality rain gear of old), just wipe them down with a damp cloth. At the end of the season, wipe them off, liquefy a tin of dressing wax in boiling water and rub in all over the jacket, especially the crevices. A hair dryer can be used to reliquefy the wax if the coating needs to be smoothed out.

When brushing clothes (or suede shoes), use a firm flick of the wrist against the nap, and then with it for a smooth finish.

Shirts

Remove any collar stiffeners, cuff links, studs, etc., check for missing buttons and then send to the cleaners. Only use starch if your employer insists, and then only on cotton collars and cuffs, as starch stops the pores of the material from breathing and cracks collars. Collars and cuffs can be replaced with white ones if worn down, although some quality shirts come with spares that can be substituted. Cotton and silk shirts should be cleaned by hand with care.

Ties

Check for and clean stains, dry cleaning only if you have to, as silk dry-cleans poorly. Iron the backs of the ties lightly, using a damp cloth.

Shoes

Change shoes daily for variety and evenness of wear. Put trees in them as soon as they are removed (so the warm shoes are pliable enough to be pushed back into shape without cracking the leather), and let them air. If muddy, let the mud dry before cleaning.

If very muddy, place the shoes under cool, running water and clean them with a knife and nailbrush. Stuff with newspaper and let them dry for a day by an open window or at room temperature somewhere away from a heat source, so that the leather does not crack. After twelve hours, replace the newspaper. When dry, insert the shoe trees and apply cream to condition the leather. When the cream has dried, apply polish, including on the instep of the sole and tongue, and let the shoes stand a while before polishing with a brush using a light motion, and buffing with a chamois duster.

For that extra shine, combine (parade) gloss with water or spittle, and work into the toes and heels with a rag, using light, circular motions with your finger. Use a cotton bud to apply a metal polish to any metal attachments.

Occasionally apply saddle soap into a lather with a sponge in order to keep the leather supple. Also on occasion, apply waterproofing to outdoor shoes. It is advisable to alternate wax with cream polishes, as wax protects the leather while cream softens it. If lacking the correct color of polish, use neutral to at least create a shine.

Keep Wellington/rubber boots out of sunshine, which deteriorates them; hang waders upside down.

Sweaters

Fold sweater carefully in the same way jackets are folded into a suitcase. Clean only if needed, following instructions.

Belts

Roll or hang up like ties; use a transparent polish on occasion.

Hats

Brush hats with a bristle brush. Felt and velvet hats can be rejuvenated by brushing them while holding them in the steam of a kettle. Store them individually, rather than one inside the other.

Various (underwear, pajamas)

Launder daily. A clean, pressed handkerchief can be placed in the jacket pocket daily, although this is rarely done these days.

Cleaning

As a valet, one sometimes has to wash or iron clothes. Understanding the signs and symbols used on the labels of clothes is therefore imperative. Maybe you learned this the hard way as a student when your favorite sweater shrank three sizes after being put through a hot wash. You can't really afford to repeat that error with a $2,000 sweater made by monks in the Italian Alps, who only have enough wool to make one hundred such sweaters a year.

Apart from the self-explanatory temperature signs, you will see triangles, which refer to bleaching. A "Cl" within a triangle means that chlorine bleach may be used. A triangle on its own means that the article may be bleached. Obviously, a triangle with a cross through it means that bleach may not be used. A square with a circle in it means that the garment may be machine-washed. An iron shape with one, two or three dots within it means that piece of clothing may be ironed cool, medium or hot.

Know before you iron!

As for ironing, the good news is that the less one does, the better it is for clothing. Often, creases fall out of heavier garments, such as suits, during hanging. If not, a steamer can be used, or a dampened brush stroked first against and then with the nap will smooth out wrinkles.

General tips include using a dampened, uncreased and lint-free cloth between the iron and garment, to avoid any shininess (or use a steam iron if you have to, but it does create a slight sheen). Iron in the direction of the nap of the cloth, follow the contours of the garments and always move toward the cuffs. Iron linings first, and avoid ironing against the outer garment in such a way as to leave an outline there of the lining. Always check the base of the iron to ensure it is clean.

If the original crease is hard to locate in trousers or pants, simply line up the seams on both legs and then iron each leg, starting with the front seams.

There are certain tools that make the job of looking after clothes easier, and these are listed in *Appendix 7B*.

Purchasing Clothes

Likewise, a sample format is provided in *Appendix 7C*, which can be used to fill in the measurements needed for the purchase of clothes for your employer and family members. This list obviously needs to be updated quite regularly, as waistlines and such forth tend to come and go like tides at the beach, and children constantly sprout in all directions.

As you may well be called upon to shop with or on behalf of your employer, or a friend or family member may need to know a measurement so they can purchase something for another family member, this list can prove most useful.

In the event that you are doing the purchasing on your own, obtain the manager's agreement that the item being purchased will be replaced, altered or refunded in the event that the recipient requires it.

If shopping with your boss or a family member, take account cards, credit cards, check book and cash. It is a good idea, if you are escorting guests through shops, to discover from your employer what he will cover and what the guest will have to pay for himself or herself. Also take a "Past Gifts" List, which shows who gave what to whom for as far back as records go. If asked for your opinion of an item, be tactfully truthful. And if in a large store or mall, fix a rendezvous point in the event of separation—or better still, supply all parties with a walkie-talkie or trade cell phone numbers.

The valet is a close cousin to the personal assistant, which makes the next chapter an appropriate place to describe this often high-paced profession.

Chapter Eight

The Personal Assistant

Just as one might trace the development of the butler from the cellars to the supervising of the male members of the house and later the whole house as the butler administrator, it is possible to see the development of the personal man servant into the valet, and then combining with the personal secretary into the personal assistant. This is, in fact, the title given to the female valet today, so the term can be a bit confusing. Whatever the title, the focus is on personal service and the administrative supporting of the employer, in contrast to the butler administrator or household manager who focus on the managing of the home and its occupants in general.

The personal assistant is particularly valuable for a busy employer, who may already have a staff to run his house, but who needs someone to run his personal affairs, such as social diary, travel arrangements, personal memberships, financial dealings and records. At the same time, the personal assistant can double up as a more intimate valet and perhaps a sounding board. These are functions a butler would find hard to cover if he's also running a household, and which a personal secretary could not perform, being neither exposed to nor trained in the household aspect of the duties.

It therefore is its own niche, usually very rewarding—not only in terms of remuneration, but also in terms of rapport with the employer and satisfaction of being able to service him or her so thoroughly.

The character required for the job is no different than the valet or butler; obviously the employer and personal assistant have to have a liking for each other, in addition to respect: they will probably see more of each other than their closest friends.

Whereas the personal assistant should be familiar with all the duties of the butler, especially the valet duties and the keeping of the Butler's Book, there is one additional area of skill, which a butler may also practice but rarely does—arranging travel for the employer and keeping him company.

The butler is more fixed at one or a few locations, looking after the running of households, while the personal assistant is in the business of looking after just one individual's needs twenty-four hours a day. As most affluent individuals are highly mobile, the personal assistant's life can be quite vigorous, as well as exciting.

Your employer may well have his own jet and various villas and mansions around the world, which makes travel arrangements very easy. Many, however, will want to use commercial airlines and hotels for their travel. In this case, you need to know his or her preferences in travel and hotels - special seats, rooms, food, etc.

You need to develop close ties with travel agents and the concierges at hotels around the world, and possibly with local dignitaries in areas often visited. Your Butler's Book would be heavily loaded with information about those areas and is best kept in a portable electronic format for easy access.

You should be familiar with all the electronic, wireless gadgetry that can make an instant office away from home. The ability to speak foreign languages may be highly desirable, so if you lack any, maybe a foreign language course would be a good idea—or at least an electronic talking translator for that language.

International travel can be quite exhausting, so the personal assistant would do well to predict and organize for every eventuality, while maintaining a low-key presence. The question of airplane seating can be tricky. Do you sit with the employer or alone? Normally the employer flies first class and you would fly economy, for financial and status reasons. Where the employer is a loner, this would be an obvious choice and you would let the employer know which seat you were in. Also alert the stewardess in first class that you are a traveling companion, should anything be required. In the case of two employers traveling, such as husband and wife, this is usually the seating plan.

However, the employer may want or offer that you sit with him or her for companionship, or because they need to work over some business matters with you. The key to being low-key and not grating on nerves in this kind of situation, is to "speak when spoken to," so to speak. In other words, speak freely when the employer talks to you, and possibly originate on occasion yourself. But do not offer or feel compelled to offer non-stop chatter. Observe all the time the mood, actions and intent of the employer, and act accordingly.

One small point: it might be advisable to refrain from referring to the employer by "Sir" or "Ma'am" in enclosed public areas, as it might not create a relaxed atmosphere.

While traveling or sojourning, you will have stewardesses and room service and maids providing service to the employer, and these should not be interrupted. The personal assistant has a supervisory and supplementary role; requesting and ensuring that the service provided is specifically what the employer wants; and filling in the missing service that those personnel do not cover, but which your employer expects.

For instance, you might ask for a morning-tea tray at the hotel, and when it is delivered, take it at the door and carry through with the usual morning routine. Or you might double-check with the stewardess that the special food ordered is actually on the plane before take-off.

If the employer were living alone, then the personal assistant would most probably also cover the butler functions and be a busy man or woman indeed. The personal assistant is in an ideal position to also act as a bodyguard and would be well advised to obtain training as one. As well as being more economical and convenient for the employer, it would probably be a good deal less tiresome for the employer to have a bodyguard who was gainfully employed. The alternative being a muscle-bound gorilla hovering around constantly with nothing to do except wait for the worst to happen, a constant reminder that it might well.

If acting as bodyguard while traveling, the task becomes much trickier to accomplish. The carrying of weapons on flights and into foreign countries is restricted, while the opportunities for exposure to hostile environments increases, so the best defense is low-profile traveling and defensive behavior, as well as constant alertness to the environment. There are obviously still many steps that can be taken for the safety of the employer, the main ones being the observation of local customs and working together with the local authorities in the case of a higher profile visit.

Meanwhile, back at home, let's take a look at one of the key duties of the butler: the orchestration of fine eating experiences.

Chapter Nine

The Orchestration of Fine Eating Experiences

Traditionally, a butler is in his element at formal dinners. By the choice of drinks, decor, table settings, silver, crystal, and even entertainment, the butler seeks to create an elegant and refined ambiance that complements the food presented and provides the makings of a highly pleasing evening for all the diners. During the meal, the butler adds an almost invisible service that foresees and satisfies each individual need just before it arises; that cares for and comforts each guest in a low-key manner.

A butler is like a true artist on stage who so knows his instrument and the piece being played, that he communicates the message directly, without the distraction of misplayed or mistimed notes, to an enthralled audience.

Whether providing a wake-up tea in the morning or a full banquet, the butler concentrates on the quality of the presentation for the enjoyment of his guest or employer.

There are various types of service, and it is perhaps helpful to differentiate them:

Silver Service—Employed at better restaurants and hotel dining rooms, guests are served from a tray by a waiter using a spoon and fork. The food is served and dishes are cleared from the left.

Banquet Service—Swift, smooth, silver service for many guests.

Ballet of Service/Synchronized Service—Serving and clearing by multiple butlers/footmen or waiters, each serving one or two guests in perfect synchronization.

Buffet Service—Guests help themselves from a selection of hot and cold foods at a buffet table. The chef is sometimes present to carve roasts and assist guests with hot dishes. Waiters may also be in attendance.

Plate Service—Most common in restaurants, where the entire course is put on the plate by a chef and served by a waiter.

Butler Service—Employed in homes staffed by butlers. Guests help themselves from a tray proffered from the left by the butler, and one or more under butlers or waiters if service needs to be speeded up. With two dozen or more guests, the butler supervises. Soup, gateaux, melon and hot drinks are not "self-serve" for the guests. Drinks are served from the right.

Russian Service—The term used in America for what is essentially Butler Service.

French Service—A combination of Butler/Russian Service and Plate Service, wherein the butler uses a tray to convey a plate of food to each guest, rather than the guest serving himself or herself.

Gourmet Service—Served from a trolley at the table (e.g. flambé) in finer restaurants and hotel dining rooms.

Service en Famille—Meat served by a waiter and vegetables placed in tureens on the table.

Hospital Service—Where a guest passes out at a meal, two waiters may carry the unfortunate person out, using the chair as a stretcher, so that recovery may not interrupt the meal. The cover (the place setting) is removed (unless the person will be able to return) and the neighbors are asked to move closer together. Of course, if for any medical reason the person should not be moved, hospital service would not be employed.

Meals to Remember

Let's start at the beginning of the day and move through the presentation of each possible meal.

First of all, you iron the newspaper and take up the morning tray, as discussed in Chapter Six. *Appendix 9A* gives the list of items that might be needed for a breakfast tray. While most people would be happy with a mug of hot coffee in bed from a loving spouse, the butler pays close attention to the quality of the presentation, making sure that the drink is exactly as the guest or employer prefers, comes with the required additives, such as cream, and is accompanied by the newspaper and a flower. And all delivered smoothly so as to gently waken the person to a new day.

Breakfast

A valet or houseman looking after one or two people would prepare and present a breakfast, usually of modest proportions. It is the attention to detail and absolute care for the every need of the person eating the breakfast that makes the meal special.

It is customary, after the butler has poured the second cup of coffee, to approach the employer and ask for any instructions for the day or days ahead, which he then notes on a small pad.

For a butler looking after a full complement of staff and a large household, breakfast is prepared by the chef and presented by the butler. It can be quite an affair; *Appendix 9B* gives an idea of the scope of food and drink offered, as well as the cutlery and china required. Breakfast is served buffet style (or plated - i.e. food placed on the plate by the chef if only a few guests), with the butler in attendance, clearing dishes, pouring drinks, making fresh toast and tea.

Attention to detail includes observing when a guest leaves the table temporarily, and either keeping his food hot in the kitchen until his return, or providing him with fresh items such as toast and coffee on his return.

Luncheon

Luncheon would be similar to the dinner presentation that follows below, or the breakfast buffet, and so receives no individual write-up.

English Afternoon Tea

This social occasion is as much a part of England as its green fields, and as much a ritual as a Japanese Tea Ceremony. While English tea houses around the country do a fine job of creating an afternoon tea for their clientele, nothing comes close to the experience of an afternoon tea delivered by a British butler in the sanctity of the drawing room of some fine house.

There can be as many as eight courses, all bound together by the ever-present cup of hot tea, optimally a different tea for each course. *Appendix 9C* lists the suggested items needed for a full English afternoon tea.

To prepare the room, chairs are placed around one table for small numbers, or several smaller tables when many people are present. If possible, guests have small side tables available by their chairs to place their teacups and plates.

The butler has the tea, cups and extra plates on a sideboard. He takes a salver around to the ladies with the teapot, strainer and its base, hot water pot and milk. Sugar, honey, sweetener and lemon slices are on the table. Just as there are two opposing camps disputing whether one should let a red wine breathe before serving it, so there are two camps concerned over whether one pours the milk or the tea into the cup first. Some swear there is a difference in taste. Certainly, if one pour the tea first, one can then regulate how much milk to dispense. But some say that if one pour the milk in first, the milk will be better distributed, the cup will not crack, or the scalded milk will bring out the flavor of the tea. Whichever sequence one prefer, it is best to check with each guest, "Milk, madam?" and pour the milk if that be her preference.

The butler pours the tea unless there are four or less guests, in which case the lady of the house pours tea brought to her by the butler. The pot of hot water is available in case guests find the tea brewed too strong.

The butler then brings in the food, which is served either butler style, with the guest helping herself with a pair of tongs from the platter proffered by the butler; or the butler places the food on the table, on triple-tiered trays with doilies.

The butler brings in the next course when some have stopped eating the food available, and he only clears away the food when no other guests avail themselves of any particular platter.

The butler changes plates between courses where plates have become dirty. He boils a large kettle of water in the kitchen for each course, which he uses to make regular fresh pots of tea. If a guest has allowed the tea in her cup to turn lukewarm, the butler will provide a clean cup and remove the old one.

How does one properly brew tea?

1) By using the finest quality teas, in bulk, not bags.

2) By running the water for a minute or two in order to aerate it before filling the kettle (water that has been sitting unaerated in the pipes tastes dead)

3) By bringing the water to a rolling boil.

4) By immediately pouring the water into the teapot, because boiling water loses oxygen and any tea made with over-boiled water will also taste flat. Timing becomes so critical that one should bring the teapot to the kettle and pour in the water as soon as it reaches a rolling boil.

5) By using bottled spring water in preference to any tap water that is full of minerals or toxic chemicals.

6) By heating the teapot with hot water that is then discarded before placing the tea leaves and boiling water in the pot.

7) By using one teaspoon of tea per person, with one teaspoon for the pot. For a pot that holds more than four cups, the ratio should be lessened.

8) By letting the tea sit for 3 minutes before stirring once and then pouring in the case of small-leaved teas such as Assam; 4-5 minutes for medium-sized leaves

such as Ceylon/Orange Pekoe; and 5-6 minutes for large-leaved teas such as Oolong or Earl Grey.

9) Once tea has been poured from the pot for all guests, the butler pours any remaining tea into a second heated pot so it does not stew (become bitter) in the leaves of the original pot. This second pot is covered with a tea cozy (a pot-shaped warming blanket) and used for any refills (removing the cozy first!).

After tea has been served, sandwiches are brought in. The chef cuts them into bite-sized finger shapes, de-crusted and thinly buttered. They contain a variety of savory fillings, from crab to gentleman's relish, paté to cucumber.

The plates are then changed and hot crumpets served, dripping with butter. Next come toasted muffins with currants and at least two types of jam.

When the guests have had their fill, single-bite pastries are provided. And when the guests are no longer sampling those, coffee and chocolate éclairs are brought in. Tartlets follow, and then cakes (Madeira, cherry, fruit).

When the guests have done these courses justice, scones are provided with fresh clotted cream and jam.

And just as the guests think they can manage no more, the grand finale is served: fresh strawberries and cream.

Given today's health-conscious, low fat, low-sugar dietary inclinations, such teas are a rare experience indeed. But for an occasional splurge, set inside on a cold winter's day, or in the garden on a balmy summer's day, it takes the cake (so to speak).

After a tea like this, a good three to four hours should elapse before dinner is served.

Dinner

Where dinner is prepared and presented by a valet or houseman, there is probably a limit on how much he can do without the quality of presentation suffering. Where he or she is a skilled cook, and adept at serving, too, then appetizers followed by a four-course dinner for six people with relatively complex recipes can be professionally prepared and presented in one day, and he or she can still clean up and collapse into bed before midnight.

But planning and purchase of the food would have to occur the day before. The food may be presented slower than optimum, and perhaps only one wine would be offered. The bar would probably have to be managed by the gentleman of the house.

With more than six guests, help would be needed in the kitchen, or else the recipes simplified. Either way, this scenario is definitely the economy version, and not the true butler and chef combination that provides Rolls Royce service for guests. *Appendix 9D* provides a checklist that such a houseman or valet (or any host) can use to set up for a dinner party, or indeed, any meal.

A formal dinner party or banquet is an entirely different proposition, requiring a good deal more work and resources.

The first step is to establish with the employer or host, certain material facts, such as:

- when and where (s)he wants the event to take place;
- what guests are to be invited by whom;
- what food and wine is to be served;
- should bar or cigars be made available:
- are any presents or favors to be given;
- any special theme desired;
- seating arrangements;
- type of service to be provided;
- the nature of the budget.

The more you iron out at the first meeting, the less your need to disturb the employer subsequently and the easier will be your task. *Appendix 10A* provides a list of possible points to work out at such a meeting.

If you are overseeing the invitations, then you can use the Printer Checklist (*Appendix 10B*).

You need a list of potential guests (the "B" list) who can be contacted and invited in the event that some of the original guests cannot make it. Some of the people on this list should be old friends of the family or family members, who will not feel snubbed if they are brought in at the last minute to fill in for any cancellations.

Contact guests or their staff to confirm travel arrangements, any needed facilities at the house, special diets or forms of address.

Then see the chef and order any needed food, such as Kosher, non-fat, non-wheat, vegetarian or vegan meals or items. If any of the recipes are new or tricky, arrange for the chef to conduct a trial tasting for the employer, which you and the chef also sit in on, making recommendations for improvement as needed.

Bearing in mind the number of guests and the proposed menu, check the bar and wine cellar; select the wines for each course and make sure you have enough in stock.

The host may like the idea of sitting at each table during different courses, in which case, you will need to select one person from each table willing to play musical chairs. He or she would be introduced to the host, and then move to the table that the host had just vacated, allowing the host a chair at a new table. For each move, a photographer could be on hand to photograph the host with his guests, and the butler would see to the smooth transfer of plates and glasses, obviously using waiters to assist.

In this case, a photographer would have to be hired (*Appendix 10M*) and instructed on the routine, as well as two waiters drilled on their roles.

Next, contact an agency or use your own contacts and staff, to arrange for qualified and proven temporary staff as waiters, sommeliers, cloakroom staff, and so forth (*Appendix 10G*).

Use *Appendix 10J* for arranging a valet service if needed. Place any orders for special uniforms, fancy dress or decorations as required.

Use a magnetic seating plan to show each guest if there are only a few of them. If there are no more than two dozen guests, then arrange for a seating plan to be printed and handed to each guest before they enter the dining room.

If there are more than two dozen guests, arrange for the seating plan to be printed, as well as a table plan showing where each table is located; and an index, listing each guest in alphabetical order and indicating at which table and seat he or she is assigned.

These plans would be handed to guests and can be augmented by a large representation of the table plan, seating arrangements at each table and the index, and displayed on a board near the dining room entrance.

Finally, consult your dinner file in the Butler's Book to remind the hostess what she was wearing, including jewelry, the last time she entertained the expected guests, so that she can plan accordingly.

Setting the Table

On a day-to-day basis, it is wise to keep an eye out for damaged or soiled tableware, linens and furniture and have them repaired or cleaned, so that sets are complete and you do not have any unpleasant surprises when you need them.

On the night before the event, have the dining room cleaned, especially any chandeliers, and have any dud bulbs replaced at the same time.

Then, on the morning of the dinner, use the checklist of items needed for a dinner (*Appendix 9F*) to bring all the items for the table into the room, with 25% extra to be kept in the sideboard as spares.

Then count the number of chairs for the number of guests, and position each chair two feet out from the table, at the location of each cover (place setting). Doing so anchors where each place is to be set, while allowing you access to the table to lay it.

Lay a felt under-cloth on the table, and then the tablecloth on top of that, allowing a six-inch overhang. The tablecloth can then be given a final, light ironing if needed.

Don a pair of white gloves (to prevent fingerprints) and set the table in the following sequence: centerpiece, china, flowers, candlesticks, and figurines. It is a good idea to use recent acquisitions or heirlooms to act as a talking point at the meal. Strive for a different setting with each dinner, looking for themes to tie the table setting together.

The word "cover" used to refer to the cloth that was placed over a place setting in medieval times, to signify that the place had been set and was verified as void of poison or other booby traps. Now it refers to the place setting as a whole. Lay a sample cover, therefore, for the staff to emulate, using the largest plate to establish how far apart to set the cutlery.

The cutlery should be brought to the table on a silver salver with a cloth placed on top of it to prevent scratching and noise. Lay the first-course cutlery furthest from the plate, and the last course cutlery nearest the plate. All cutlery should be measured at a thumbnail distance from the edge of the table so that a straight line is formed along the length of the table by the ends of the handles.

If the seats are too close together to allow all of the cutlery to be laid, then place some before the meal (usually three deep) and the rest halfway through the meal.

The middle of the side-plate should be placed level with the tip of the largest fork. The salad plate is placed above the setting unless there is no side-plate. Ashtrays and silver matchboxes are placed in front of smokers when they begin to smoke (or after the host announces that guests may smoke, usually after all the eating and speeches are done). Mustard and cruets (bottles for vinegar and oil) are placed in front of each setting or shared between two.

Place cards and menu cards are positioned in front of each setting, with names and titles checked for accuracy in spelling.

Glasses are placed diagonally from the right of the largest knife in the sequence in which they will be used. Napkins are folded simply so as to minimize hand contact by those setting the table.

The above is merely a suggested and classic layout for the cover. There are many other formats, equally aesthetic and/or functional.

It is then a good idea to air the room, verifying that the ventilation (or air-conditioning or heating) will be adequate for the number of guests over the expected time period. Also check lighting levels.

The butler uses a sideboard to the side of the room as a base or relay point from which to provide items quickly for diners. As well as nuts and chocolates for each guest, and extra cutlery, napkins, etc., he keeps cigars, cigarettes, ashtrays, coffee cups, saucers and spoons, sugar, sweetener and finger bowls there.

Then ensure the cream and butter dishes are ready in the refrigerator, the coffee is set up, the bar fully stocked, and all the wine is available at the right temperature, decanted if necessary.

Late Afternoon and the Reception

Now is a good time to take a shower, change and double check everything you have already done to pick up anything missed or not fully done. Ensure the rooms in the public eye are spotless and serviced (i.e. flowers on display, rest rooms). Ensure the valets have arrived and that they know what to do, where to park.

Call the staff together and ensure they are all there, looking clean and sharp. Brief them on the ground rules, the schedule of events and give each a copy of the menu ingredients (*Appendix 9E*) so that they can answer guest's questions as to ingredients when taking the food around.

If possible, have the serving staff sample each dish so they can describe it if called upon to do so by a guest. Have the staff eat so they will last the night without eating half the guest's food. If some of the staff are temporary, take them on a tour of key areas, so they know where they will be working and where to direct guests for rest rooms, exits, etc.

Have all staff locate for themselves the coatroom, rest rooms, seats in the reception rooms, bar, ashtrays, table/seating plan. Ensure, meanwhile, that all functions are covered and everyone knows what to do.

The ground rules set the pace for how waiters go about their duties when working for a butler at a private dinner. These would need to be covered for any staff or temporary staff not used to the requirements, which are as follows:

Service is at a casual but dignified tempo. Waiters are minimal in number and always in the background so as to obtrude as little as possible. Complete silence is observed, which means only two plates are cleared at a time to a station outside the dining room to avoid clashing of china. If cutlery or a napkin is dropped, it is swiftly and silently replaced.

Complete silence extends also to the staff. The American habit of chatting to diners is a complete error in the private household. I once tried to enjoy a four-course meal in a four-star-hotel restaurant and was interrupted no less than fifteen times by five different employees wondering how I was, how the meal was, if I needed anything. The fact that I was engaged in conversation each time I was interrupted with these questions escaped each one of these waiters, maitre D's and busboys. They all had their policy: make friends with the guests, talk to them at least three times each meal. Whoever made this rule never sat on the receiving end. He or she also tried to replace intelligence and observation with rote procedures.

The basic violation is that a waiter should be interested in the guest, meaning he or she observes the guest. Is he happy, does she look like she needs anything or is about to need anything? The waiter then acts invisibly to provide that item or service. Ideally, the guest would not even notice the item arriving. In all this, the flow of attention is outward from the waiter to the guest.

In the American way, however, all the attention is inward upon the waiter. "Look at me, I am here doing my bit, 'How are you doing?' did you notice me?" The guest's attention is yanked off what he or she is doing and onto the waiter. The waiter becomes the focus of attention. Most people do not eat out to applaud or notice the waiter, but to enjoy the food and company. It is the skill with which the waiter ensures the guest enjoys his or her meal without distraction that makes a meal memorable and enjoyable.

Centuries of this service in Europe have resulted in this invisible service as the ideal, and that is why butlers continue the tradition. This one point will be the hardest to drill into temporary staff who have some experience in waiting, but it is probably the most vital to communicate.

Each waiter is expected to be able to answer questions, however, as to the menu and its ingredients, and to swiftly, without fuss, obtain an alternate meal from the chef and present it to a guest who does not care for the offered dish.

When you have drilled the staff on this idea of being invisible, clarify the sequence of service.

In America, the female guest of honor seated to the right of the host at the head of the table is the first to be served, and then guests in counter-clockwise order, finishing with the host. If two butlers, the second would start with the guest of honor to the hostess' right and continue counter clockwise. Or some would start with the hostess.

Butlers in Europe tend to follow the traditional serving of the guest of honor and then proceeding in a clockwise direction past the host. Others still will serve the host first, then the guest of honor to his right, and then reverse tracks in a clockwise direction. If two butlers, the second generally starts with the guest of honor to the hostess' left at the foot of the table, and continues clockwise.

The anticlockwise theory is based on the fact that you come in from the left side naturally as you walk around, thus obviating the need to walk past the person and swing in on their left side, which is required in the clockwise direction. The differences above were pried apart by protocol consultant, Mr. John Robertson, after much heated discussion with butlers around the world. Follow the sequence your employer prefers, and if no strong opinion on his or her part, that is used in the country you are serving; or if no strong protocol exists, which you find to be the most workable.

If someone is eating an alternate meal, serve him/her in sequence. If a guest does not want to eat a dish and does not wish for an alternative, then move on to the next guest but leave the cover set up in case the guest changes his or her mind.

If a guest continues talking and does not notice the salver, say in a low voice (this is about the only occasion one would interrupt or speak to a guest, on the basis that not to do so will delay service for the other guests and allow the food to cool), "Excuse me, Sir/Madam," and if they do not divine why you have interrupted them, "Would you like to help yourself?"

With many guests, a butler taking a salver round on his own would have cold food on the plates before he had finished the rounds. In this case, he enlists the help of waiters. If there are many small tables, then one person could be assigned to each table.

If there is one large table, then either the table is divided into sections between waiters or the whole table is managed by the butler, followed by three waiters. Each carries a different dish: for instance, the butler would go first, carrying the meat, the second in line would carry the sauces and gravies, the third would offer the vegetables, and the fourth would present the starches.

If a guest is eating slowly and will finish more than a few minutes after the rest of the guests, alert the host, who will decide whether to delay the clearing of the plates. If guests use their fingers, immediately present a finger bowl from the sideboard, with rose petals or a lemon slice in warm water.

If a guest is extremely happy with a dish, you might ask for the chef to write down the recipe, place it in an envelope and give it to you for relay to the guest when she leaves at the end of the evening.

Dealing with certain problems

Should a guest spill food or drink on his or her clothes, a cloth dampened with cold water is usually effective if applied immediately. Do not attempt to clean any item if unsure how to treat it. If the clothes are unusable due to the spill, give the guest a change of clothing and have the dirty garment sent for dry-cleaning accompanied by a note stating what was spilled.

Do not pour into one glass over another and never touch napkins in use. Do not educate a guest making a mistake, such as using the wrong spoon, but make up for any shortfalls, such as replacing the wrongly used utensil without fanfare when it is time for it to be used.

If a guest is being greedy and apologizes, put him at ease with such as, "The chef will be delighted, Sir," or "It's good to see someone with a hearty appetite."

This may seem like a lot of information to impart to temporary waiters, but it only takes five minutes for an alert crowd.

Before the guests arrive is the time to see to the final points of organization. Ensure that the chauffeur and valet room is set up with entertainment, food and drink. Check with the chef on his progress. Have some staff meanwhile wash the fruits for the meal by dipping them in iced water and allowing to drip-dry on a towel. Remove the cheeses and butter (one for each guest) from the refrigerator to warm to room temperature by the time they will be needed, and open the red wines so they can breathe. Young and tart wines can and should be aired for a couple of hours to mellow. Old wines should be aired for just a few minutes to lose any unpleasant odors from being cooped up for years or decades.

Let the host and hostess know that everything is ready and the chef on schedule. Alert them to any items of interest concerning the food, drinks and guests. Satisfy any last minute wishes they may have.

As the guests start to arrive, open the door and welcome each one. Take any invitation card they may have brought with them (without checking it!), Take their coats and hand them to the housekeeper, who hangs them up and may give tickets back to you. If so, give the gentleman the tickets. Then announce the guests to the host, who will be standing nearby.

After speaking briefly to the guests, the host would direct them into the reception room, where a waiter takes orders for drinks/aperitifs and serves them, while another circulates with hot canapés. Cold canapés are brought out by another waiter and kept in circulation until there are either no more takers or dinner is announced.

As the guests are entering the reception room, and before they give their drinks order, they can be given the seating, table plan and index, as well as being shown the location of the table and seating chart near the dining room door. In this fashion, they can determine their seating location early on and confusion will be minimized when dinner is announced.

If there are only a few guests, the butler would circulate once all the guests had arrived, and show each guest the magnetic seating plan. He would tell them any information of interest about their neighbor(s) (in the event that they do not know them) and where they will sit in relation to the entrance.

For a large gathering where "musical chairs" will be occurring, the butler circulates, speaking to those guests at each table who will be changing places with the host or hostess, securing their cooperation and letting them know after which course they will be changing.

In the event that a guest has not arrived, telephone them and liaise with the chef and host for a possible delay. Or if the guest is unable to come and no immediate and willing replacement from the "B" list can arrive in time, clear the guest's cover and seat and close the gap between the seats.

If the guest will be arriving very late, move his name card to the bottom of the table, and let the host and new and former neighbors know. Co-ordinate the chef's needs with the host's wishes concerning the start of the meal. There are some dishes, such as soufflés, which cannot be delayed, so the chef's needs sometimes take precedent over the host's. Check with the host and then a likely guest (such as a Bishop) whether grace will be said.

When the chef is ready, and with the host's blessing, announce clearly, with adequate volume, (bearing in mind the hubbub of guests talking and the size of the room): "Ladies and gentlemen, dinner is served." For a lesser number of guests, say twelve, a more appropriate announcement would be, "Ladies and gentlemen, when you have enjoyed your drinks, dinner is served."

The difference being that you do not want the start of the meal delayed too long, and you have more control over a dozen people being slow about moving into the dining room, so you can be a bit less "pushy" at the outset. But with one hundred guests, you want to give them as little leeway as possible for delay.

Two waiters can open the doors into the dining room and stand there with trays to take aperitif glasses. In the event that a glass is still full, they can ask, "May I take your drink in for you, Sir/Madam?"

A minute later, if there is no motion in some groups, ask individuals in those groups to proceed to the dining room. For any die-hards, you can say something like, "The host and hostess are seated and have requested your presence; would you please move through *now*?"

Have waiters standing by to help seat the female guests or VIPs by pulling out and then pushing in their chairs, perhaps asking, "Are you comfortable, Ma'am?"

Serving the Meal

The serving now begins. Start by pouring the water, offering fizzy or still, and remove any table numbers at the same time.

If a grace is called for, stand behind the host and announce, "Ladies and gentlemen, pray silence for (guest), who will be saying grace." If several religions are present, a non-denominational grace you could suggest is, "For food and good fellowship, we give thanks."

Bring in the first course and then pour the wine for that course. Keep the chef briefed on progress, so that he or she knows how long before the next course needs to be ready.

Clear the plates when everyone has finished, or the few stragglers are almost complete. If musical chairs are to occur, ensure the photographer has taken a picture of the host (and/or hostess) at his table, give the host a nod, and then alert the guest at the next table to the impending move. Waiters stand by to remove and replace napkins and transfer glasses as soon as the host and guest stand up, and switch before they sit down at their new seats. This sequence is repeated after each course, at each table.

Next, serve the main course and pour the wine for that course.

If a guest arrives late, take his or her coat, ask if he or she would like to use the rest room to freshen up, and ask if they would like an aperitif, offering to bring it to the table. Show him or her the menu, explain what he/she has missed and persuade if possible to have all courses anyway. Tell him about his neighbors, show him to his seat and introduce the neighbors. Alert the chef, fetch the guest's aperitif, and smoothly plate-serve his courses without rushing, until he has caught up with the other guests. Where possible, you slow down the serving and clearing of the other guests' courses, by such devices as topping up the drinks, clearing one plate at a time.

Top up wines and water and, before offering second helpings, ensure you have about half of what was taken in the first round, so that you don't run out on the second round before everyone has been offered more. The better wording for seconds is, "Can I tempt you with some...," rather than "Would you like some more _____?", which can suggest the guest is being greedy.

Unless cheese and celery follow, clear away the condiments and bread with the main course plates, and remove crumbs from the tablecloth.

If cheese is being served, place butter, margarine, celery, grapes, radishes and four or five types of crackers and breads on the table. Then take around the cheese board with eight or ten cheeses. If you cannot recognize or remember each cheese, then affix small labels to the backs of each, so that you can answer any questions as to name, origin and description. Cut the amount of specific cheese(s) they ask for, placing them with the knife on a plate that an assistant carries on a salver.

Have a fresh cheese board brought to you if any of the cheeses are running low, and have the first one replenished in the event that the second one also runs low. Then top up their wines, or offer port. If someone asks for more cheese, bring it to him or her and then offer all other guests the board.

When done, clear everything away and crumb down.

Serve the pudding and clear the dishes. Then serve the fruit as follows: place a doily and finger bowl onto a side plate and place on top of a pudding plate, which has a fork on the left, spoon to the right and knife across the top. Place this set in front of the guest; if he or she does not place the side plate and finger bowl above the setting, then do so yourself. Then offer the fruit bowls. As with the cheese, if a guest asks for more fruit, offer it to that guest and then all the others. Once again, clear everything away.

Then put out the petit fours (bite-sized cakes, pastries and chocolates) and nuts. This calls for another procession: the first waiter puts down side plates for the petit fours and asks if the guests would like coffee, offering tea if not. The second waiter, who is listening for the answer, puts down either a coffee or teacup, saucer and spoon, or none at all. The butler follows, pouring the coffee for those with coffee cups, but first checking whether decaffeinated is required. If so, the third waiter provides it. The fourth waiter follows with the cream, milk, sugar and sweeteners. By the time the first two waiters have put down the cups and side plates, they immediately bring around the tea, milk, sugar and sweeteners for those taking tea.

The port is then served by the butler, who recognizes that its consumption is no less a ritual than the English afternoon tea, and treats it with appropriate decorum, not to mention reverence. He has earlier secured the cork from the bottle around the decanter by means of a silver chain, and placed the dusty bottle on the sideboard, with extra decanters as needed. He then places the decanter in front of the host, and removes the stopper with a flourish, placing it by the decanter. As the first decanter is about to dry up on its rounds, the butler replaces it with a fresh decanter.

By tradition, the host pours the port for the guest of honor to his right, then fills his own glass and slides the decanter to the left with the right hand. The decanter thereafter continues in a clockwise direction, always being slid with the right hand. This custom originated in the days when all knights were right-handed and had to be restrained from using their swords to skewer their fellow diners by requiring that they keep their right hands gainfully employed in the passing of the port. Port decanters, unlike others, have a smooth base to permit sliding across table surfaces without scratching. If not, the butler would ensure some felt or other buffer were placed under the decanter to facilitate sliding without scratching.

Should the butler notice the decanter unmoving, he gently whispers to that person, "You have the port, Sir." Any guests who pass on the port without partaking are asked if they would prefer a liqueur or other drink, and it is brought if so.

The port is customarily for the men who stay at the table after the ladies retire to the (with)drawing room; but if the ladies are still at the table when the port is served, they are also offered other drinks as required.

If a toast is to be proposed, or a loyal toast (the loyal toast in the United Kingdom is made to the Queen and in America to the President), or a speech to be given, position yourself behind the intended speaker. Rap the table sharply twice for quiet, and announce, "Ladies and gentlemen, please may I have your kind attention," or, "Pray silence for your host/Mr./Mrs./title____, who would like to say a few words."

Pull out his or her chair, stand behind him during the speech, and help seat him or her afterwards. At this point, the host may announce, "You may smoke if you wish." In this case, quickly place ashtrays by known smokers and those who light up.

Offer cigars in a humidor, leaving an ashtray with any who take cigars, as well as lighter and cigar cutter.

Offer refills of tea, coffee, and liqueurs; ensure the port is making the rounds, or pour it yourself. Ashtrays are replaced when they have extinguished stubs in them. Placing a clean ashtray over the dirty one to prevent ash flying over the guests, remove them both from the table, return the clean one to the same spot and move the dirty one behind your back—three deft movements.

When the dining room is finally empty, have the waiters clear, clean, polish and stow everything (dealing with the glasses last). Have them replenish the condiments but empty the salt containers, if they are made of silver, to prevent tarnishing and corrosion.

While clean up is proceeding quietly, keep an eye on the guests, topping up their drinks and generally seeing to their needs. Ask the guests to sign the Visitor's Book if the host has requested it.

What does one do with leftovers that the employer might not want served again the following day? Give them to the staff or local soup kitchens, but on the understanding that the food must be consumed straight away before it spoils.

Charity is a fine virtue, but do not let the modern-day phenomenon of frivolous litigation sour the act.

If guests are staying overnight, buttonhole them while escorting them to their rooms. Ask how the evening was, when they would like to be awoken, what they would like for breakfast, which newspaper they prefer and if there are any travel or other arrangements you need to attend to the following morning. Note this all down, not just for action that night and the following morning, but also for your records for their future stays. It is always impressive to guests when they return five years later and you ask if they still prefer that particular breakfast and paper.

Also noted in your Butler's Book is a record of that dinner: guests who attended, food and drinks served, how they were liked, gifts given or received, clothes and jewelry worn by the hostess and special diets required by different guests.

The follow-up for the dinner includes sending any letters of thanks needed, as well as any photos of the musical chairs, with a compliment slip from the host and hostess.

If all this seems like a performance to you, you are right. It's also a lot of work, but therein lies the difference between a meal and an occasion to remember. Select whatever works out of the above chapter for your own dinners. Whatever extra effort you put in will not go unnoticed or unappreciated by your guests.

Chapter Ten

Other Social Occasions

There are naturally a good many alternatives to dinner for a social occasion or function. This chapter covers the broad outlines of organizing such occasions, but relies mainly on checklists in the appendices to give the exact actions required. The checklists include steps that you may want to omit, and on the other hand, may also omit some actions that you consider necessary. However, they do provide a sequence of actions which, when followed intelligently, allow you to organize and produce a function smoothly.

The first step is always to determine exactly what type of function is wanted, its venue and time, who will be invited and how, and a host of other questions, which can be found in *Appendix 10A*. It is important to thrash out as many details as possible at this time, so that correct planning can occur. Is the planned event in keeping with the message or occasion? Is it too ambitious for the existing resources? You will want to do justice to the event, and with that in mind, it may be better to produce a more modest but professional celebration than attempt a complex one that flops.

Having completed the checklist in *Appendix 10A* and established exactly what is wanted, you then select the required checklists referred to in this chapter, and mark against each target who will get it done, and by what time. As each step is completed, mark it "Done" with the date, so that you can keep track of the progress and see clearly where you may need to wade in and sort out any blocks delaying a step from timely completion.

As soon as the guest list is decided upon, and any celebrities on the list are confirmed as being available that day, you will want the printing checklist (*Appendix 10B*) completed, so that invitations can go out. Ideally, invitations should be sent out at least six weeks ahead of the planned event. Otherwise the rest of the guests are likely to have their engagement calendars booked up already.

It could be that the planned event is as simple as a dinner at a restaurant; in which case an "investment tip" may have to be made if the restaurant is heavily booked and/or hard to book. Find out the going rate and present cash in an envelope to the manager, asking him if a table is available. It will be, if your actions are discreet enough. If your employer is unknown at that establishment, you could give the manager a small photograph with your employer's name on it, so that the manager and headwaiter can recognize and greet your employer by name.

Next, organize with the manager the procedure you would like followed for the dinner party. If this is a restaurant that your employer likes, and visits on a regular basis, it is a good idea to give occasional sweeteners throughout the year to the manager. *Appendix 10C* gives the checklist for arranging a dinner party at a restaurant.

If the function is too large to be held at the house, or is to be held in an area where your employer does not own a house, then a hotel may well be required. *Appendix 10D* gives the steps to accomplish this.

Possibly the function is too large to be held inside the residence. If the weather is generally fine, a marquee could be rented. *Appendix 10E* gives the necessary steps for renting one and hosting a function in it. Sometimes it is possible for the marquee to remain on the premises an extra day, in which case you could propose to your employer that one of his charities or clubs might utilize it that day. If he agrees, contact the charity or club and brief them on the dos and don'ts. It would be sensible to have a legal agreement drawn up that clears your employer of any liability for any phase of their activity.

Most probably you will need to bring in a caterer to provide the food, in which case *Appendix 10F* would be valuable in hiring one. If possible, assign your own staff to oversee and act as liaisons for each catering function. Otherwise, act as a liaison yourself, troubleshooting when required to ensure the event is serviced smoothly. One of your staff could act as a gopher to assist you.

If a caterer is not to be called in, then you will be using your own staff to handle food and beverages. You may need to call in additional temporary staff for the function. *Appendix 10G* delineates the actions you could take to hire staff from an agency.

Appendix 10H can be used to hire any uniforms that may be needed.

A valet service becomes vital when many guests will be arriving in their own cars, otherwise they will be obliged to park their cars at a distance, possibly in an unsafe place, and walk to the residence and back. *Appendix 10J* provides the steps for the smooth hiring and supervision of a valet service.

At larger functions, especially outdoor ones, security may well be an issue, so *Appendix 10K* provides a simple checklist for hiring a security firm that will provide the service you require.

Some form of entertainment is invariably required at functions, and so *Appendix 10L* shows you how to organize it.

Some other services may be necessary, and these are listed in *Appendix 10M*.

There are several events or functions which can require quite some organization to pull off professionally, such as a champagne reception (*Appendix 10N*) and a dinner that is broken off in the middle to attend the theater, opera or some similar event (*Appendix 10P*, used in conjunction with *Appendices 9E, F and G*).

For outdoor events, barbecues are covered in *Appendices 10Q* and *10R*. Picnics and similar events are covered in *Appendix 10S*.

The checklist on *Appendix 10T* organizes anevent many families celebrate: Christmas, the English way.

Lastly, Appendix 10U provides a checklist for hiring a limousine service

For events not covered here, I strongly advise you to make up your own checklists—from experience, I have found they provide a fixed point of certainty in what may seem like a sea of confusing motions. They also allow forward and orderly progress to occur that can guarantee your goal of a successful and pleasurable occasion is reached.

An event that rarely occurs, but when it does, is possibly the largest single project any butler undertakes, is moving house. How to do so smoothly is covered in the next chapter. Many of the actions listed can also be applied in the more common scenario—the employer adding another residence to his holdings.

Chapter Eleven

Moving House

When one has to move house, what a blessing it is to have a butler to organize and carry off the whole affair! This chapter aims to make such a move, whether for oneself or an employer, as smooth and stress-free as possible.

The first action for a butler is to obtain assistance in covering his normal duties while organizing and executing the move full-time.

Preparations at the Old House

As the next step, preparations need to be made for leaving the old house. At least three removal firms should be contacted and the firm hired which best fits the following criteria:

- uses new packing cases, covers, tissue papers, wardrobe boxes, as well as using mattresses when needed;
- is properly insured for theft, injury, damage and loss;
- has experienced movers who are bonded and security cleared;
- offers the best price and provides a written contract, rather than an estimate.

Arrange for the move to start on a Monday with no national holidays in the week ahead. This will ensure no weekend overtime charges are called for, nor will the company be obliged to call in less experienced and reliable temporary staff.

Break the news to any staff in such a way as to minimize upset, perhaps having first obtained brochures and information from the chamber of commerce for the area you are moving to, if far away. Let them know that their interests will be taken care of and concerns consulted. Those staff staying with the employer can make their own moving needs known, and start preparing for that move, such as schooling, social ties and so forth. Those staff not staying can start finding alternative living quarters and vacate tied houses (accommodation provided by the employer) in time, as well as looking for new positions.

You may need to recruit new staff at this point, possibly contacting agencies in the area you are moving to.

At this stage, it would probably be wise to draw up a separate staff program, once each staff member has determined what he or she needs to do. This will allow you to keep track of progress and ensure that by the time the actual move starts, the staff are there and helping, rather than still involved with problems relating to organizing their own moves.

Change-of-address cards need to be ordered that give the move date, new address and phone number(s). These need to be sent to the same friends, relatives, suppliers, subscription magazines, local authorities and so on, who have the present address. Send out these cards one week before the change.

The inventory of all movable and valuable items then needs to be updated, assigning numbers to each item according to the room it was located in. An additional column would also be made, so that the room number the item is being assigned to in the new house could be indicated.

The insurance would have to be amended to include the transport of possessions and insurance for the new premises. The insurance should be kept on the old house until the new owners take possession. It is advisable to insure for fractionally more than the actual worth to cover markdowns by the insurance company.

A security company could be engaged to transport very valuable items, and to escort the actual movers (in the case of very valuable possessions).

If your employer owns many cars, hire drivers to convoy them or engage a car transporter to drive them to the new location, once the garages are available for parking at the new house.

Engage for a vintner to move the wine cellar if its size and worth warrant it. Wine does not travel well and old wine can be ruined by rough handling.

The post office needs to be alerted to forward mail from the day after you leave. Utilities and phones should be cut off as you leave the house.

Arrange a holiday for the family (or at least some accommodation somewhere else to keep them happy and busy until the new house is ready to receive them). Arrange lines of communication with the employer in case of emergency.

Arrange for at least one staff member to be stationed at the new house, with utilities, security system, phone etc. turned on, from the moment the house becomes the property of the employer. This person acts as a caretaker, chef to any workmen there, and also cleans and upgrades while there. Likewise, arrange for a couple of staff to stay behind and clean the old house top to bottom, and then fly out to the new house if they're staying with your employer.

Arrange for the moving of the staff's possessions. Arrange overnight motel stays for movers, security, staff and their families along the route, if moving a long distance.

Preparations at the New House

You need to visit the new house and locale well in advance, in order to determine the existing situation and program various actions that will need to be taken. Having obtained your employer's go-ahead on the recommended programs, execute the steps needed. Some of the points listed below may already be in hand through other professionals, but you may want to provide a fresh perspective where something may have been overlooked.

The kind of points to look for inside the house are: interior design; renovations of existing systems, such as plumbing, electricity, gas; installation of such as water softener and purification systems, fire and security systems; energy source upgrades or going "green"; emergency generator; kitchen equipment; sports facilities; telephone and cable lines, and satellite dish; new carpets and curtains; new paint work, woodwork; built in furniture.

It is a good idea to call in a firm from several states away to install a security system. The reason for this is simple: being further removed from your location, they will be less likely to be connected to someone who can return at a later date to burglarize the home. Put them up in a local hotel, drive them to the new residence where they will change the key-ins for the locks, install the new security system and install a safe in the floor of the pantry and the employer's office. They are paid from the office address and retained to change key-ins at the old address after the move.

The kind of things to look for outside the house and in the grounds are: any needed upgrades to the outside of the buildings; any additional buildings planned or built (i.e. garages, sports facilities, etc); driveways improved; a perimeter fence upgraded or built; garden landscaped or otherwise upgraded.

Obviously, if the house being moved into has just been built according to specifications, most of the above work would not be required.

It is also expedient to draw a plan to scale of all the rooms, numbering each. When you return home, you can make cut-outs of already existing furniture and then go over these with your employer to find out which piece of furniture will go where, bearing in mind the intended decor. You can then list new furniture needed and either purchase or arrange for it to be purchased with the employer's authorization. Have each new piece delivered directly to the new residence and placed in the proper room.

While at the new locale, take the time to establish the availability and location of local services such as recommended doctors, hospitals, dentists and chiropractors. Also get information on police and fire stations, local, state and federal agencies;

various suppliers, services such as staff agencies, security firms, caterers; malls and department stores, quality shops; entertainment and sports facilities, libraries; transportation systems; clubs, churches, banks and schools. Input all this information into your computer.

If you have any sort of training in public relations, try to discover the local customs, likes and dislikes. The information so gathered may necessitate some changes if moving into an area where you, or your employer, are a minority by color, background or religion.

Whether or not there is a wide divergence between your employer's life-style and the local populace, it is always a good idea to create a safe landing for your employer's arrival by contacting the locals, finding out what they do or don't like, and then acting appropriately. An open house for the opinion leaders in the community might be in order and acceptable to your employer, or at least a house-warming party on your employer's arrival.

You can prepare the paperwork for your employer's or his family's membership in any organizations they may want to belong to in the new community.

You can arrange for the purchase and delivery of basic food and dry goods items to stock the house, as well as for the use of the staff caretaker, any workmen, and staff and movers when they arrive.

Make sure that the movers have access at the new (and old) house—that they know there is no driving over the lawn, etc.

Arrange for all work on the new house to be complete before the arrival of the furniture, and for the whole house to be given the Navy "white-glove" (so clean that a white glove worn by an inspecting officer finds no dust or dirt on being slid over any surface or crevice in the house).

Lastly, ensure any new staff are interviewed and hired (and arrive before the employers do) so they can be instructed in their duties and the peculiarities of the household.

Several trips may be required to the new house to accomplish and see through all of the above, which is why a move, to be done properly, requires your full-time attention.

The Actual Move

There are a few basic rules to follow, to ensure proper care of the items being moved, as well as their orderly transfer to the new house.

First of all, each item to be moved needs to have a number attached to it that designates the room it should be moved to in the new house.

You position yourself at the front door, where you check large items as they are taken out, using a copy of the inventory. One staff member accompanies each packer so as to inventory each item put into each box, and ensure the box is properly labeled as to contents and room destination. Any breakage can then be noted (if pre-existing) or reported to you if they occur during the packing.

Clear from the ground floor up, in order to avoid carrying large boxes or furniture over items on lower levels. Lay down plastic sheeting over well-traveled areas, and have the movers wear overshoes so as not to track dirt into the house.

Staff possessions go in a separate truck(s), as do garden and garage items.

Provide refreshments for staff and movers from the kitchen, so as to maintain the move's momentum; work through the foreman to control the movers.

Double check everything has been taken away before sending off the convoy. Ensure the utilities and telephones are cut off and the locksmith arrives to change the key-ins, and then leave. Have the house white gloved by a couple of staff who then fly out to the new house (or go on to their new jobs, if they are not leaving the area).

You can either join the convoy or fly out, using cell phones to monitor progress if the trip is long.

When the convoy arrives at the new house, plastic sheeting is already in place and the movers again use overshoes in the house. Post-its and French chalk are already in place, marking the positions for each item of furniture. Again, you position yourself by the front door and repeat the procedure but in reverse, including moving in from the top of the house down.

Have one staff member connect all electrical appliances, ensuring that they work, setting clocks, etc. Other staff can help put away silver, porcelain, clothes, etc.

Ensure each truck is empty before being allowed to leave. When everything is in and checked off, go around with the foreman and his crew, using the inventory and house plan to double check everything has been delivered and properly positioned. Check for any damage to walls, floors, etc and have the foreman sign to that effect. Receive confirmation that any move into separate staff quarters has gone smoothly. When you are fully satisfied, give the foreman a suitable tip.

Having Arrived

The first action is to white-glove the house again using any newly-hired, local staff while the staff who just arrived settle into their own quarters.

Then orienting the staff in the new house and becoming acquainted with any new staff becomes a necessity. Tour them around the house, the grounds, and also the locale. Ensure each has a map of the area and knows the locations of each facility they are likely to need or be interested in. Also make sure they know the local customs and likes and dislikes, so that they do not inadvertently create poor word-of-mouth for your employer. Then dummy run all the lines and procedures, checking for missing items or unexpected problems in presenting the services your employer is used to receiving. This should include fire drills and security drills. Also ensure the house is properly stocked with victuals and supplies.

When your employer and any family arrive, correct anything that they find unsatisfactory. Send out any house-warming invitations and hold the party.

Finally, as a follow up, ensure the staff has moved in fully, their children are at school and that they are happy. Check on any new staff, making sure they are settling in well with the rest of the team. Give all the staff a party of their own, including a bonus if authorized by the employer.

Moving house is no small feat, therefore this chapter may well omit some steps that are considered important by some. If you manage the above, at least, I am confident that your employer will be pleased, as you will have done all the work, leaving him free to turn his mind to other things.

To make your job easier in the event that you do have to move house, *Appendix 11* gives a checklist that is based on the points covered in this chapter.

While it is entirely possible you will never have to use any of this information in your duties, it is also possible that the following chapter falls outside your employer's needs. But if your employer is in the public eye, then the information and expertise can only be useful. John Lennon did little to make any enemies, but he became the target of a madman crazed with psychiatric drugs, and we all lost a very talented musician. A butler/body guard could have prevented that unhappy incident from occurring.

Chapter Twelve

Security and the Odd Job Factor

To any litigation-happy readers, I give formal notice to ignore the information in this chapter. Contact the police for all the information you need. When you inevitably mess up, you can take it out on them.

I am sure butlers through the ages have jumped to the defense of their lords and ladies wherever required and possible. Their weapons would have been whatever came to hand—possibly the silver tray they carried, itself a heavy and formidable weapon.

However, in recent decades, events such as the 1992 riots in neighborhoods adjoining that jewel of Los Angeles, Beverly Hills, have understandably created a demand for butlers who are somewhat better prepared for all eventualities. This concept of a butler/bodyguard is not entirely new: "Oddjob" of James Bond fame seems to have played this role to some degree.

Any person willing to learn the skills and assume the responsibilities that being a bodyguard entails, will be able to provide an extra service to his employer that can only be an asset in a society where the odd automatic-wielding kook has been known to create mayhem at random.

There are various ways to protect self and others. Prevention and deterrence are the best ways. But given an intruder situation, how does one best respond?

As a first step, one would simply try talking to the person and escorting him/her off the premises. The next level would include various degrees of martial arts. And only as a last resort would a firearm be produced or used.

There may be a romantic or macho image to carrying a gun, but in truth, it is a nuisance to have a hard and heavy lump rubbing against one's chest. I can almost guarantee it will never be used, but it has to be carried anyway, according to the old umbrella principle.

In the event I would have to use a gun, the grim reality of the destruction those bullets would wreak leaves no room for posing and creating an image. It's sweaty business ducking behind cover, being deafened by the blasts and scared out of ones wits by the near misses.

As a bodyguard, one is obliged to physically interpose one's own body between one's employer and any assailant, so that one can take the bullets. If that is not an appealing thought, then read no further.

If you are still with me, fine. I won't comment on what kind of perverse streak we share, other than to say that possible consolation lies in the fact that most people have rotten aim when it comes to shoot-outs. The average exchange of fire lasts just a few seconds and the average number of shots fired by each person is three, with usually none of them connecting. Obviously, if some trigger-happy criminal is discharging an Uzi from point blank range, chances of a hit are high. But most homicides do not follow that pattern.

To become a bodyguard, you have to obtain a firearm legally, train on its use at a firing range, and then obtain further training from a bodyguard trainer. The firing range can probably connect you with such a person or school.

Different states and countries (?) have different laws concerning the carrying of a concealed weapon. There are still some places, such as Alaska, where one can walk around town with a gun in a holster, like in the old frontier days. Obviously, as a bodyguard butler, your weapon would have to be concealed. So you have to ascertain the laws concerning the carrying of concealed weapons on private property, in public areas, and so on.

Different states also have different laws concerning the owning of a gun. In some states, permits are required and tests have to be passed.

Where body guarding is a formal part of the job description, one becomes a paid or working gun and therefore may well need to have insurance and be licensed.

The employer would cover the insurance, and it would have to include death or injury by accident or design to guests or intruders. You might injure a maniac who was peppering the decor and guests with lead and some jury somewhere could be counted upon to award him damages.

One may also need to obtain a security license (much like a business license) for about $200, and an armed security license for about $100. The local police would be a good starting point for finding out about the various requirements covered above.

My own preference for weaponry is a 38 Magnum revolver, as they are lighter and more compact, easier to care for, easier to operate, and more economical than semi-automatics. They chamber five shots, two more than the average three per incident.

Let's look, then, at the actions you would take in the event of a hostile and/or armed intruder coming onto the grounds or into the house.

The first step is to call the police, describe yourself and let them know that you are armed. Then coral the family members with a view to taking them off the property if that can be done without exposing them to the intruder. Otherwise, take them to a safe area and stand in front of it.

With your back to walls at all times, and from a position of cover, talk to the intruder to establish intentions and any other information. Keep him talking, because that allows the police more time to arrive, as well as increasing the possibility of defusing the situation. If not armed, or if you can persuade him to throw down any weapons, have him kneel and then lie face down, legs and arms spread-eagled, palms up.

When the police arrive, they may have you do the same until they can establish for themselves who the white hats and the black hats are in the situation.

Like military plans that fall apart on the battlefield, your intruder may not obligingly follow your plan. Maybe he will jump out from behind a potted palm, while you have your hands full of that soufflé the chef spent hours sweating over, and demand that everyone aerate their armpits while he punctuates his words with staccato bursts from his semi. In this case, you are on your own, but I would start off by gently putting down the chef's soufflé and then doing as bidden. I know the chef would definitely be in a killing mood if the soufflé collapsed!

If you do end up in a shoot-out, then make sure your field of fire is clear (i.e. that anyone you are trying to protect is not located between you and the intruder, or behind the intruder you are shooting at), and aim before you pop off any shots. If possible, do the old "Israeli dodge," which involves quickly peeking round a corner to locate the intruder, ducking back and then from a different level, coming out from behind the same or a different corner, aiming and firing.

The question of when to shoot needs to be clarified. I once read that a would-be burglar in New York broke his leg when the roof of a building he was about to break into collapsed under him. He successfully sued his intended victims, the owners of the building. That kind of logic seems to highlight the complete inanity of the modern U.S. justice system, where technicalities and abstruse precedents take priority over common sense. For this reason, you need to know when you are legally in the clear to shoot another human being.

The basic idea is that you only shoot in self-defense, where not doing so would reasonably result in injury to yourself or another.

This means that you should only shoot if the intruder has any sort of weapon that you can see, and is either advancing on you, or otherwise about to use it.

If he is advancing on you without a weapon, and an extreme disparity in strength exists, warn him that you will shoot. If he ignores your warnings and you fear for your or another's safety, then you may shoot.

In any event, shooting is only a last resort to defend yourself or another from personal injury. It cannot be used to protect possessions or to stop someone who is fleeing.

Your view is to immobilize your adversary as swiftly as possible; he is behaving psychotically and can be regarded, if somewhat callously, as a sort of "weapons system" that has to be "neutralized." So if you have already tried the reasoning approach and he is still in attack mode, then it is time to overwhelm him hard and fast. Bullets do just this, but only if you direct them to the right spot.

You always aim for the chest, shooting two bullets as fast as possible.

If he still does not go down, then he is probably wearing body armor and you have to go for the headshot.

Do not try to wing the assailant by shooting for his limbs like actors do in movies. Your adrenaline will be flying all over the place, as will your aim and the assailant's, too. In this kind of situation, you have to aim for the biggest target that offers the best chance of a hit, and one which will also be effective in stopping an attack. A shot in the arm or leg will probably do little to stop a maniacal attacker.

You do not shoot to kill; you shoot only to end his attack. As soon as the attack is ended, you have no right to use the gun any further.

The above gives an idea of the worst-case scenario—actually having to use a weapon in defense. I have given only a thumbnail sketch of the response you might initiate.

I mentioned earlier that the best form of body guarding is deterrence and prevention. These two subjects account for ninety-nine percent of your activities as a bodyguard.

The first lesson is to be unpredictable in the scheduling of your activities, and the routes and motions you go through during the day. This makes it hard for intruders to observe and plan any attacks. Such randomness may be difficult to maintain, as being a butler often requires a very set schedule and pattern of actions. Do what you can to satisfy the requirements of both sets of duties.

The second is to make the house and grounds as impregnable as possible. Just as Houdini proved there was no way to stop a really determined person from breaking out of something, I think enough law-officers will tell you that there is no way of preventing a really determined person from breaking into something. The emphasis then becomes making it as uninviting and difficult as possible for a would-be intruder to break in. You want him to see that he will be slowed down circumventing all the barriers you have erected, to such a degree that he will think, "Oh, the hell with it."

The way you accomplish this effect is by touring the house and grounds looking for points of entry that are easily broached, and then having them changed. A sampling of the types of upgrades includes:

* installing thick, hardwood or metal outside-doors and frames;
* trimming greenery that can act as a screen by lower windows and doors;
* putting several screws along the top edge of sliding doors so they cannot be popped;
* using Lexam glass in doors with windows or adding hurricane film;
* installing one or more burglar alarm systems, tied into a security firm with response resources.

The existence of:
* out-of-reach lights and cameras;
* deadbolt locks, window locks, walls, fences and bars that will slow his entry;
* guards and guard dogs;
* moats and signs about mine-fields in the lawn that keep the burglar guessing,

generally serve to put off all but the most determined assassins and assailants.

If you refer to Chapter Five, specific information is given concerning the security aspect of letting people in and out of the grounds or front door.

Thirdly, you should also sit down and imagine what the purpose of a criminal might be, double the viciousness of any scenario you might have come up with, and then take a tour of the house and grounds, looking for:

* possible break-in sites;
* ways to alert authorities (portable phone is a must);
* escape routes for family and self;
* cover for family and self in case of a fire-fight with firearms.

Security with vehicles is another issue. Be aware, when driving, of escape routes as well as situations engineered to bring you to a stop. Be aware of vehicles following yours and people doing suspicious things around you. Drive in an armor-plated vehicle if your boss does have enemies, and have jet engines, machine guns, laser guns, battering rams, ejection seats and other high-tech gadgets designed into the vehicle if it makes him happy. On a more mundane level, buy and use a mirror on wheels to check for possible bombs underneath the vehicle.

If there *is* a real or known threat of attack, then you would be advised to call in an armed security service. Also, run through some drills with the family so they become familiar with the actions they should take and locations they should proceed to in the event of trouble. But possibly this sort of scenario is best left to Hollywood.

You would, at least, be reasonably well prepared with a realistic plan, and like my symbolic umbrella, never have to put it to use.

So what else does the Twenty-first Century butler do? Let's have a look in the next chapter.

Chapter Thirteen

The Twenty-first Century Butler

How to Manage and Remunerate a Butler

Butlers are run according to the ideas of their employers. Most English employers have very definite ideas on the place and activities of the butler, grounded in a millennium of slowly evolving duties and experience.

The butler looks after the wine, the table, the silver, the male household staff; he can act as a valet. He sometimes administers to the running of the house. He is the stiff-upper-lip type who says little and is gracious in public; "a bulwark of sound advice and sensible conduct in any crisis."

In other parts of the world, some employers are known to treat their butlers and other household staff much in the way they have been for centuries—as chattels. Slaves formed the bulwark or roots of household employment in America and this legacy has survived even until recently.

While I paint these pictures with a broad brush, they have some truth to them. In all cases, no one has analyzed what makes a butler uniquely a butler or what his purpose is. The duties, therefore, have never been fully outlined, and certainly not in a modern context. As a result, butlers have been viewed as two-dimensional figures, caricatured and limited in scope. If a three-dimensional picture were drawn in full Technicolor of the duties a butler could undertake, then an employer would be much better served.

Currently, people who employ butlers act like someone who has just bought a Bentley Turbo for a quarter of a million dollars and never taken the owner's manual out of its soft leather binder. They may be able to drive the vehicle down the road, but they have no idea how to operate any of the other controls, and so the ride is far from the exquisite one they paid for and could have.

Whether you want a butler because it is the only thing left that you don't own yet— the ultimate status symbol, now that everyone else owns a yacht and homes dotted across the world—or because you need someone to free up your time, a butler needs to be run with the same courtesy as you would like to be run if you were in his or her position.

He has to be told exactly what is wanted and then allowed to deliver it without being micro-managed. A daily conference, perhaps a closer liaison during times of intense activity, should suffice. If you cannot depend on the butler to do what is required after enough time has elapsed for him to know, then you should find another one.

If you are genuinely in need of someone to take over the running of a household or your personal affairs, then work out what the butler could be entrusted with, and go ahead and hire one.

If, on the other hand, you want the butler for a status symbol, or because it would be nice to have one, then you really have to find something that you want him (or her) to do which you consider worthwhile. Each employer and household has different actions that have to be performed; so it is really important for you to list them and decide which can be relinquished to a butler. Once that's established, you can hire a butler, show him what it is you want done, and then gradually phase out of those activities. Then you can travel the world, write a book, support a pet charity, sponsor a sport team, throw yourself into a hobby, take up political office, or tend the rose garden. The world is yours…spread your wings and fly, as the saying goes.

The point is that the butler is someone who is allowed into the family, while not actually being a member. He knows how to behave under these circumstances, leaving everyone at ease about having a stranger so intimate to their affairs. As such, he or she can be used for personal, household and business chores. If you consider the kind of things a butler can do (based on this book) and then ask yourself the question: "What do I spend my time doing or planning, which I could hand over to a butler so that I can concentrate on _____?," then you would probably compile a sizeable list.

In any event, it would probably be more than the limited, "cooking, cleaning the silver, waiting on table," list that makes up the job descriptions of most housemen/butlers, while the employer does all the other chores. My response to that is, "Why buy a Bentley Turbo when all you really want is a Lincoln Town Car?"

Gone are the days when the butler would expect a bed, a salary of $200 per annum, and the right to the gentleman's cast-offs, the left-over candle wax and one-in-every-six bottles from the cellar. A butler worthy of his salt is invaluable to you in terms of freeing up your time and attention for more exciting adventures in life, or for making more money, or whatever it is you want to do. He should be well remunerated, on a level with any professional manager. He should be receiving an executive salary in the range of $50-$150,000 a year, with health insurance, room and board, and a car if one be needed for the position, which is usually the case.

For this, he or she works on a flexible schedule, according to your requirements, averaging fifty hours and working on occasion far longer hours as needed. He or she is entitled to two full days off per week, which are also flexible according to your schedule. The butler is available to service your every need. The only difference between him and the slave of olden times is that the butler works for you because he wants to, and therefore he will display initiative and go the extra mile in caring for you, as long as he is treated accordingly.

If, however, he is treated with a poor attitude and inconsiderate demands and if he's remunerated as if money were a problem, he will likely clam up, do things because he *has* to, and look elsewhere for employment after a while.

Future Markets for Butlers

So what are the possible future uses and markets for the butler?

The more affluent household, of course, has a use for the butler, as always. A large percentage of millionaires in America today acquired their wealth within the last generation or two. That means that there is no real tradition or understanding in these families, as there is in England, of how to establish and run an estate beyond hiring some maids to clean it and gardeners to maintain the grounds. Similarly missing is an education on how to act and interact with society. With several hundred thousand such households worth over ten million dollars in the United States alone, there is plenty of need and no shortage of demand.

Corporations can use butlers in houses run for the benefit of employees and clients from out of town; embassies have a similar need. Hotels can use them as personalized valets/room service/concierges. Single professionals can use them to take care of the home front. Butlers already work in these fields to varying degrees.

Homes and communities for the retired or the vacationing could have butler-trained managers who provided the service and quality of care that is peculiar to the profession. Larger or high-end restaurants could adopt Butler Service for formal dinners. High profile politicians can certainly use butlers, paid for by the public exchequer in the same way that chauffeurs or bodyguards are. Companies can also provide them for their higher-paid executives, as an additional perk that directly assists them in their work.

Maybe as more women move into the business world, the butler will become the official representative of the family unit and its interests—a surrogate, or at least supplementary mother and father figure, like Mr. Belvedere.

And for those families unable to afford a butler, the houseman or housekeeper could be developed and remunerated in kind in some fashion or other. The current market for the lower-end, untrained houseman in America runs between $25,000 and $50,000, plus the benefits listed above.

Perhaps the Twenty-first Century butler could best be described as a synthesis of all household professions, who is also sublimated into an intelligent personal assistant for his or her employer. Instead of having a cook, a maid, a gardener, a chauffeur, a butler, they will all be rolled into one person, who sub-contracts the chores as needed.

However the butler profession develops, as long as butlers continue their tradition of excellence in personalized service within the family unit, combined with integrity and trustworthiness, they will always find work and their employers will always find a need filled.

Chapter Fourteen

For the Beginning Butler

The Tools of the Trade for the Twenty-first Century Butler

The primitive tools of an Eleventh Century bouteiller would not stand today's butler in good stead. A damp cellar, poorly made bottles and jugs with wax or other tops, and metal or clay goblets, may have been high-tech and de rigueur in a long-since collapsed castle. But today's demands include instant communication, the orchestration of events over great distances involving many people and much materiel, and lives packed with an extraordinary variety of activity.

As such, a butler is well advised to become "office literate," able to operate a computer, printer, fax machine, cell phone and copier machine. An electronic Personal Digital Assistant is also recommended. The functionality of PDAs increases in leaps and bounds, currently offering wireless Internet access, telephony as well as networked computerized capability. What else should the butler have in his armory?

A digital camera is handy for taking photographs of inventoried items or the employer's exploits.

Phone and credit cards, cash and bills, round off the pecuniary picture.

A butler needs an office where he can keep all his tools and equipment. He should have access to a large safe to secure valuables.

He should have a supply of packaging and mailing items, as well as gift wrap accessories.

An iron and ironing board are required equipment, especially if he is also being the valet, and perhaps even an industrial steamer.

A hygrometer and thermometer are needed if he runs a house furnished with antiques that need just the right temperature and humidity.

He should carry with him his PDA, keys, bottle opener, cigar cutter/lighter combo, credit and phone cards, coins and bills and paper handkerchiefs. These can be discretely secreted about his jacket without turning him into the Michelin man, so that he can service most of the immediate needs of his employers and guests.

If traveling with his employer in a foreign country, local currency and an electronic translator could be added to the list.

Formal day-to-day wear includes a black single-breasted jacket and waistcoat, gray pinstriped trousers (pants), white shirt and gray or black tie. Otherwise, gray trousers and blazer with a shirt and tie or cravat, or whatever the employer prefers or provides. Informal evening attire might include a variation of gray tie and waistcoat. On formal occasions, an evening suit or tails are worn, but with a white bow tie or white waistcoat to distinguish him from the normal wear of the guests. If a houseman, appropriate smart-casual clothing would be better, including an apron if cooking!

If being a toastmaster, the usual dress would be crimson tails with a white waistcoat, and evening-suit trousers.

For the ladies, a female equivalent would do, with make-up, perfume and jewelry that are low-key: if she draws more eyes than the employer or his wife at dinner, she will not be winning any brownie points or accomplishing her mission!

If also being a bodyguard, he would probably require a handgun and/or mace spray.

Appendix 14A provides a fuller checklist of items a butler needs.

The Hiring Process

There are two major steps involved for the prospective butler; first, letting the right people know you are available in the right way; second, closing them (to borrow a sales term) during the job interview. Many texts have been written on these two subjects, some of which are helpful. I offer my two bits based on my view of both sides of the hiring game.

Let us look at intentions, first. The prospect needs a job, the agency needs prospective employers and employees so that it can make a living, and the prospective employer needs staff so that he or she can be free to party or retire or work on more pressing or interesting matters.

The agency is only in the picture long enough to collect a commission, although some of them are genuinely concerned with providing the right match of client and employee. The employee wants a boss who is fair, reasonably generous, and in the long run, is pleasant enough to like. The employer wants a staff member who can be trusted with his or her more intimate affairs, and who will stay with the family, rather than seeking greener pastures. He or she would also like someone who will be able to perform his duties competently.

Personnel difficulties usually arise because the interests of the employer or employee are not aligned. Employees falsify their resumes to cover up for earlier indiscretions or lack of adequate experience. They claim they want to stay with the family, while intending to stay only as long as they themselves want. The employers treat their staff with little respect or try to pay them a pitiful wage. These kind of situations often are the result of people's fixed ideas—their own particular solutions to problems long gone. All sorts of shifts are engaged upon to become employed and then unemployed; to check up on staff or keep them under control. This kind of climate is unpleasant for one and all while the relationship exists, and frequently results in departures and recriminations.

It is the employer who sets the pace, really, but employees have to play their part in furthering the relationship. Agencies can perform a vital role in bringing the two sides together in a more compatible frame of mind.

Let's paint an idealized picture. An employer who needs and wants domestic staff invariably has a good deal of funds at his or her disposal. Maybe while growing up, this employer was not wealthy at all, but instead had to scrimp and save. Of course that modus operandi really has no place in later years, when wealth is the existing condition. Yet so many wealthy people, such as the legendary Paul Getty, are known for their miserly handling of money. I do not advocate waste, but only the passing on of a small amount of that wealth to those under one's care that deserve it. Whether one paid a maid minimum wage or two to three times that amount makes a difference of a few thousand dollars a year to the employer, depending upon how many staff one has hired, but it can mean a world of difference for the maid. These figures, even over the whole lifetime of an employer, would not even come close to one percent of his or her total wealth. When lying on his or her deathbed, does the employer gain satisfaction from having helped his staff, or from having saved an extra few thousand dollars by being tight and keeping the staff in a lowly position financially? In effect, is it the size of his bank balance alone, or its size plus the knowledge of having helped his fellow man to also prosper, that counts?

If staff members are treated well, they will generally respond positively. Very few will take advantage of a kind employer. And being treated well means with dignity, not just financially. They should be told what their jobs are and then be allowed to get on with them, with thanks given on occasion, and without continual instruction and fault-finding.

The whole business of being a boss is incredibly easy once the elements of trust and mutual respect are in place. The staff in such a household will feel comfortable about being there, and will be unshakably loyal. Staff will not be coming and going as if there were a revolving back door. They will go the extra mile willingly, and the house will be a pleasure for all to live in; not all roses and moonshine, to be sure, but certainly few lasting problems will be generated within such a household.

119

If, instead of blaming agencies and complaining of the difficulties in finding good staff, employers inspected all their own ideas on the management of staff, and possible instances of their mismanaging of them, and then corrected these issues, then perhaps staff would get with the program and find it easier and more gratifying to actually provide the employers with what they want.

On the other side of the coin we find that employees, in particular those new to the profession, have an especially difficult time and give employers plenty of reason to complain, unless they have completed formal household manager or butler training.

The prospective butler can sort out for himself what kind of employer would be acceptable to him, as well as what remuneration would be fair. Don't then compromise with these standards by accepting a position with someone who views himself or herself as the arbiter of a staff's destiny and upholder of Nineteenth Century master-servant roles. It would be a mistake to rush into such a position, as it would not only be untenable, but would likely further sour the employer while embittering the butler.

Keep yourself on the market until you find someone you can service with all your heart—that way you will both come out smiling. I have turned down billionaires, famous people, aristocracy and high salaries, rather than accept a position that I might wish to leave again shortly thereafter.

For the employer, how to find a butler is essentially covered in the first few pages of Chapter Five. For the prospective butler, the existing avenues for advertising are also listed in that chapter. Send your résumé to domestic staff agencies in the country and even abroad.

Rather than trying to reach as many agencies as possible, narrow down your options to one or two agencies that you trust and work closely with them. If you are trained and qualified, you will have no problem being placed in today's market.

You do not need to pay an agency to write a resume for you—do it yourself. Make it brief and to the point. State clearly that you want a position that requires certain skills and characteristics, then highlight those skills that you have without leaving out any material facts. *Appendix 14B* provides a sample resume.

Some agencies anyway do not present your résumé to prospective employers, but create their own version of it. It's always better to visit the agency in person, not just because some require it, but also because you will become more real to agency personnel and thus more marketable as a result. Your agency contact will be able to help you fix up your résumé as needed so it fits their clientele, and agree on the best strategy for you. He or she will subsequently also be able to talk more forcefully to clients about your specific qualities.

If you cannot manage to visit the agencies, at least establish a phone contact and keep calling every once in a while. As a caveat, agencies are sometimes not too terribly well organized and some of them suffer from a heavy staff turnover. It is not unknown for résumés, faxes and letters to be lost, or for the agency to have no record of you at all, even though you have been dealing with them for months. The answer to that problem is repeated contact, thus reminding them of your presence, and making sure they have everything they need from you. The old adage, "Out of sight, out of mind," becomes truer in proportion to the length of time they do not hear from you.

When an agency calls with a possible position, they will describe some of the duties and the salary. This is to determine if you are still in the market and willing to try this particular job, and to give you some information about the character of the employers. If you have developed a good rapport with the agency representative, they will not bother contacting you about a job that does not fit your parameters.

The next step is to go for an interview and this requires some skillful work on your part. You may have spent months and many dollars contacting agencies and waiting for a job offer (or you may be fortunate and have one within a week of putting yourself on the market), so this interview may assume terribly important proportions, upon which your whole life depends. That's the first attitude you have to blow out of the water. You need to be relaxed but alert during the interview. Having a procedure to follow, as detailed below, should help put you at ease.

The Interview

It is normal for the agency to arrange for the employer to cover any room and board and travel expenses in interviewing a prospective butler, where they involve more than a tank of gas and a meal away from home. It is better that return plane tickets are pre-paid, rather than being reimbursed to the applicant on arrival.

Dress in a smart, well-fitting, neutral-toned suit and black shoes. Some agencies recommend dressing in the uniform one would normally wear, but generally this is not necessary.

Arrive half an hour before the appointment, well fed and watered. Find a place to freshen up, clean your shoes and suit of any dust and lint. Present yourself at the appointed hour.

On entering the room, greet the employer with a "Sir" or "Ma'am" and only shake hands if offered. To end any nervousness, look around the room and the people in it until you feel at ease in the surroundings.

You want to be alert, rather than too relaxed, however, so on invitation, take an upright seat, or sit upright in a soft seat. Likewise, decline any offer of food or drink, as you want to present a professional, low-key demeanor—which isn't enhanced by lounging in a chair, sipping a soda or chomping on pretzels.

When "scientists" are given exorbitant grants and quoted in papers, it is sometimes for inane studies that have little bearing on reality. One such study looked into how someone conducting a job interview formed his or her impression and image of the applicant: apparently, 55% do so by appearance, 38% by the way the candidate speaks, and only 7% by what he says. I do not know how important or true these claims are. It's far more useful to follow the procedure outlined here, otherwise you might feel justified in speaking utter nonsense.

Let the employer ask the questions and make the statements, while you sit, listen and observe. Keep your own motion to a minimum, especially any nervous mannerisms. On a one-to-one basis, you have to eyeball and listen to the employer, and see what he likes or does not like, and then accommodate him or her. You won't do this if you are busy talking instead of looking and listening. In other words, if you really are a butler and have learned your lessons well, you won't have any trouble coping with the situation.

The employer will probably provide a job description. Listen, ask questions only to clarify points you really do not grasp, and take notes if needed. Ensure you clearly understand his requirements and your responsibilities; who else is employed and their responsibilities as distinct from yours; and the chain of command in the house. Other questions you could ask during the interview, if appropriate, are whether you would do the food purchasing; if there is a chef in the household; what kind of travel might be expected with the position; whether you would be handling finances for the household; what kind of entertainment the employer is used to giving; whether you would hire, supervise and fire staff.

The answers will help you evaluate whether you want the position, or feel capable of doing it justice; but the asking of the questions also serves to show the employer that you know what you are talking about. When the employer asks questions, give concise answers, and don't be tempted to say more if he doesn't respond to your answer. Just wait for the next question, or if not forthcoming, ask him if he minds you asking a question.

There is one type of employer whom no one in their right mind wants to work for, as covered in Chapter Four. The time to find this out, if possible, is at the job interview. It is the response to the asking of the questions above that will show you whether the employer is open to communication and considers others worthy of his or her attention, or has an attitude that would freeze water at twenty paces and make "underlings" cringe from his or her very shadow.

Usually the salary will be made clear by the agency. If not, only discuss it after you have been accepted. It's a moot point until then, and can serve to turn off employers if brought up earlier.

One important "don't" is to avoid bad-mouthing earlier employers; it often signals a bitterness and untrustworthiness to the prospective employer that most prefer not to have in their own home. Whatever openings are made during the interview or afterwards to harp on perceived problems and upsets with earlier employers can be skirted around easily with charitable, or at worst neutrally phrased, statements. There is an old adage you would do well to follow:

> *"There is so much good in the worst of us*
> *And so much bad in the best of us*
> *That it ill-behooves any of us*
> *To talk about the rest of us."*

Answers to anticipated tough questions should be worked out and drilled in advance, perhaps with a friend, until you know you will not be thrown for a loop when asked. "Why did you leave your last job?" might be embarrassing to some, while: "How long do you expect to stay on the job, if accepted?" might cause stammering and foot wiggling for others. In general, if you have gone to the interview with an honest heart, it should be easy enough to answer any tough questions smoothly, as long as you have worked out for yourself what the answer really is. You may need to have the answer pre-packaged into something that, while still being true, is stated in a manner that is acceptable to an employer. "So, why do you want to be a butler?" is a key one to work out for yourself. And if the only answer is, "because it pays well," or, "because I like driving your fast cars," then try a different profession. If you insist on being a butler despite that, then give those reasons—there's an outside possibility that your honesty may land you the job with some employers after all.

When the interview is concluded, thank the employer (or the employer's agent) for his or her time, and leave. You will hear back from the agency if you're accepted, but until you do, keep up the pressure on the other agencies.

Where to Start once You Arrive on Duty

Without a set plan of action, starting on a new job can be quite a harrowing experience. Your new employers may cut you some slack for jobs undone or poorly done at the outset, but usually not for too long. The tendency of the new appointee to waltz in and change everything is sometimes over-riding and can create upset. Old staff sometimes resent new bosses, feeling threatened or unacknowledged.

The first steps in a new position involve finding out what the existing procedures are. Getting to know the family and staff members there, what each requires of you and what each likes and does not like. And then working hard to satisfy those demands which fall within the legitimate duties of your position. *Appendix 14C* provides a checklist to assist you in making all the right moves in a new position.

As you continue to focus on improving your performance, your employers will be increasingly pleased and rely on you more and more. After a while, you will be worth your weight in gold to them.

Your value may increase even further if you can perform the duties delineated in the next chapter, on the occasion your employer decides to host a formal party or occasion with speeches.

Chapter Fifteen

The Toastmaster

What is a toastmaster? What does he (or she) do?

A toastmaster's basic duties are the introduction of speakers to an audience and the proposing of toasts.

What is a toast? It is a stated wish for success or good health for a person who is named, and then the symbolic downing of alcohol by the whole gathering, to show agreement with that wish. The chairman of a meeting could perform these two functions.

A master of ceremonies usually just introduces speakers or performers. He does not propose toasts. If one wanted a formal figure, usually clad in red tails and evening wear, who both introduced the speakers and proposed (some of the) toasts, then a toastmaster would be hired. As a toastmaster would also take on much of the organizing of the event itself, he can prove to be a valuable facility for an otherwise busy chairman, quite in addition to the extra authority, grandeur and spectacle he will impart to the occasion.

Very few butlers are also toastmasters. Perhaps one reason is that butlers tend to be low key, always in the background, whereas a toastmaster is most definitely in the limelight—even if only for a short while and merely in a supporting role.

Given that you are asked to act as a toastmaster, whether a butler or not, there are a few standard actions that should be undertaken to organize the event. The first is to establish the time and venue for the occasion, and that there is a worthwhile subject or occasion around which to structure the event.

It is then up to you to contact speaker(s) who are experts on the subject and secure their agreement to speak on that date. You may be lucky and have already received the names from the person organizing the event. Establish a schedule with exact times for each speaker, leaving the best or key speaker until last. Allow time for a short introduction by the toastmaster before each speaker, and if a lengthy schedule, for a break in the middle.

It is up to the toastmaster to keep the speakers on schedule. You make travel, accommodation and meal arrangements for the speakers and agree with them on fees. You will need to instruct them on the subject of the conference, the subject of their speech, and the time allotted to them. They will need to know the venue, the exact time they will speak, who the other speakers are and the composition of the audience. In turn, you need them to send you some biographical material for your promotion of the event and introduction of them as a speaker.

Arrange for hosts and hostesses to look after the speaker(s) while they are in town. See the chefs and caterers to arrange the menu and decor for the event, and use the checklist in *Appendix 10A* as a starting point to organize any other functions that have to be covered, such as valet service.

Inspect the room or space in which the event will actually take place. Is the ventilation, heating and cooling system adequate? How are the acoustics? Too much echo, or are sounds swallowed up? Do kitchen, street or other noises such as airplanes intrude into the room? Are the microphone and speaker system of top quality, by actual test? Is the building properly licensed, of sturdy construction and with adequate fire safeguards and so forth?

You may or may not have picked the venue yourself, but these matters are certainly of concern to you. Many people will be convening under your direction at this one place, and you don't need to deal with the roof caving in on top of them. You should aim to send out promotion and invitations at least six weeks before the meeting, so that calendars will not already be full by the time people find out about it. Speakers should receive copies as a courtesy.

Compile a list of guests, with correct pronunciations of their names established, and some brief information on each for introduction purposes if needed. Debrett's book on etiquette and Letitia Baldrige's book on manners both contain the more common forms of address for dignitaries, and these should be part of any butler's library. Have table and seating plans drawn up and place cards made, so that you and the guests know where they will sit.

Making Toasts

If you are expected to propose a toast for the occasion, or if you suspect you may be so called upon, then prepare some toasts suitable for the occasion and audience.

Be alert for the use of words that may have an (embarrassing) meaning other than the one intended, and be sure to verify that the context of any piece you may have extracted a quotation from, is also in keeping with your intended message and audience.

When toasting, do so, and do not say anything else. Toasts are usually offered while standing, even though the practice of standing up for a toast was no longer mandatory after both Charles II and William IV of England bashed their heads on the beams of navy vessels while attempting to stand for a toast. Even though low ceilings are rarely a problem these days, I suspect a toastmaster who proposed a toast while seated would receive little sympathy from his audience; so you would be better off standing.

Keeping the Occasion on Track

Make sure that the guest speakers and those at the speaker's table meet each other before the event. Give each speaker a list of the key guests attending. Answer any questions each speaker may have about the audience or event.

Security checks are often a requirement these days and should be made as guests enter an established foyer area. As the toastmaster, you then introduce each guest to the host(s). If the guest hands you an invitation card, take it and bring it to your side without looking at it. If you do not know the guest and/or partner, ask their name and introduce them in a clear voice. An alternative is for each person to be introduced by announcing their name to the room as a whole.

The toastmaster is responsible for the smooth running of the event, in close contact with the host, organizer and headwaiter. If formal toasts are to be made, the earliest would be after the main course; the sommeliers should ensure that each guest has something to drink (not necessarily wine) before the toast is offered.

Informal toasts, of course, can be made during the meal, either by the host or any of his guests. You should already know the name and title of any speakers, or those proposing toasts. If, however, you are unsure, pick a time when that person is not eating and ask, "I understand you will be saying a few words, and I'll have the pleasure of introducing you. How do you prefer to be introduced?" Fix a time for the person's speech/toast if needed, preferably after dessert when the waiters are not distracting the guests.

The toastmaster should stand behind the person who is going to propose a toast. He raps sharply on the table twice and says, for example: "Excuse me, ladies and gentlemen, may I please have your attention, Mr. _____ would like to take wine with Mr. _____." Or "Your host, Mr.___, would like to say a few words." Or "Pray silence for...." A loyal toast is usually proposed after the last course.

When introducing the speakers, introduce yourself first of all to the guests, and then introduce each speaker to the rest of the audience. The best approach is a light touch with some humor; a chance for some showmanship that adds sparkle to the event. The idea is to please everyone and offend nobody while smoothing the way for the speaker and making him or her feel at ease. Let the audience realize why it is a treat to hear this speaker, without hyperbole (exaggeration) that the speaker cannot hope to live up to. Be brief without being curt.

Make sure the speaker sticks to his allotted time, and when he has finished, thank him on behalf of the audience without repeating his speech. It is a pleasant touch to personally thank the speaker afterwards, handing him/her a small gift as well as their fee or honorarium where agreed upon beforehand.

The butler-as-toastmaster remains low key and in the background when not actually speaking. Even if he is wearing a crimson coat, he is not the center of attention or the star of the show. The reason, by the way, for the crimson coat, is so that he can be easily spotted in a crowd and summoned by his employer. The practice originated, I believe, during the Middle Ages in Italy when a distraught employer couldn't find his butler at a large affair.

So we have come to the final point in our review of the butler's world. Hopefully, you will take these points to heart, enroll in a school and join the profession. Or if on the other side of the salver, consider what a butler can do for you and hire one.

Whatever you do, I wish you well.

The following appendices appear in the order in which they are introduced in each chapter.

Appendix 5A

Names/Phone Numbers of Suppliers and Services

	First	Second	Third
Staffing agency			
Florist			
Gardener			
Landscape gardener			
Tree Surgeon			
Swimming pool maintenance service			
Electrician			
Heating, cooling and refrigeration engineer			
Plumber			
Window cleaner			
Mobile car wash and detailing service			
Tailor			
Dry cleaner			
Pest control service			
Vintner (visit)			
Grocer (visit)			
Fishmonger (visit)			
Butcher (visit)			
Furniture and fine art restorer			
Uniform supplier			
Linen supplier			
Fancy dress supplier			
Stills photographer			
Video photographer			
Paramedic (for large, especially outdoor functions)			
Master of Ceremonies/ Toastmaster			
Caterer (*Appendix 10C*)			

Security service (*Appendix 10D*)			
Valet service (*Appendix 10E*)			
Printers (Appendix 10J)			
Marquee and portaloo rental (*Appendix 10L*)			

Appendix 5B

The Butler's Book

The book is mostly computerized, but includes some ancillary hard files. The book is compiled over the years, kept up to date and handed over to any successor.

SERVICE STRUCTURE PROGRAMS

- Family's needs and wants
- *Employer's Schedule*
- All checklists (listed in this book)
- Job descriptions for self and staff positions
- Schedule of functions for staff
- Programs for the upgrade of the estate
- Cleaning and maintenance task sheets
- Rules of the house
- New staff briefing sheet
- WQSB (Navy term for Watch, Quarter, and Station Bill, meaning a large board showing at a glance what everyone's main and subsidiary duties are, when they are on shift, their contact info etc. Used in houses with many staff and more than one shift)
- Rolodex of family, employees, suppliers, contractors, etc.

INTRODUCTION FROM THE TELEPHONE BOOK, including:

- Local Maps
- Underground/bus plan
- Museums and art galleries, etc.
- Libraries
- Theaters, concert halls, stadiums, sports venues, etc.
- Local outings and attractions
- Churches of all denominations
- Sources of information

TELEPHONE LOGS AND COSTS

CLOTHES

- Clothing standards
- Inventory
- Dry-cleaning record
- Usage and repair record

LISTS AND RECORDS (by subject, but also cross-referenced as appropriate on the computer's calendar function)

- Telephone message form
- Credit card order format
- Full birthday list (with info on presents already given)
- Christmas presents list (with info on presents already given)
- Christmas and New Year cards received/sent
- Forthcoming events
- Long term Diary Planner
- Christmas bonus list
- Religious festivals/seasons, with do's/don'ts and which guests/ staff/ family members follow them
- Presents in stock
- Publications with renewal dates and details of payment
- Wine cellar stock list
- (Shopping) list of foods and dry goods normally stocked
- Going away reminders
- (Suitcase) packing list, including sponge bag contents
- List of clocks (for power failure/time changes)
- List of files in cabinets and archives
- Menu and Guest Book (giving the occasion; date; guests; menu; wines; seating plan; flowers; decorations; dress and jewelry worn by lady of the house; comments)
- Instruction books, receipts and guarantees for appliances and other purchases (hard copy)
- Own resume
- Files on employees with HR information on employment history, wages/bonus history, sickness, disciplinary actions, vacations taken/owed, etc.
- Consent for Treatment form for minors

SUPPLIERS: addresses, phone/fax numbers; contacts; records; account numbers; comments.

FINANCIAL

- Orders and purchases made and well received
- Bills Paid book
- All financial records, disbursement vouchers, bills etc. in weekly and monthly order (hard copy)
- Monthly and annual summary of household accounts
- Bank account details for transfers, etc.
- Property tax assessment records
- Utilities records

- Insurance data
- Inventory (including suppliers and their addresses)

TRAVEL

- Agency information
- Names, addresses and phone numbers of airline, cruise, train, cab and limo companies
- Frequent flyer and other account cards upkeep, numbers and mileage summary
- Insurance and emergency numbers abroad
- Copies of passports

PERSONAL INFORMATION

- Clothes sizes of employers
- Favorite items of employers, family, guests, from forms of address to newspapers to drinks to foods/recipes to pastimes.
- Family members
- Addresses and phone numbers of all family and friends
- Cultural, ethnic and religious traditions honored by family, guests and employees
- Medical concerns, such as allergies, for family, guests and employees
- Doctors and dentists, phone numbers and addresses
- Dietary and drink requirements of employers, family, friends
- Videos/films/plays seen
- Telephone/fax lists (printouts for various rooms in house)
- Speed dialing lists
- Long distance area codes, time zone map, international dialing codes
- Addresses - all ever used.
- Scrapbook of articles on employer, family and friends (hard copy)
- Working file for each major function put on (hard copy), with salient points noted as applicable on the computer.
- Correspondence (hard copy)

In a hotel setting, one would also note points such as:

- Nationality
- Purpose of the guest's visit
- Company name and position if a corporate guest, and contact information
- How many times they have come
- Preferred arrangements of their room
- Smoking/non-smoking rooms, and what are their favorites smokes
- Amenities already given, special ones preferred
- Preferences in butler and butler service
- Activities engaged in, restaurants visited with comments on outcome
- Issues and concerns and how resolved in the past

Appendix 5C

Ordering and Taking Delivery of Merchandise

Supplier's Name_____

Date of Order_____

Ordered by letter_____ phone_____ fax_____ in person_____

With whom dealt _____

Item ordered_____

Description_____

Quantity/weight_____

Catalog number_____

Quoted price_____

Their order number_____

Delivery Date_____

How paid/to be paid (i.e. credit)_____

Running balance with supplier_____

Action taken if late delivery_____

Remarks on arrival_____

Any action taken on receipt_____

Payment entered in Bills Paid Ledger_____

Format for Bills Paid Ledger

Date   _____

What purchased_____

_____

Quantity_____

Charge_____

Paid to_____

Paid by: (state total owed to the credit card)

     AMEX   _____

     Diner   _____

     Visa   _____

     MasterCard   _____

     Cash   _____

     Check   _____

     Other   _____

Appendix 5D

Phone Memo
(Use for calls other than for purchase of merchandise)

Number called _____Date_____

Person spoken to _____Time_____

My request_____

_____

Person's response_____

_____

_____

Action promised by them_____

_____

_____

Action needed by me_____

_____

_____

Appendix 5E

Stocking The Bar

BEVERAGE NEEDED	TYPE	APPROX. QUANTITY for 100 guests
Beers	Various	36 bottles
Lagers	Various	36
Bourbon		2
Rye whiskey		2
Scotch	Various Blended	12
	Various Malt	12
Campari		3
Gin	Strong	3
	Aromatic	3
	Popular	3
Vodka	Various	9
Pernod		1
Rum	Light	3
	Medium/dark	1
Vermouth	Sweet	2
	Dry	2
Brandy	3 top brands	6 of each
Sherry	Sweet	2
	Medium	2
	Dry	2
Wines	White sweet	3
	White medium	3
	White dry	3
	Red	10
	Rose	5
Champagne	Pink sweet	25
	White dry	50
	White Medium Dry	25

For a champagne reception, bank on one bottle per person per hour; or if a full bar is available, half a bottle per hour. Then add 25% to that final figure and return any unused bottles. For champagne during dessert, one glass per person + 25% should suffice.

BEVERAGE NEEDED	TYPE	APPROX. QUANTITY for 100 guests
Liqueurs	Selection of all types	1 bottle each
Non alcoholic wines	Selection of various reds, whites and rosés	5 of each
Non alcoholic beers	Selection of various brands, US and European	42 bottles

Mixes, Sodas and Juices:

Angostura bitters	2
Bitter lemon	12
Canada Dry-Ginger	36
Clamato Juice	3
Various sodas Diet	24
Regular	36
Lime juice	2
Mineral Water-Carbonated	75
Still	25
Orange Juice	12
Soda water	36
Tonic Water	36
Tomato juice	25

FOODS	APPROX. QUANTITY FOR 100 GUESTS
Ice, crushed and cubed	10 bags
Maraschino Cherries	
Lemon/lime slices/wedges	
Olives	
Cocktail onions	
Nuts	
Horseradish	
Worcestershire sauce	
Salt	

GLASSES TYPE	APPROX. QUANTITY FOR 100 GUESTS
Champagne flutes	300
Sherry (small)	50
Martini	30
Manhattan	100
Cocktail	60
Highball	100
Whiskey	100
Water	100
White wine	40
Red wine	40
Port	25
Brandy	40
Shot	25

ACCESSORIES

Cocktail sticks
Blender
Cocktail shaker
Pitcher and long-handled stirrer
Different types of bottle and can openers
Cutting board and knife
Decanters (for wine, whiskey, spirit and liqueur)
Ice buckets
Ice tongs
Measures
Silver trays
Soda siphons
Wine coolers
Coasters
Long spoons
Purified water
Large fridge
Ice machine
Bar towels

With a hundred guests, it is better to set up at least two bars with a minimum of one bartender at each, and have three waiters circulating with drinks and canapés.

Appendix 5F

Checklist on Seasonal Departure from a House

1.   Perishable food given to staff, soup kitchen or disposed of

2.   Florist alerted

3.   Car-washer alerted

4.   Dry cleaner alerted

5.   Newspapers canceled

6.   House cleaned

7.   All appliances in house checked and operational

8.   Timers for lights/spraying set and operating

9.   Chimney flue closed

10.   Parasols and garden furniture cleaned and stored inside

11.   Swimming pool covered and/or heat turned off

12.   Service schedule set up for cars

13.   Internal thermostats adjusted

14.   Alarm set

15.

16.

17.

18.

Checklist on Arrival

1.   Pest spray done a few days before arrival

2.   Food, drinks and cleaning supplies purchased

3.   Florist scheduled

4.   Cars serviced and operational

5.   Cars cleaned/detailed, and schedule set up

6.   Staff there and doing fine

7.   House cleaned

8.   Pool serviced

9.   All appliances in house checked and operational

10.   Timers for lights/spraying set and operating

11.   All light bulbs working, inside and out

12.   Garden well groomed, furniture put out

13.   Bedrooms serviced

14.   Newspapers ordered

15.   Windows cleaned

16.   Dry cleaner alerted

17.   Water-purifier cleaned

18.

19.

Appendix 6

Suggested (Guest) Room Checklist

1. Flowers _____
2. Sparkling & still water _____
3. Drinks cabinet clean and stocked (lemon, etc.) _____
4. Ice _____
5. Candies and bars _____
6. Fruit (washed and ripe) _____
7. Glasses _____
8. Clothes and lint brush _____
9. Writing paper, pens, pencil and stamps _____
10. Alarm clock (working) _____
11. Radio (working) _____
12. TV and Video and video tapes (working) _____
13. Gift (champagne, chocolates) _____
14. Bathrobes _____
15. Towels, bath mat, flannels _____
16. Toiletries, such as shampoo, soap, toothpaste, toothbrush, his and her deodorants, razor and blades, mouthwash, sun block, hand and body cream, hairspray, all unused or looking unused _____
17. Hairdryer, hair curlers, comb and hairbrush _____
18. Insect repellent, plasters/bandaids, aspirin, analgesic _____
19. Trash cans clean and empty _____
20. Carpets, curtain, furniture cleaned/polished _____
21. Beds clean and made _____
22. Windows spotless _____

23. Bathroom spotless, mirrors, too _____

24. Toilet paper, tissues, cotton buds and balls _____

25. If fireplace, spotless, and fire ready laid, with log baskets
    and coal scuttle full; dry pine for kindling. Use hawthorn,
    oak, beech if possible, otherwise ash, holly, birch,
    hornbeam, sycamore or hickory _____

26. If a shoot or golf, game cards and invitations displayed on
    the mantelpiece _____

27. Heating, ventilation, A/C, lights all working and adequate_____

28. Books, magazines suitable/requested for guests/occasion _____

29. Playing cards, jigsaw, games (toys for kids) _____

30. Ashtrays if a smoker (plus favorite smokes, and a lighter)_____

31. Humidors full and serviced _____

32. Clocks properly wound up _____

33. Guide books _____

34. Schedule of events put on by the host _____

35. Local events, attractions at that time _____

36. Hypoallergenic pillows _____

37. Extra blankets _____

38. _____

39. _____

40. _____

The housekeeper keeps supplies of all sizes of tights/panty hose, sanitary napkins and diapers. She also keeps children's items such as playpens, baby seats, carry cots, prams/strollers and toys.

145

Appendix 7A

Sample Checklist for Packing a Suitcase
(for a male, for two days and one night away)

Evening suit	_____	Bow tie	_____
Three ties	_____	Trousers (pants)	_____
Business suit	_____	Three shirts	_____
Two matching pairs of cufflinks			_____
Waistcoat	_____	Sweater	_____
Patent leather shoes	_____	Two office shoes	_____
Three sets shoe trees	_____	Three underpants	_____
Three vests (under shirts)			_____
Five pairs socks	_____		
Pair gloves	_____	Raincoat	_____
Dressing gown	_____	Slippers	_____
Pajamas	_____	Belts/braces	_____
Any Sports Gear	_____	Lint brush	_____
Steamer	_____	Spare spectacles	_____
Cigars/cigarettes	_____	Calculator	_____
Laptop	_____	Mobile phone	_____
Phone cards	_____	Pens/paper	_____
Stamps, envelopes	_____	Reading materials	_____
Some cash	_____	Trip schedule	_____

Addresses going to   _____

                      _____

                      _____

SPONGE BAG

Mouthwash   _____   Toothpaste   _____

Toothbrush   _____   Shaver   _____

Sponge   _____   Flannel   _____

Lather/Brush   _____   After shave   _____

Shampoo   _____   Conditioner   _____

Deodorant   _____   Dental Floss   _____

Medication(s)   _____   _____

Other   _____   _____

Appendix 7B

Equipment Checklist for Caring for a Wardrobe

1. Clothes brush   _____

2. Lint brush   _____

3. Steam iron (cordless)   _____

4. Padded ironing board, or large table, padded _____

5. Steamer   _____

6. Trouser presses   _____

7. Portable sewing kit   _____

8. Sets of hog bristle shoe brushes, 2 for each color shoe _____

9. Short haired bristle brush to remove mud/dust _____

10. Knife and nail brush to remove mud _____

11. Kiwi polish of all colors   _____

12. Meltonian brand shoe creams of all colors _____

13. Wren's Dubbin brand shoe waterproofing _____

14. Saddle soap   _____

15. White spirit (to de-crust applicator brushes) _____

16. Cotton buds   _____

17. Small sponge   _____

18. Cotton rags   _____

19. Meltonian grease and tar remover _____

20. Brasso   _____

21. Suede fabric shampoo and a weather-proofer _____

22. Spare shoe laces   _____

23. Old toothbrushes   _____

24. Wooden shoe and boot trees (plastic for travel) _____

25. Shoe racks   _____

26. Hangers (wooden, shaped and unvarnished) _____

27. Shoe and boot bags for each pair   _____

28. Trouser cuff hangers   _____

29. Plastic hangers for travel   _____

30. Padded hangers for ladies   _____

31. "U" shaped shield to use for polishing brass buttons   _____

32. Barbour material thorn-proof dressing   _____

33. Acid free tissue paper (art supply shop)   _____

34. Stickers for hangers, shoe bags, for labeling/inventory   _____

35.   _____

36.   _____

37.   _____

38.   _____

39.   _____

40.   _____

Appendix 7C

Measurements

NAME _____

Collar _____

Sleeve _____

Body Length _____

Waist _____

Hip _____

Chest _____

Bust _____

Cup _____

Dress Size _____

Leg (inside) _____

Glove _____

Fingers _____

Head _____

Left Foot _____ Right Foot _____

Appendix 8

Checklist for Booking Airfares and Hotels
and Traveling with the Employer

1. Know employer's preference in travel and hotels—special seats, rooms, food, etc. Update the Butler's Book

2. Utilize travel agency that is creative in finding best quality, schedule and prices:

Flight Numbers:	_____	Connections:	_____
Seating: 1st Class:	_____	Business/Economy: (for self)	_____
Visa/passport:	_____	Aisle/Window:	_____
Health Requirements:	_____	Insurance:	_____
Hotel:	_____	Film:	_____
Limo:	_____	Food:	_____
Restaurant:	_____	Drinks:	_____
Entertainment: Magazines/paper/games:			_____

3. Follow up travel agency bookings with calls to any known managers and concierges to ensure the usual high standard of personalized service afforded to employer.
   Note: if a booking is canceled at a late date, ensure the hotel is reimbursed if unable to occupy the room. Also, it is sometimes a good idea to book a popular hotel for longer than the expected stay, in case the employer has to extend his visit

4. Confirm arrangements with employer, make any changes

5.   Use *Checklist 7A* to pack, adding on-board items:

- Foreign currency, including coins
- International phone cards
- Passport with visa
- Health requirement documentation
- On flight toiletries/medication
- Magazines and papers
- Games/portable video machine
- Phone numbers and addresses
- Portable office items

6.   On the day before departure, confirm flights, hotel, limo, food on flight, and write down details for the employer

7.   If sitting with employer, compile up-to-date information on the running of the household or the employer's affairs, as well as on subjects of interest to him or her (i.e. sports, shares, fashion etc.) for conversational purposes

8.   Ensure on boarding that employer's food is also on board

9.   Offer employer first choice of seats if seated together

10.   If you are in the economy section, tell the employer your seat number and location; tell stewardess you are a traveling companion and ask to be fetched if anything is needed; then ensure employer receives his special food, etc.

11.   At hotel, develop manager and concierge (usually has crossed keys on uniform shoulder) as well as managers and Maitre D's at restaurants as future contacts, giving investment Tips

12.   Purchase thank-you gifts on behalf of the employer for any managers known to employer, with his or her authorization

Appendix 9A

Checklist for the Morning Tea or Coffee Tray

NAME:_____

Room:_____ Wake-up time _____

Coffee and type _____

Tea and type _____

Fruit juice and type _____

Cream and type _____

Milk and type _____

Sugar and type _____

Sweetener and type _____

Cereal and type _____

Cup and saucer _____

Doily for cup _____

Spoons for: Coffee _____ Tea _____ Cereal _____

Juice/milk glass_____

Napkin _____

Newspaper(s) and type _____

Flower and type _____

Flower vase _____

Tray_____

Cloth for tray matching napkin _____

Appendix 9B

Breakfast Buffet Checklist

ITEM	TYPE	QUANTITY
Coffee		
Tea		
Fruit juices		
Cream		
Milk		
Sugar		
Other sweeteners		
Cereals		
Yogurts		
Fruits		
Eggs		
Toasts		
Rolls		
Croissants		
Muffins		
Jams		
Jellies		

Marmalades		
Butters		
Margarine		
Condiments		
Other dishes		
Sausages		
Bacon		
Tomatoes		
Mushrooms		
Fish		
Kidneys		
Meat		
Mugs		
Cups		
Saucers		
Glasses		
Cereal bowls		
Yogurt/Fruit dishes		
Side plates		
Entree plates		
Knives		
Forks		

Spoons		
Teaspoons		
Coffee spoons		
Tea pot		
Strainer and bowl		
Coffee pot		
Milk jug		
Cream jug		

Appendix 9C

Checklist of Items Needed for
a Full English Afternoon Tea

1.   Large urn of boiling water
2.   Separate pot of tea for each type of tea wanted
3.   Teacups and saucers
4.   Tablecloth
5.   3" square napkins
6.   Teaspoons
7.   Castor sugar
8.   Sugar cubes
9.   Sweeteners
10.   Honey
11.   Side plates
12.   Small knives
13.   Small forks
14.   Tea strainers and bowls
15.   Thinly sliced lemons
16.   Milk jugs
17.   Hot water jug (to weaken tea)
18.   Plate and fork (for lemon slices)
19.   Small boxes for leftovers
20.   A little of every variety of tea, properly sealed
21.   A lot of the usual teas
22.   Tongs for sandwiches
23.   Cake servers
24.   Cream (double and clotted), bowl and spoon
25.   Jam bowls and serving spoons
26.   Salvers and 3 tier cake stands
27.   Doilies

NOTE: You'll need at least three of all plates, cups, napkins, etc. per person.

Appendix 9D

Checklist for Preparing for a Less Formal Lunch or Dinner

<u>FOOD</u>

- Appetizers
- Salad
- Dressing
- Soup
- Crackers
- Bread/Dinner rolls
- Meat (Sauce?)
- Fish (Sauce?)
- Fowl (Sauce?)
- Starch/pasta (Sauce?)
- Vegetable "A" (Sauce?)
- Vegetable "B" (Sauce?)
- Vegetable "C" (Sauce?)
- Pudding/Desert (Sauce/cream?)
- Fruit
- Cheese and crackers

<u>GARNISHES</u>

- Appetizers
- Soup
- Salad
- Meat
- Fish
- Fowl
- Vegetables

- Pudding
- Tea
- Coffee
- Ice/ice bucket

UTENSILS

- Place mats
- Knife & fork for entree
- Spoon for soup
- Fork & spoon for dessert
- Specialized cutlery
- Serving spoons/forks etc.
- Serving bowls/platters
- Serving tray
- Napkins
- Soup bowls & plates
- Entree dishes
- Salad dishes
- Side plates & bread plate
- Dessert plates
- Fruit bowl, plates and knives
- Coffee mugs/cups
- Water glasses
- Wine glasses
- Salt & pepper
- Coffee pot
- Butter dishes
- Ashtrays
- Bell or remote bell control
- Candles

Appendix 9E

Details of Menu, Including Key Ingredients,
Points of Interest

Appetizers_____

Hors D'oeuvre_____

Other course_____

Entree_____

Pudding_____

Fruits_____

Cheeses_____

Breads_____

Sauces_____

Wines_____

Coffees_____

Chocolates/petit fours_____

Brandy/Port_____

Cigars/Cigarettes_____

SPECIAL DIETS

What substituted for which course and for whom _____

What substituted for which course and for whom _____

What substituted for which course and for whom _____

Appendix 9F

Checklist of Staff and Material Needed for a Dinner Party

Date and Time_____

Location_____

Time of reception_____ Dinner_____ Time end_____

Special occasion/Theme_____

Guests_____

STAFF REQUIREMENTS

Chefs_____

Kitchen Hands_____

Waiters_____

Sommeliers_____

Others_____

UNIFORMS REQUIRED

Jackets_____

Bow ties_____

Cummerbunds_____

Ladies shirts_____

White gloves_____

TABLE SETTINGS
(For tableware, flatware and glasses, add 25% to number of expected guests)

Dinner service to use _____

Flatware to use _____

Glasses, number and type: 1)_____ 2)_____

3)_____ 4)_____ 5)_____

6)_____ 7)_____ 8)_____

Tablecloth #_____   Color _____   Sizes _____

Napkins #_____   Color_____

Candles #_____   Color _____   Sizes _____

Printed Menus_____   # Place Cards _____

#/Type Ashtrays _____

#/Type Vases _____

Cruets_____

Salt/Pepper shakers _____

Figurines _____

_____

Flowers for tables_____

For room/entryways_____   For guests _____

Nuts/Chocolates_____

Knives, #//type: 1)_____ 2)_____ 3)_____ 4)_____

Forks, #//type: 1)_____ 2)_____ 3)_____ 4)_____

Spoons, #//type: 1)_____ 2)_____ 3)_____ 4)_____

Other, #//type: 1)_____ 2)_____ 3)_____ 4)_____

Serving utensils: 1)_____ 2)_____ 3)_____ 4)_____

5)_____ 6)_____ 7)_____ 8)_____ 9)_____

Plates, #//Type: 1)_____ 2)_____ 3)_____ 4)_____

5)_____ 6)_____ 7)_____ 8)_____ 9)_____

Circle the following items needed, noting numbers required:

CHINA

Cereal bowls	Knife rests	Luncheon plates
Cheese plates	Oyster plates	Oval platters
Ramekins	Salad bowls/plates	Scallop shells
Side plates	Seafood cocktail sets	Soufflé dishes
Soup bowls	Soup cups and stands	Dessert plates
Egg cups	Napkin rings	Entree plates
Escargot shells	Corn-on-the-cob holders	Finger bowls
Artichoke plates	Flan dishes	Mustard bowls
Fruit plates	Fish plates	Grapefruit coupes
Hors d'oeuvre plates	Ice cream coupes	Sundae glasses
Coffee cups	Coffee saucers	Coffee mugs
Demitasse cups	Demitasse saucers	Irish glasses
Tea cups (breakfast)	Tea saucers (breakfast)	Tea cups-small
Tea saucers (small)	Tea plates	Sugar bowls
Floaters		

MISCELLANY — SERVERS

Asparagus servers	Toast racks	Cake/pie servers
Pastry tongs	Sandwich tongs	Sugar tongs
Decanting basket	Carving knife/fork/board	Fish servers
Grape scissors	Crumb brush and scoop	Kebab skewers
Wine coasters/buckets	Chopsticks	Meat servers
Salad spoon/fork	Salvers/Serving trays	Tea strainer set

FLATWARE

Spoons	Sugar	Dessert	Bouillon	Coffee
	Grapefruit	Tea (large)	Tea (small)	Egg
	Soup	Ice cream	Iced tea	Jam
	Mustard	Soup	Salt	
	Tablespoon (dessert and table size)			
Knives	Butter	Caviar	Cheese	Dessert
	Dinner	Entrée	Fish	Fruit

Forks/Tongs etc.

Lobster picks	Escargot fork/tongs	Oyster forks
Cake/pastry forks	Corn holders	Fish forks
Asparagus tongs	Dinner fork	Entree fork
Crab crusher	Table forks	Dessert forks

SERVING

Baskets (bread/rolls)	Gravy boat and stand	Salad bowl
Sauce boat/stand	Breadboard	Cheese board
Trifle bowl	Sugar bowl (un/covered)	Fruit bowl
Cake plates/stands	Chocolate container	Butter dish
Food covers (sml/lrg)	Round casseroles (.75/2.5/4 pints)	
Casserole (oval 3.5 pts.)	Condiments (salt/pepper)	Water carafe
Caviar container	Jugs (cream/milk)	Marmalade dish
Soup tureen	Cheese dish	Jam dish
Vegetable dish (un/covered)	Vegetable tureen	Pickle dish
Cheese platter	Fish platter	Meat platter
Coffee pots	Tea pots	Tea tray
Sandwich tray		

ACCESSORIES

Glass towels	Menu holders	Tray cloths
Place-card holders	Napkin rings	Waiter's cloths

Appendix 9G

Checklist for Organizing a Formal Dinner Party

PREPARATIONS

1.   Discover from host(ess):

- Date and time
- Venue
- Guests (names, numbers, B list)
- Invites
- Menu (alert to any repetitions for guests)
- Wines
- Cigars
- Seating arrangements
- Musical chairs (Chapter 9)
- Which silver/china to use
- Visitor's Book signed
- Flowers
- Any special theme
- Presents for guests

2.   If doing invites, complete Printer Checklist (*Appendix 10B*)

3.   Contact guests (or their staff) to confirm travel arrangements, any needed facilities at house, special diets or forms of address. Handle any points required

4.   See chef to fix alternate recipes and order food

5.   Trial tasting for self, chef and host if new or tricky recipe

6.   Check bar, wine cellar and humidor and make necessary orders

7.   If musical chairs planned, contact/contract photographer

8. Use checklist if hiring agency staff (*Appendix 10G*)

9. Use checklist if valet service needed (*Appendix 10J*)

10. Order special uniforms/fancy dress/decorations as required

11. Draw up and/or print table plan, seating plan and index as required

12. Alert hostess on what worn last time with those guests

SETTING UP THE TABLE

The Day before:

1. Ensure linens, chairs, cutlery, glasses in sufficient number (*Appendix 9F*)

2. Dining room cleaned, including chandelier, replacing any dead bulbs

The Day of the Dinner:

3. Bring all the items for the table into the room, with 25% extra for the sideboard (*Appendix 9F*)

4. Set the table, with a sample cover for staff to emulate
5. Air room if needed; check ventilation and ensure it is adequate for the number of bodies expected

6. Check lighting levels

7. Ensure the sideboard is properly stocked with cigars, cigarettes, coffee cups, saucers, spoons, sugar bowls, finger bowls, chocolates and nuts

8. Cheeses, cream and butter dishes in fridge

9. Ripe fruit in supply

10. Coffee set up

11. Check bar stocks; prepare the port

12. Ensure needed wine is at right temperature, decant as needed

LATE AFTERNOON AND RECEPTION

1.   Shower and change

2.   Check table, food, wines and drinks; staff and valet present, relevant rooms spotless and serviced (i.e. flowers)

3.   Red wines opened, cheeses out of the fridge

4.   Staff eat, including sampling the foods and briefing on ingredients

5.   Staff inspection and briefing on ground rules

6.   Dummy run lines for coats, rest rooms, seats in reception room, bar, ash trays, table/seating plan, easy access to dining/withdrawing rooms. Ensure all posts are manned and staff knows what to do

7.   Ensure chauffeur/valet room set up w/entertainment, food/drinks

8.   Alert host to any items of interest re: foods/drinks/guests

9.   Check w/chef on schedule

10.   Fruit dipped in iced water and drip-dried on towel

11.   Butter placed on table on ice-filled bases, one per guest

12.   Welcome guests; housekeeper/self take coats, announce guests to host if needed

13.   Seating plan handed out at reception room; waiters serve drinks, hot and cold canapés

14.   If musical chairs, clear with involved guests

15.   Keep tight line in between chef and host

16.   Phone any late guests and handle as late or no-shows

17.   Check with host and likely guest if grace being said

18.   Announce dinner and get guests seated

THE DINNER

1.   Announce grace as needed

2.   Pour fizzy/still waters and remove table numbers

3.   Serve the main course and pour the wine

4.   Handle any late guests, catching them up to the rest of the party

5.   Top up wines and offer seconds if enough to go round

6.   Clear condiments and bread with the main course and crumb down

7.   CONDITIONAL: If cheese is to be served
        - remove condiments and bread and
        - crumb down after cheese course

8.   Serve pudding and clear

9.   Serve fruit and clear

10.   Put out petit-fours, chocolates and nuts; serve coffee and tea, then clear

11.   Serve the port

12.   Announce toast and/or speech if to be given

13.   Distribute ashtrays, cigars and cigarettes if required

14.   Keep cups freshened, the brandy moving and liqueurs etc. offered

15.   Clear and clean the dining room, putting away all contents once cleaned and polished

16.   Leftovers distributed

17.   Guests sign visitor's book, if required

18.   Button hole guests staying overnight and make arrangements for the following morning's needs and requests

19.   The following day, note all information in the Butler's Book. Send any letters of thanks needed and musical chair photographs

Appendix 10A

Checklist for Planning a Function

1. Date and time? _____

2. Type of function?
Champagne Reception	____	Picnic	____
Theater/Opera Supper Party	____	BBQ	____
Dinner at Hotel	____	Restaurant	____
Supper and Ball	____	Home	____

    Other _____

3. Any theme for function, influencing dress/decor/food? _____

4. Inside or outside? Marquee required?   ____

5. Number of guests?   ____

6. Names (and addresses) of guests made available   ____

7. Any VIPs who MUST attend? (quickly confirm date/venue is
    OK with their secretaries)   ____

8. The date does not conflict with any event popular with the
    intended guests?   ____

9. Invitations need to be sent out?   ____

10. Entertainment required?   ____

    Type of Music_____

    Band/Disco/Cabaret/Chamber/Orchestra/Pianist, etc. _____

    Film _____ Play _____ Singing _____ Poetry   ____

    Clowns _____ Videos _____ Games _____ Fireworks ____

    Reading _____ Lightshow _____ Other _____

11. Caterers required, or preferred?   ____

169

12. Outside agency staff needed? What functions? _____

13. M/C Toastmaster?   _____

14. Speakers?   _____

15. PA system?   _____

16. Valet service?   _____

17. Limo hire?   _____

18. Photographer/Video?   _____

19. Guests staying overnight? At the house and/or hotel?   _____

    Who?_____

    Who?_____

20. Menu? _____

21. Cigars/cigarettes offered?   _____

22. Drinks?_____

23. Wines? _____

24. Flowers?   _____

25. Specific instructions re: special decor?   _____

26. Existing tableware and linens to use?   _____

27. Special costumes?   _____

28. Security and safety (fire/First Aid)?   _____

29. Insurance?   _____

30. Coat check-in?   _____

31. Powder/Men's Room adequate? Portaloos needed?   _____

32. Gifts for guests? If yes, purchase selection from shops on sale or return basis, or procure catalog   ____

33. Total budget?   ____

34. Access to finances for running costs, employer for consultation? ____

NOTE: Refer to appropriate checklist to accomplish each step

Appendix 10B

Printing Checklist

1. Determine: size, paperweight, color, print style, motif, design and contents for the following:

   - Invitation cards

   - Place cards

   - Menus

   - Table index, folded, wallet size for each person (alphabetical names with seat and table noted [could have a table plan with seat numbers noted, on back page])

   - Seating plan (couple of large ones outside dining room, with each person listed at table sitting at)

   - Table plan (couple of large ones outside dining room giving floor plan of tables and the entrance)

2. Contact printing company and ensure they can manage the job on time

3. CONDITIONAL: If unknown, check quality of earlier products and ask for referees to ensure reliability

4. Ensure they can accept changes on printing the seating arrangements up to the day of the event, and that they will print on that day

5. Have the invitations sent out six weeks ahead (eight weeks over a holiday period). Use a secretarial service if printing company cannot send out the invitations

6. Keep on hand a list "B" of close friends/family who do not mind being invited as back up at the last minute, to cover no show guests

7. Finalize the seating arrangements with the printer, and have him print the seating information on the morning of the event

Appendix 10C

Booking a Restaurant for Dinner

1. Investment tip made beforehand as needed.

2. Give manager your employer's (host's) photograph and clear the plans for the dinner with him.

3. All drinks at bar put on the bill, with barman asking host what guests want to drink.

4. Then guests given menus without prices, and host given the one with prices.

5. Barman checks again with host re: drink refills.

6. Head waiter draws attention to stellar foods available and waiter takes orders up to main course.

7. Party called to eat, with host seating people according to conversational optimum.

8. Once seated, host given wine list with prices and decides.

9. Butler can sit in for host if he is delayed. When host arrives, a new cover is put down and butler leaves.

10. Butler pays for meal next day, and tips manager in cash. If needed, the manager can be left a credit card as security that night. Check for and query any obvious discrepancy on the bill.

Appendix 10D

Booking a Hotel for a Function Checklist
(or Museum, Art Gallery, Church [such as St. Martin's in the Field], etc.)

1. If no preference by host, shortlist and contact banqueting managers of those appropriate hotels that are free that day, and arrange appointment.

2. Confirm the following with each prospective hotel, by looking, not listening:

   - Adequate space to handle required numbers

   - Supervised and ticketed cloakroom

   - Clean, adequate and accessible restrooms for number of guests involved

   - Cleanliness, especially in the kitchens

   - Menu planned, quality, portion sizes

   - Wines, aperitifs and after dinner drinks

   - Cigars and cigarettes

   - Flowers on tables and around rooms—state what

   - Linen, glasses and cutlery of adequate quality and quantity

   - If not, get him to hire some and check them

   - Spare table set up nearby in case of additional guests

   - Sound and PA system of adequate quality

   - Adequate stage, electrical points; room for artists to change and stay in

   - Adequate dance space

   - No late charges

   - Tips included

- Staff ratios of 1:6 waiters and 1:10 sommeliers, with the latter briefed to help waiters when not engaged in serving drinks, cigars and condiments

- Place for cars; valet service included

- Complimentary suite for employer, and a small room for self

- Complimentary tasting for employer and self (paid for if booking subsequently canceled)

- Total cost with no hidden extras (bar wines, drinks and cigars separately billed per consumption)

- Take pictures for employer

3. Brief employer: show pictures, make recommendations and set up tasting

4. During tasting, check for taste of food, presentation, color, appeal, preparation, wine combination and service.

5. Negotiate any changes needed and any reduction in price for same services. Then confirm booking with the hotel of choice, fax confirmation and receive acknowledgement from the banqueting manager. Send any needed advance payment and the fax original. Inform the rejected hotels

6. Confirm final guest numbers three days before event and arrangements all in hand

7. On day of dinner, ensure everything according to plan, sampling food

8. Announce guests as they enter the event hall

9. Ensure guests happy and event running smoothly; check with host

10. Announce speakers

11. When banquet is over, send final payment with letter of thanks and recommendation, and a small present to the banqueting manager

Appendix 10E

Hiring A Marquee Checklist

1. Contact company and ensure marquee of choice is available at prescribed time

2. If so, set up a meeting and iron out the following:

    - Necessary tents available
    - Portaloos
    - Ground covering
    - Furniture, stage
    - Electrical outlets
    - Insurance coverage, in writing
    - They obtain necessary fire, police and local council authorizations
    - They provide someone during the event to service their equipment
    - How long to set up, and when to set up by
    - When take down?
    - Restore turf, make up any damage, remove their trash
    - Complete cost quoted, no overheads
    - Pictures provided, and referees
    - Contract drawn up

3. Obtain employer authorization and contact the company with any needed changes; negotiate a reduction in price for same service

4. Fax new agreement, and once acknowledged, send any needed advances

5. Should Marquee remain unused an extra day, propose to employer he allow its use by a charity or club, or even his staff. If acceptable, contact the charity, etc., let them know the do's and don'ts; and have a legal agreement drawn up that clears your employer of any liability for any phase of the activity

6. Five days before the event, phone marquee company to re-confirm

7. When the men arrive to set up the marquee, show them the locations and keep an eye on their progress

8. Ensure they use their Portaloos; supply them with refreshments

9. Buttonhole the person who will be remaining behind and ensure he or she is able to:

    - Handle any emergency, such as fire, tent collapse, etc
    - Electrical maintenance
    - Plumbing and servicing of the portaloos

    Ensure he/she has:

    - The needed tools
    - Smart uniform
    - Schedule of events
    - Badge or other marking to be easily spotted from a distance

    Ensure he/she knows:

    - Where his food and base will be
    - To contact you if any problems
    - There's a gratuity if all goes smoothly

10. Confirm police, security, fire, insurance, council/city government permissions obtained

11. Ensure take-down occurs as promised, and any damage made good

12. Send check and letter of thanks/recommendation plus small gift, if appropriate

Appendix 10F

Hiring a Caterer Checklist

1. Phone appropriate caterers to determine availability

2. Arrange meetings and iron out the following:

    - Menu and numbers involved (+25% on portion control)
    - Experienced waiters, not students
    - Waiters/chefs uniforms
    - Flatware
    - Crystal/glasses
    - China
    - Linen
    - Condiments and their containers
    - Furniture (tables must be lockable to prevent the legs from collapsing)
    - Arrival of materiel the day before
    - Staff arriving first thing to clean, polish, set up
    - Use/non-use of home kitchen/equipment
    - Tasting for client and self (free if booked)
    - Total costs, without hidden extras
    - Obtain references and pictures of past dinners if caterers are new
    - Obtain written quote and statement of intent

3. Verify referees, arrange and hold tastings with employer

4. By phone, go over any required changes, negotiate to discount the price for same services, and then fax new agreement. Once acknowledged, send original of final fax, plus any advance needed

5. Three days before the event, confirm staff and supplies have been arranged

6. Ensure arrival and set-up in plenty of time; sample food and have any corrections made as needed

7. Assign own staff as liaisons for the caterers

8. Brief all staff on schedule, ensure they know where everything is and are ready for the evening

9. Staff shower if needed, change and eat

10. Staff inspection and briefing on food contents as needed

11. Rove around during the event, ensuring guests are happy and everything is running smoothly in the following areas:

    - Bar tending, bottle opening
    - Drink distribution and top-up
    - Glass, ashtray, napkin and trash collection
    - Canapé distribution
    - Buffet set-up and running/table set-up and laying
    - Plate/silver service
    - Clearing tables
    - Taking coats w/tickets
    - Checking rest rooms (sign-posted)

12. Ensure clean-up, and later take-down, occurs rapidly and smoothly

13. If all went well, tip the person in-charge

14. Send check and letter of thanks/recommendation, and present if appropriate

15. Thank/reward own staff

Appendix 10G

Hiring Casual Agency Staff Checklist

1. Determine what staff are needed and how many of each:

    - Chef
    - Sous-chef
    - Kitchen hand
    - Waiter/ress
    - Cloakroom Attendant
    - Sommelier
    - Bar staff

2. Determine:

    - Time period:
    - Location:
    - Occasion/dress:

3. Contact agencies, arrange for staff to be hired

4. Check two days before that those trained staff are confirmed

5. Five hours before the event, call roll, introduce yourself, instruct on schedule, menu and drinks; their food arrangements, rest rooms, shower and uniform provisions; parts of house out of bounds, tips (and wages, if needed). Assign duties and drill

6. Have them help with preparations and polishing of glasses, flatware, etc. (for dinner, show them a cover, and have them set them up)

7. Let them eat, shower and change as needed, and then do final inspection

8. Supervise the staff at work

9. At end of day, retrieve uniforms, any cutlery, gloves, linen, etc.

10.   Give wages/tips as indicated

11.   For any good staff noted, take their names and addresses, for future casual personnel pool, or future staff, if interested (remember to give the agency a commission if you do take one of their current staff)

12.   Send check and letter of thanks/recommendation to agency

13.   Next time you use that agency, negotiate a discount

Appendix 10H

Hiring Uniforms/Linen
(In the event that caterers or staff agency do not have correct items available)

1.   Determine items, quantity and sizes needed of:

- Jackets, shirts and bow ties (color?)
- Gloves (color?) (five per person)
- Special theme uniform
- Chef's uniform
- Other
- Table cloths
- Tray cloths
- Napkins
- Waiter's cloths
- Glass cloths

2.   Place the order, to arrive two days before the event itself

3.   Upon arrival, check for dirt, tears, missing or wrong-sized items and have supplier correct immediately if any found

4.   After the event, ensure all items are collected, checked for damage, and returned with payment and letter of thanks

Appendix 10J

Valet Service Checklist

1. Contact companies to determine availability

2. Arrange meetings with those available to iron out:

   - Adequate resources (three drivers per ten cars)
   - All drivers insured and properly licensed
   - They find location for cars and properly patrol locations
   - All drivers uniformed
   - Two-way radios between house and car park
   - Two vans for transporting drivers back to car park
   - Cleaning of cars during the event, if host would like that courtesy for the guests
   - Total cost, without hidden extras
   - Negotiate discount without reducing service
   - Procedure they follow; ensure it aligns with employer's needs

3. Fax agreement; once acknowledged, send original and any needed advance

4. The day before the event, ensure all drivers will be in place one hour before event

5. When drivers arrive, show them their room with television and refreshments; brief them on the event and the schedule

6. Check with the foreman on insurance, licenses, vans and two-way radios; check over procedure they will follow, and what they will need

7. Check over drivers for uniform, attitude, manners, and correct via foreman as needed

8. Check over selected ground for parking, correct any problems; give foreman a list of VIP cars that may stay on the grounds

9. When guests have arrived, arrange for roster of drivers not engaged in security or cleaning, to return for food and relaxation

10. Before guests start to leave, alert foreman to send drivers back

11. Where possible, alert foreman of those about to depart for minimal delay in delivery of their car

12. As remaining number of guests dwindles, allow some of the drivers to leave

13. Tip the foreman when all done if gone smoothly

14. Send check and letter of thanks/recommendation to the company

Appendix 10K

Hiring a Security Firm Checklist

1. Contact firms and check if unknown:

    - Availability

    - Referees and credentials

    - What services they provide

    - Any insurance

    - Bonded and experienced personnel only

    - Small walkie talkies, with one for you

    - Complete price, no hidden extras; negotiate reduction

    - Fax confirmation

    When acknowledged, send any needed advance with original of the fax

2. Two days before the event, phone to confirm

3. Ensure they have food/beverages, rest rooms and base set up, if needed

4. They arrive beginning of the day, show them round, brief them on sequences, guest names and vehicles, staff expected, locations, VIPs.

5. End of the day, tip and return walkie-talkie

6. Send check with letter of thanks/recommendation

Appendix 10L

Checklist for Engaging Entertainment

1. Unless specific artists are named by employer, track down requested type of artist by word of mouth and yellow pages

2. Discover when and where they are playing and go look and listen: video or tape the performance if possible; check for professionalism in performance/dress/conduct; determine overall attitude, communication ability, adequate equipment. Judge whether they conform to your employer's requirements

3. If applicable, play video/tape to employer and make proposals for guest and back-up performers

4. Contact managers and ensure the performer(s) picked are available on the event day (meaning the key artists, not fill-ins)

5. If so, hammer out contract as follows:

   - They arrange economy travel to city, billing us on arrival
   - You arrange local travel
   - Bed and breakfast only at motels/hotels (mini-bars and other items like phone calls not covered)
   - You feed them
   - What do they need in terms of electrical outlets?
   - They provide all equipment, but changing room, rest rooms and stage provided
   - What is cancellation fee?
   - Insurance covered by themselves; get what, in writing
   - Failure to perform clause
   - Non-alcoholic beverages; no eating/drinking on stage
   - Total fee, free of any hidden extras

6. Fax the agreement to manager and receive acknowledgement
   - Iron out any problems
   - Follow up by sending him original of final fax and any advance

7. Draw up a list of actions to implement the points brought up in (5) above, and get it done

8.   Check with manager that everything is going according to plan one month and again one week ahead

9.   On arrival of artists, brief them on outline of the event; its schedule and purpose

   • Show them their rooms and facilities, where to go for food, etc.

   • Introduce them to staff member looking after them (if not self), and to relevant contractors

10.   Find out any further needs and wants and satisfy them if appropriate

11.   Have artists set up beginning of day

12.   Ensure everything is smooth for the artists before and during the performance and audience appreciating them

13.   At the end, give tip, ensure travel arrangements set and they are happy

14.   Send final check to manager with letter of thanks and recommendation, and some gift/memento, if appropriate

Appendix 10M

Checklist for Miscellaneous Services Needed for Functions

1. Arrange for the following as needed:

    - Florist

    - Gardner and landscape gardener

    - Electrician

    - Vintner

    - Grocer

    - Butcher

    - Fishmonger

    - Stills photographer

    - Video photographer

    - Paramedic

    - Master of Ceremonies/Toastmaster

    - Trash collector (for extra pick up)

    - Fire Marshall (for standby truck)

2. Contact and confirm those companies available, briefing them on what is needed and wanted. Arrange for them to visit

3. When they visit, do full planning, work out agreement, negotiate discounted fee and pay any needed advance

4. Confirm by phone two days before

5. When they arrive, groove them in and ensure they have everything they need to produce. Show them their "office," including food and restroom arrangements

6. Ensure they are doing their job during the function

7. Send letter of thanks with check

Appendix 10N

Champagne Reception Checklist

1. Ensure sufficient bottles in cellar, or purchase one bottle per person per hour on sale-or-return basis

2. Order three fluted champagne glasses and two china plates per guest as well as serving plates and trays, to arrive the day before

3. Arrange with chef or caterer for the purchase and making of fifteen eye-appealing canapés per person

4. Staff arrive day before or beginning of day and are briefed on the event purpose, schedule, highlights, tips and out-of-bounds areas; arrangements for their own food, rest and changing rooms. Give each a specific function, which you run them through the motions of, and make sure they know what everyone else is doing

5. Glasses polished and checked for breakage

6. Three hours before event start, oversee final clean-up and set-up, including champagne chilled in fridge for at least two hours

7. Drill the staff together on the procedure and iron out any snags

8. Staff fed and changed into uniform one hour before

9. Final staff inspection for appearance & cleanliness of nails, face and hands twenty minutes before

10. Champagne poured fifteen minutes before first arrivals

11. Sequence: Valet service; security service if needed; two people taking coats, with tickets; toastmaster introduces guest to host while clicking a counter to check numbers arrived

12. Guests file through pink-jacketed waiters on one side, with pink champagne, and white jackets/champagne on the other side

13. The front waiters peel off, replenish and join the line at the back, the other waiters moving forward one

14. Others circulate arrived guests, topping up, "May I freshen your glass, Sir/Madam?" Only change glass if champagne now warm

15. Canapés available, and also distributed with another waiter in tow with clean napkins

16. When most of guests have arrived, assign waiters at the entrance to top up (no tray used), canapé rounds, trash policing, clearing glasses, checking rest rooms. Ensure all areas of the grounds are covered if guests outside

17. Bar tenders give away no unopened bottles

18. Chill more bottles if needed, twenty minutes upside down in ice water is the fastest way

19. If guests request non-champagne drinks, then waiter ascertains where guest will be and brings drink to them

20. As guests leave, decrease number of bottles being opened, and toward end, your authorization is needed to open any more (to prevent waste of partially used bottles of champagne)

21. If an (urgent) call comes through for a guest, track him or her down in a low-key manner—no tannoy/PA system announcements!

22. Rotate staff for breaks as needed

23. Ensure clean up and set-down rapidly and smoothly done

24. Ensure return of glasses, trays and china

25. Staff thanked and paid upon return of uniforms

26. If the event continues into the night, give a couple of trusted staff a bonus, taxi fare home, some nice food and drink and extra time off, and have them stay overnight to make the place spotless by the morning

27. Secure left-over champagne and return, or keep if good quality

28. Extra food given to staff to consume there and then

29. Send checks to staff agency and caterer, with letters of thanks and/or recommendation

Appendix 10P

Theater-supper Party
(Use in conjunction with checklists 9B, 9E, 9F and 9G)

1.   Briefing from employer to include:
     • Guests by name
     • Date (possibly subject to any VIP's availability
     • Theater and performance
     • Menu, including drinks (motif'd on the play?)
     • Intermission drinks

2.   Invitations printed and sent out

3.   Purchase tickets, programs, souvenir brochures; find out about the schedule. (If guests not able to be seated together, purchase in twos at least and let employer allocate seating.)

4.   In the event tickets have been sold out, contact concierges, ticket agencies and touts and pay over the odds according to your employer's expectation

5.   Book limo service as needed *(Appendix 10U)*

6.   Alert chef on the required menu

7.   Check stock levels of food/drink, and order/purchase as needed

8.   Order and have (Belgian) chocolates delivered

9.   Phone guests to determine how arriving, special diets, preferred drinks for intermission (unless employer has specified which drinks to provide)

10. Alert chef on any food needed for chauffeurs, limo drivers, and also special diets for guests

11. Have menu copies and place cards printed off for each cover

12. Set up entertainment rooms for chauffeurs

13. Day before play, see the head bartender at the theater, order and pay for drinks, arrange their location, and pay him a tip (if any drink choices are not known, arrange to phone the orders through after asking the guests before dinner)

191

14. On the day before the event, confirm:
    - limo
    - food is in
    - drinks are in
    - chocolates are in

15. Using the dinner checklist (*Appendix 9G*), lay the table for the first two courses

16. As needed/required alert the lady of the house on what she wore last time she went to the theater/opera, and entertained same guests

17. Staff and rooms inspected

18. Limo drivers arrived, briefed on schedule and on confirming arrival and departure at theater by phone; limos numbered if required

19. Tickets in envelopes with guest's name on and their limo number, and placed ready with brochures, programs, chocolates

20. Welcome each guest, take coats

21. Give aperitif, circulate with dinner board giving the seating arrangements and information on their neighbor(s); ask for intermission drink choice if unknown and phone through to head bartender at the theater

22. Ensure dinner starts on time, and keep host informed of the time

23. Serve first two courses

23a. CONDITIONAL: If guests not eating very fast, ask if food is to their liking. If yes, then tactfully alert to deadline

24. Give tickets to host to hand out

25. Give chocolates to the ladies, "Compliments of (hostess)"

26. Give programs and brochures (and tickets, if sitting individually) to the men, "Compliments of (host and hostess)"

27. Remind them of the limo numbers on their envelopes, and to return in same limo

28. Tell the host where the drinks will be placed during the intermission

29. Check (visually or verbally) that they all have their tickets if they do not leave straight away with them

30. When they have gone, air the room, completely clear the table and re-lay for the dessert etc. (seat assignments will be random on their return)

31. On their return (heralded by call from limo drivers), greet them at the door, take their coats, programs, brochures and remaining chocolates and use their old place cards to identify which items belong to whom. Ask "Did you enjoy the show, Sir/Madam?"

32. Show them through to the dining room, and serve up dessert/wine

33. Meanwhile, pay off limo drivers, ensuring nothing left in limos

34. Guests through to the withdrawing room for coffee, liqueurs

35. On departure, ensure they take their brochures, etc.

Appendix 10Q

Checklist for a B-B-Q

1. Go over menu with chef or caterer; based on this, work out food needed, plus 25%

2. Have chef or caterer order food or do so yourself

3. Work out and order drinks, plus 25%

4. Glasses, cutlery and plates ordered

5. Portolets/Portaloos and BBQ gear ordered

6. Supplies in 1-4 above all arrived on time

7. Staff arrived five hours before the event and briefed on schedule, event, menu, drinks, their duties; as well as their food, drink, rest room, shower, changing and uniform arrangements; house out of bounds; tip

8. Have the staff:
   - Polish cutlery and glasses
   - Set up tables and chairs
   - Establish pits
   - Move food, drinks, ice chests, charcoal, lighters and tools into place, as well as napkins, plates, cutlery, glasses and wet-wipes
   - Erect signs showing locations
   - Erect lanterns if night event

9. Staff eat, shower and change into uniforms (chef uniforms for pit attendants) and final inspection done

10. Valet service in place and operating

11. Coats collected and tickets given

12. Butler introduces guests to host on arrival

13. Guests offered any drinks they would care for

14. Canapés served

15.   Start cooking; queues will form as smells permeate

16.   If any line is overlong, have less busy chefs cook that item and let guests in long lines know about alternative lines

17.   Staff circulate in all areas, collecting dirty glasses & dishes, replacing with new; providing drinks as needed; servicing portaloos

18.   Ensure clean up done swiftly and smoothly. Pay a couple of staff extra, if late at night, to make everything spotless

19.   Staff thanked, tipped, and given leftover food

20   Double-check everything spotless first thing in the morning

21.   Agency/caterer sent check and letter of thanks/recommendation

Note: Variations on barbeques can be as exotic as spit roasts, Hawaiian pits and large Paella pans.

Appendix 10R

Checklist of Items Needed for a B-B-Q

- Grates
- Bricks
- Lighters
- Charcoal
- Tongs
- Spatulas
- Lanterns
- Torches
- Napkins & wet wipes (five per person)
- Very thick cardboard plates (three per person)
- Knives/forks/spoons (three per person)
- Quality plastic glasses (three per person)
- Trash bags
- Chef uniforms
- Portaloos
- Fire blankets and extinguishers (one per pit)
- Tablecloths (three per table)
- Locking tables (so they do not collapse)
- Chairs
- Balls
- Frisbees
- Boules
- Volleyball and net
- Horseshoes
- Other games:

Appendix 10S

Checklist for an Outdoor Event, Such as a Picnic

1. Find locations, such as an old barn for a shoot, a pretty place for a picnic; draw clear map on how to get there and distribute copies to different drivers before leaving

1a. Find an alternative location in case of rain or other problems, such as mosquitoes, etc. so the event can continue

2. Obtain phone numbers and addresses/map of doctors, hospital, police, veterinarian, garage, hotel, rest rooms, etc in the area. Contact and ensure open that day

2a. Ensure any necessary permits are obtained, including permission to serve alcohol

3. Use four-wheel drive wagon for supplies; dress appropriately

4. Obtain needed supplies:
    *   Foods that are easy to eat and serve
    *   Thermos for hot/cold soups and drinks
    *   Ice chests and ice for drinks
    *   Plates
    *   Cutlery
    *   Cups
    *   Napkins and tablecloths
    *   Seats and tables
    *   Cheese board
    *   Trash bags
    *   First aid kit, fire extinguisher
    *   Primus stove and pan
    *   Golf umbrellas
    *   Change of clothes and towels
    *   Wet wipes, kitchen rolls
    *   Portable phone
    *   Games for picnic (balls, volleyball, frisbee, etc.)
    *   Hampers (individual ones for kids maybe)
    *   Bug and bear sprays
    *   Plastic sheeting, blankets

5. Precede party to the location and set up

6.　　Serve everyone with drinks to start

7.　　Give everyone plate and cutlery wrapped in a napkin

8.　　For a shoot, use Butler Service; for a picnic, buffet service would be more appropriate

9.　　After meal, collect utensils (check they're all there, if valuable)

10.　Collect up trash (one bag for paper, one for food)

11.　At home, unload, wash and store everything

12.　For a shoot:
- Prepare drying room for wet/muddy clothes
- Clean clothes and boots
- Ensure guests have their pheasant brace (male and female) wrapped in newspaper before leaving
- Do not serve same food type for dinner as the items shot, unless specifically requested

13.　If it rains, cover food with plastic sheets while family takes shelter. If it thunders, move everyone into cars straight away

Appendix 10T

Christmas

PREPARATIONS
BETWEEN JULY AND SEPTEMBER

1. In July, see employer and determine what he/she needs and wants:
    - Home or away?
    - Number of family, guests, how long to stay? (And secondary list of guests to cover any no-shows)?
    - Travel/pick up for family/guests, who to pay?
    - Outside 5* accommodation if too many guests for house?
    - Meals at home, or in restaurants? Which?
    - Timetable of events?
    - Presents to be bought, for whom and what (refer to earlier gifts bought)?

2. Xmas tree, decorations, Father Xmas, Magician, disco, dance, other?

3. Printing of invites, special Xmas cards, Thank you cards, menus, schedule of events, local events?
    - Commissioning of special presents?
    - What gifts in room, stocking gifts?
    - Staff Xmas party, presents and bonus? What, how much?
    - Special themes, i.e. staff in fancy dress, song/play?

4. Book as needed:
    - Hotel(s)
    - Restaurants
    - Theater, concert
    - Flights
    - Limos
    - Temp agencies for waiters, extra valets/maids/drivers
    - Father Christmas, other uniforms/costumes
    - Conjuror/magician
    - Marquee in hot climates
    - Disco/cabaret/band
    - Caterers

5. Draw up checklists for staff use

6.   Hold meeting with chef and housekeeper; brief them and give them their checklists; adjust checklists according to their input

7.   At the next weekly staff meeting, brief the staff on Xmas plans and schedule (extra time off later, week extra pay, Xmas bonus and party for families as well, including Father Christmas, band or whatever; if they have already committed themselves financially for other plans, these will be reimbursed on presentation of a receipt if person willing to change plans)

7a.   If any staff really cannot make it, cover with agency staff/contacts you have

8.   Determine and arrange any special transportation/accommodation needed for staff, and iron out any further problems or objections, enlisting their superiors or those they look up to, for assistance in resolving

9.   Arrange someone to organize the staff song/play/caper

10.   Chef to propose menus for whole period, including staff meals

10a.   Employer's approval obtained

BEGINNING OF SEPTEMBER

11.   Order:
   - Food
   - Wine
   - Non-alcoholic drinks
   - Spirits
   - Dry goods
   - Specially commissioned works
   - Flowers (calling florist in to advise)
   - Printing job
   - Videos
   - Confectionery
   - Xmas tree
   - Christmas crackers

BY OCTOBER

12.   Purchase:
   - Decorations for trees, rooms, outside house
   - Wrapping paper, ribbon, bows, tape, tags
   - Games to play
   - Purchase (or arrange purchase of) presents for:

- Family to family
- Family to guests
- Family to friends
- Family to staff
- Family to suppliers, etc.
- Presents for surprise guests (two for each of male/female child/teenager/young adult/old adult)
- Yourself to family and staff (quality and thoughtful, but not extravagant)

BY NOVEMBER

13. Send off invitations to guests (with information on having to stay at hotel and any travel reservations made as appropriate) at the beginning of the month

14. Check all guest rooms and ensure they have any needed upgrades/re-decorations done

15. Investigate Church, community, cultural activities, listing out on a schedule basis, with details and addresses
    - Add to proposed schedule of events for Xmas
    - Obtain employer's approval, make necessary reservations
    - Have schedule printed

16. Bring in maintenance men to service fridge, freezer, extractor fan, all electrical, gas and fire appliances

17. Have the household cars serviced as needed

BEGINNING OF DECEMBER

18. Send gifts and Christmas cards at the very beginning of the month

19. Confirm all orders and bookings and handle any problems

20. Contact all guests who have not yet responded, confirming arrival and departure times, special diets, and needs (i.e. pets)

21. In the event of any guests unable to come, confer with employer and contact the secondary guest list as needed

PRE-CHRISTMAS

22. Advent calendar up and in use

23.   Family to decorate tree (if family tradition; if not, have staff do it)

24.   Presents put under tree, stuffed into stockings

25.   Ensure arrival of:
   - Drinks
   - Food
   - Flowers
   - Printed menus, schedule, etc.
   - Presents
   - Tickets, etc.
   - Dry goods
   - Costumes
   - Confectionery
   - Decorations
   - Videos

26.   Sit in on rehearsal of staff caper and ensure of adequate standard

CHRISTMAS EVE

27.   Guests picked up and brought to house

28.   Those staying at hotel taken directly there to unpack and freshen up. Phone them on arrival to ensure everything all right and to arrange their pick up and transport to the house

29.   Try to remain at the house, but if a guest has to be put in a hotel and was not told about it before, meet them at the airport to explain, drive them to the hotel and arrange for their pick up and transport to the house, as above

30.   Put on a buffet dinner

31.   Put out Christmas stockings

32.   Set-up breakfast, tea and lunchrooms (prepared and cleaned)

CHRISTMAS DAY

33.   Give staff a very good breakfast before nine in the morning

34.   Do the usual morning teas, etc, with some Christmas twist

35.   Breakfast is a leisurely affair, with a very wide selection. During the meal, show the guests the lunch menu, and take note of any special requests, letting chef know of them as soon as possible. Butler or employer might excuse self just before presents are opened, at tail end of the breakfast.

36.   Father Xmas then comes in, presents are distributed and unwrapped, the housekeeper standing by, noting who received what from whom (for thank you cards). After a short while, the butler or employer re-enters and wishes everyone happy Xmas (the assumption having been that he was acting as Father Christmas)

37.   The guests go their different ways: take walks, play, Church, etc., and are offered refreshments when they appear at random

38.   While the breakfast room and tables are cleared and laid for tea, the lunchroom is laid for lunch

39.   Half an hour before lunch, punch is served hot, with a fruit punch for the children

40.   At lunch, serve the wine first, and accept yourself, if pressed. Lunch is also a very leisurely-paced meal

41.   When the bird or roast is ready for the main course, dim the lights and have the chef present it to the host, hostess and guests, and then carve it after letting the employer do the initial carving

42.   Warm the (good quality) Brandy, pour it over the Christmas pudding and bring it in ceremoniously, all a-fire

43.   Staff do their performance

44.   Serve mince pies, cream, port, brandy, cigars and nuts

45.   Washing up/clearing of tables done on all-hands basis, and lunchroom set up for dinner buffet while guests go for walks, etc.

46.   Hold staff Christmas lunch and party w/father Xmas, usually eating and drinking the same as the guests. But ensure those needed to serve tea/dinner do not take too much alcohol

47.   Butler may give a speech on behalf of boss and self, delighted with work all year, especially at Christmas, and give bonus (same for everyone). Celebrate with champagne and open presents

48.   Very informal tea served, buffet style at 4.30 p.m., then cleared away

49. Dinner buffet set up (no leftovers), with first course at both ends so no bottleneck. Chef stands by to carve. Ensure plates and cutlery are swiftly cleared when anyone goes up for more/new course

50. Bring out the cold/iced puddings once main course is wrapped up and place them on empty buffet table

51. Announce that coffee will be served at the table

52. Once all guests have gone, clear and clean room and prepare for next day

53. Ensure thank-you cards are sent on behalf of employer/family for presents received

Appendix 10U

Checklist For Hiring Limousine Service

1. Contact limousine companies in your area and arrange a visit. ____

2. Eyeball their offices, the vehicles, the drivers and dispatchers, and determine if they are well organized, well groomed/uniformed and professional in demeanor. ____

3. Their resources are adequate ____

4. All drivers are insured and properly trained and licensed ____

5. They have cell phones for communication between house and car ____

6. Procedure they follow; ensure it aligns with employer's needs ____

7. Total cost, without hidden extras ____

8. Negotiate discount without reducing service ____

9. Narrow down the best three limo companies and enter them into your butler's book ____

10. When a limo service is needed, contact your chosen limo companies and find book the one that is available. ____

11. Fax an agreement and once agreed upon, send original and any needed advance ____

12. The day before the event, ensure the drivers will be in place one hour before event ____

13. When drivers arrive, review their instructions for the day/night/trip, give them your cell phone number and tell them to call you at significant points in the trip (i.e. when they reach the destination, or if they need any assistance). Get their number. ____

14. At the same time, confirm their appearance and attitude and correct on the spot or ask for a replacement ____

15. If the driver is picking up someone and you will not see them, then do target 4 at the same time as target 3. ____

16. When the limo driver has completed the trip, check with the person being driven how the trip was. Pick up and resolve any problems so they are happy. ____

17. Ensure nothing has been left in the limo and then TIP the driver ____

18. If the guest was mistreated or unhappy, take it up with the limo company (or the driver if minor). ____

19. Build a file of reliable drivers and ask for them when ordering service, or keep them in mind if you need to hire a chauffeur. ____

20. Send check and letter of thanks/recommendation to the company. ____

Appendix 11

Checklist For Moving House

PREPARATIONS AT OLD HOME

1. Obtain assistance to cover your normal duties while supervising move fulltime ____

2. Contact at least three removal firms and hire the firm which:

    a) Uses new packing cases, covers, tissue papers, wardrobe boxes; and mattresses ____
    b) Is properly insured for theft, injury, damage, loss ____
    c) Has experienced movers who are bonded and security cleared ____
    d) Offers best price and provides a written contract ____

3. Alert staff so that:

    a) Those staying with the boss can make their moving needs known and start taking action for their move ____
    b) Those not staying can vacate tied houses in time and arrange for other jobs ____
    c) You can recruit new staff as needed ____
    d) A staff program can be drawn up and executed ____

4. Order change of address cards ____

5. Send these cards one week before the change ____

6   Update inventory of all movable items of value in the house and number each by the room it is in ____

7. Update insurance to cover the move and new house (keep insurance on old house until new owners take possession) ____

8. Engage security company to transport very valuable items as well as to escort the movers ____

9. Engage drivers to convoy boss' cars (or a transport carrier) ____

10. Arrange for forwarding of mail from day after leaving ____

11. Arrange for utilities and phone to be cut off on the actual day you leave _____

12. Engage for a vintner to move the wine cellar separately if its size and worth warrant _____

13. Arrange a holiday for the family during the time of the move (or at least some accommodations somewhere else to keep them happy and busy until the new house is ready to receive them.) Arrange communication lines between yourself and them in case of need while they are gone, during the move itself _____

14. Arrange for at least one staff member to caretake the new house, with utilities, security etc. turned on, from the moment you take possession _____

15. Arrange overnight motel stays for movers, security, staff and their families _____

AT THE NEW HOUSE

1. Inspect, submit a program to boss and fix-up any problems with:

    a) Interior design work _____
    b) Renovation and redecoration inside, including:
        i) Water, softener and purification systems _____
        ii) Energy: improving efficiency, utilization of natural energy sources, emergency generator available _____
        iii) Fire alarm and protection system _____
        iv) Kitchen equipment _____
        v) Sports facilities _____
        vi) Telephone lines _____
        vii) New carpets and curtains _____
        viii) New paint work, woodwork _____
        ix) Built-in furniture _____
        x) Wiring _____
        xi) Plumbing _____
        xii) Satellite dish/cable TV _____
        xiii) Security _____
    c) Any needed upgrades to outside of building _____
    d) Additional buildings planned or built (i.e. garages, sports facilities, etc) _____
    e) Driveways improved _____
    f) Perimeter fences upgraded and/or built _____
    g) Gardens landscaped or otherwise upgraded _____

2 Draw plan of all rooms, numbering each   ____

   a) Make cutouts of already existing furniture   ____
   b) Go over with employer planned decor for each room, and
     which old/new furniture goes where   ____
   c) List out new furniture needed   ____
   d) Purchase after consultation with employers   ____
   e) Have each new piece delivered and properly positioned ____

3. Discover local services as follows and compile card file or put on
   computer:

Doctors	____	Hospitals	____
Chiropractors	____	Dentists	____
Schools	____	Department stores	____
Police	____	Fire	____
Various Suppliers	____	Libraries	____
Banks	____	Sports facilities	____
Churches	____	Clubs	____
Transport systems	____	Entertainment	____
Various Services	____	Quality shops	____
Government Agencies	____		

4. Discover local customs and likes/dislikes by survey   ____

5. Take public relations actions to make your employer's arrival
   known to and accepted by the locals   ____

6. Gain entry & handle enrollment as appropriate/required to those
   schools/clubs/libraries etc. as indicated by employer ____

7. Order basic food/dry goods items to stock-up, especially for staff
   movers, decorators, etc.   ____

8. Ensure access at (new and old) house for movers; no driving over
   the lawn, etc.   ____

9. Whole house white-gloved   ____

10. Ensure new staff are instructed on their duties and the family
   they will be serving   ____

11. Before arrival of the actual moving convoy with household items and
   furniture, have plastic sheeting put down in all major walkways

and rooms so movers don't track in dirt or damage carpets/flooring _____

12. Where known, have each room marked with post-its and French chalk to show which furniture items go where, so when movers arrive they can simply follow those directions to unload. _____

ACTUAL MOVE

1. Clear from ground up, with staff member accompanying each moving team, listing contents of each box, marking the boxes and supervising the movers _____

2. Butler stands at front door, ticking off master list _____

3. Each box or item is numbered with a note indicating which room it is going to in the new house _____

4. Staff possessions go in separate truck, as do garden and garage items _____

5. Food and refreshments are provided from kitchen _____

6. Confirm everything has been taken away, before sending off convoy _____

7. Utilities and phone cut off _____

8. Locksmith arrives to change key-ins _____

9. Have old house white-gloved by a couple of staff who then fly out to new (house or possibly by staff who will not be moving with the household to new location) _____

10. Escort the convoy or fly out, using portable phones to keep in touch with the convoy _____

11. When they arrive at the new house, plastic sheeting is already down, and the movers use overshoes in the house _____

12. Already have post-its and French chalk to mark positions for the furniture _____

13. Position self by front door and repeat procedure at the old house, but moving in from top down _____

14. Pictures are put up last by movers _____

15.   Have staff member connecting up electrical appliances   ____

16.   Have staff putting silver/porcelain/clothes, etc. away   ____

17.   Ensure each truck empty before allowing to leave   ____

18.   When all items are in and checked off, go around the house with the foreman and his last crew, using the inventory and house plan to double check that everything has been delivered and properly positioned   ____

19.   Check for any damage to walls, floors, etc and have the foreman sign to that effect   ____

20.   When all OK, and staff move confirmed as satisfactorily completed, tip the foreman   ____

HAVING ARRIVED

1.   White glove house and furniture   ____

2.   Dummy run all lines, check for missing items; check that everything works and handle as necessary.   ____

3.   Do new fire drills and security drills   ____

4.   Take staff round for orientation on house, estate, and then local town and amenities   ____

5.   Ensure stocks of food, drinks, dry goods up to par   ____

6.   When employer arrives, make note of any dislikes   ____

7.   Fix anything they want changed   ____

8.   Send out house-warming party invitations   ____

9.   Hold the house-warming party   ____

10.   Ensure the staff are all properly moved in, children at school, etc.   ____

11.   Acknowledge staff with a party and possibly bonus   ____

12.   Ensure new staff are settling in well with team   ____

Appendix 14A

Tools of the Trade for the Twenty-first Century Butler

1. Telephone

2. Portable telephone, with computer hook-up capability

3. Pantry

4. Fax machine

5. Xerox machine

6. Computer, with laser printer with graphics

7. Software for calendar, book keeping, word processing, data base and rolodex functions

8. Polaroid Camera

9. Large safe in ground of pantry room.

10. Table board for table settings

11. Petty Cash Disbursement Vouchers

12. Furniture polish & brushes

13. Hogs hair bristle brushes for different ceramics/metals

14. Pony hair fitch for gilded items

15. Plate brush for silver

16. Cotton and plastic gloves

17. White gloves for serving

18. Goddard's silver dip; Long Term Impregnated cloth; Long Term Silver polish.

19. Hygrometer

20. Thermometer

21. Acid free tissue paper

22. Superonic-N or other silver dip

23. Brown wrapping paper

24. Envelopes, large & small

25. Gift wrapping paper, matching tags, ribbons & bows

26. Scotch tape

27. Pictures of employer

28. Boxes for presents and also cakes, chocolates, etc

29. See also the clothes checklist (Appendix 7B)

30.

31.

32.

33.

34.

WHAT A BUTLER CARRIES ON HIS/HER PERSON

1. Several pens

2. Note pad

3. Paper handkerchiefs

4. Keys

5. Personal Digital Assistant

6. Butler's friend

7. Coins and bills

8. Credit cards

9. Phone cards

10. Cigar cutter/gas-lighter combo

11. Digital camera (can be part of a PDA or a pen)

IF GOING ABROAD, ADDITIONALLY:

12. Foreign currency

13. Portable Translator

Appendix 14B

Sample Resume

PERSONAL DETAILS:

Peter Jeeves   SS: 123-45-6789
123 W 45th St.   Green Card: A12345678
New York, NY 10001   Phone/Fax: (212) 323-4334
British; DOB 1/23/45; single, no children

Non-smoker; good health; like children, animals, etc.

EDUCATION/SKILLS:

Private schools in England were successfully graduated. MBA from Sussex University, 1970. Further education over the years, including small arms and bodyguard training; advance driving techniques; and butler training at the British Bureau of Better Butling in Bognor Regis, England, Spring 1981.

OTHER SKILLS:

Continental and American cuisines; fluent in Spanish and French

EMPLOYMENT HISTORY:

8/81-6/93	Employed as a butler/houseman/valet for a socially active gentleman in New York. My duties included managing two households, purchasing, supervision of contractors and fifteen household staff; some cooking; waiting at table; looking after silver, wine cellars, etc., some driving. Employer recently deceased, hence need for new employment.
6/72-2/81	Chauffeur and estate manager for business owner in England
9/70-5/72	Peace Corps volunteer in Brazil and Nicaragua

Two references attached.

Appendix 14C

Outline of Actions for Assuming a New Position

For homes with a structure, the following sequence of actions followed will enable you to discover it and insert yourself successfully into the household. As may be clear by now, it is vitally important that you compile a written record of the information unearthed in doing these steps, adding them to the Butler's Book, so that the information is not just verbally stated and then almost immediately lost. The profession has suffered in the past from a lack of written materials at all levels—whether in the form of textbooks or written records at the household level. The result has been non-uniformity and lost technology, both of which have conspired to undermine the profession. By keeping records, you will make it easier not only for yourself (especially when the employer inevitably forgets some things he or she had said before), but also for your successor.

1. Introduce yourself to each of the staff, let them know about your title, duties, and roughly what you might need from them to carry out your duties. Find out what they need from you to carry out their duties. Make sure they understand what you have said, and feel fine about your being there   _____

2. Find out the existing service standards and policies for the home:

   - who the friends are   _____
   - preferred suppliers   _____
   - who is allowed into the house   _____
   - what visitors are allowed to be served   _____
   - religious affiliation   _____
   - customs and observances   _____
   - taboos   _____

3. Find out the family's preferences and likes/dislikes:

   - food   _____
   - drink   _____
   - entertainment   _____
   - manners   _____
   - forms of address   _____
   - uniform   _____

4. Determine any already existing schedules, programs and plans for the year ahead and start to work on those still valid   _____

5. Contact each supplier/service person, and let him/her know of your duties.

Let them know what you need from them, including the service standards of the house. Make sure they are happy and provide them with anything they might need from you to do their jobs properly   _____

6. Work hard to provide each family and staff member, as well as suppliers, with what they need from you   _____

7. Have them provide you with what you need from them to do your job per the service structure of the household   _____

8. Purchase a computer and start in-putting the Butler's Book, using *Appendix 5B* as the model   _____

9. Purchase needed items per *Appendix 14A*   _____

10. Inspect the security situation at the house and remedy any weaknesses with your employer's consent   _____

11. Do the same for matters of hygiene   _____

12. Do the same for fire safety and first aid   _____

13. Hire more staff if below complement   _____

14. Work to improve staff matters, such as morale, health, discipline and ethics, understanding of their jobs   _____

15. Improve administrative matters in the household, such as computerizing the accounts (with a view to streamlining paperwork, rather than increasing it)   _____

16. Complete an inventory; make sure that all valuables are insured   _____

17. Inspect and submit a program to upgrade the house and grounds   _____

18. Review this book for ideas on what else can be implemented to improve service to your employers   _____

Addendum

The following supplementary articles (and one speech) were published (or delivered) in various industry magazines and newsletters after the first edition of this book was published. They are included here for the reader's enjoyment and use, as they contain valuable information covering recent industry developments.

Household Professionals Code of Ethics

Integrity

Always act in the best interest of your employer. Placing their interest above your own, perform and maintain the highest level of professional standards in all relationships and duties.

Confidentiality

Keep all confidences regarding employer and staff.

Service

Serve the employer as the employer chooses to be served. Actively seek to determine their preferred style of service, while maintaining a comfortable, safe, and secure environment at all times.

Lawful Behavior

Be knowledgeable of and ensure compliance with all applicable local and national laws. Abide by the highest ethical, moral and legal standards.

Dedication

Perform your duties diligently, impartially and responsively, to the best of your ability. Activities outside working hours must not diminish confidence in you or your ability to perform your duties.

Personal Development

Endeavor to improve and enhance both personally and professionally. Strive to increase your service knowledge and improve your skills through training, study and the sharing of information and experiences with your peers.

Respect

Work towards achieving a strong foundation of mutual respect between the employer and all employees. Educate and instill a healthy respect for all persons and property associated with the employer.

Professional Relationship

Strive to maintain appropriate relationships and boundaries in all aspects of service. Avoid discrimination based on age, disability, gender, sexual orientation, race, national origin or family politics.

Promotion

Commit to the promotion of superlative service, through personal and professional example, mentoring, establishing industry standards, and consistent, active involvement.

July 2001

Ask Not What The Butler Did, But What He Could Do For You

The Hotel Butler - Recognizing the Value Butlers Bring to the Bottom Line

We all know the cliché, but what was it the butler did? Sometimes in movies or board games, he was the one the police wanted to question further. In the hotel environment, the butler can be a failed experiment or a service facility that keeps high-rack occupancy rates at 100%.

Where he fails, it is because he is cast in (frankly) degrading-to-the-profession roles such as "bath butler," "fireplace butler, "technology butler," "baby butler" (who provides rocking chairs and watches children), "dog butler," "ski butler," and "beach butler." The idea being that anything that offers superior service in some small area is called "a butler" in an effort to siphon some of the prestige of the profession.

At least when the term valet was extended to "dumb valet," that furniture item upon which one lays out clothing for the following day, there was no pretence that this was the real item. Fortunately for the profession, the public were not fooled or taken in by these "dumb butlers" and the practice has faded relatively rapidly before it could sour the public mind on the concept of butlers. And fortunately so for the butlers working in top hotels around the world, who do justice to the profession, and the hotel managements who have recognized the value butlers bring to the bottom line and the repute of their establishments.

In an industry that is completely premised on the idea of service, and in which service is a key differentiator, it's a no-brainer to institute butler service. Butlers have always represented the pinnacle in service quality. After the initial required training, the running of a butler service is not much more expensive to provide than regular service, yet it allows rack rates to be raised and creates a loyal following of repeat visitors, as well as enhancing word of mouth and thus new business that make the investment very sound.

Once management has decided to institute butler service, the next question is: how to bring it about.

The first step is to bring on board the most service-minded of your employees to undergo training. The second: Bring in one of the handful of butler trainers who can train hotel butlers (as distinct from butlers in private residence, as the hotel environment is very different and requires fewer and different skills than the traditional butler).

In putting together a training program, it is important to know the four main elements that hotel butler trainees and hotel butler programs need in order to succeed.

First of all, there are the mechanical actions, the skills that butlers need, such as how to clean shoes, how to greet guests, tour them around their suite, how to arrange events for their stay, etc.

Then there is knowing and adopting the psyche or mindset of the butler. It is a truism that in order to do something effectively and with conviction, one has to be able to be the role that one is playing fully. Unless a butler has this as a starting point, he or she will never be able to carry off the role convincingly or handle guests and even fellow staff with the aplomb that makes butlers such quintessential service professionals.

This is why the training has to include the history, rationale, characteristics and communication skills of the traditional butler, and enough drilling-in of these elements so that when the novice butler is faced with a tricky or embarrassing situation, he or she is not left tongue-tied, upsetting guests, or proving that he is not the smooth, low-key character that guests expect in their butlers.

Thirdly, having covered the theory and done copious drills on applying the skills in a classroom environment, the trainer needs to move out with the butlers and expose them gradiently to guests in the actual areas they will be providing butler service. By gradient is meant the trainees using each other and then senior staff as guest guinea pigs, and then servicing known-to-be-easy guests, and then VIPs and known-to-be-difficult guests. The trainer should correct them on an internship or apprenticeship basis until the trainees can confidently do their duties.

Finally, for training to be practical and workable, it needs to tie the general actions of butling into the specific hotel environment in which they are being instituted. This means the trainer has to work with hotel management and butler trainees to adapt existing SOPs (standard operating procedures) and propose new ones that align with existing SOPs. These SOPs would be developed during the training and then drilled and corrected and used during the apprenticeship period and then fine-tuned. The result would be a butler manual that would be referred to regularly, and used to train new staff to be butlers as the program will probably expand and there will always be some attrition.

The end result of the whole program as outlined above is generally employees with high morale who competently carry out their duties, wowing guests and resulting, as stated before, in 100% occupancy, a very high rate of return visits, and the opportunity to increase rack rates while enjoying stellar word of mouth.

Perhaps it would be better to ask then, not what the butler did, but what he (or she) could do for you.

August 2004

Spa Service Has One Key Flaw
It Ends the Moment a Guest Leaves the Spa to Return to His or Her Room

Many high-end hotels and resorts offer spa services and are looking for a way to excel even further and so differentiate themselves in the minds of their guests. The same could be said of the butler service offered by many such institutions. Both programs add value and prestige, but is there a way to improve these service offerings? The short answer is, "Yes!"

Spa service has one key flaw: it ends the moment a guest leaves the spa to return to his or her suite. The way to make a guest's experience a complete one, and offer a total immersion in the "get away from it all" relaxation and rejuvenation, is to make the butler service an extension of the spa experience, wherein spa-trained butlers provide their usual high-end service in the hotel, but with the added knowledge and techniques that enable the spa environment to continue in the guest's own suite.

A guest, for instance, may well undergo a catharsis or detoxification as a result of his or her spa experience‹knowing how to deal with this with understanding and empathy can create quite an impact on guests. Moments of drama aside, when a butler knows and understands the spa program of a guest, he can converse about the guest's experiences with good reality, should the guest so desire, and can also take actions to enhance that program‹such as adding a complEmentary (not complImentary!) bath salt to the bath, rather than one that conflicts with the spa program.

The spa butler is really the architect of the ultimate spa hospitality experience, designing and arranging the entire spa guest experience. The spa still delivers the spa services, but the butler acts as the main point of contact before, during and after the guest's stay. Because he understands and knows what the guest is going through, and the basic spa methodologies, he can be there for the guests and extend the entire stay into a smooth experience for them. That's the simplicity of the program.

Translated into the real world, this program means the butler asks and cares about the guest's goal in coming to the spa; he cares about the guest's room, ensuring that the space reflects the guest's needs and wants. The butler supports the guest by being a sounding board and conversing with understanding and empathy. He introduces the guest to the people, places and services he or she will be experiencing at the spa, answering all questions and resolving all concerns. He smoothes the preparations for each spa experience and helps the guest through the ramifications of each spa treatment, asking the right questions.

The spa butler understands the mechanism of each spa treatment in order to give accurate and convincing explanations of treatments to the guest. The application of hot or cold therapy to the body may seem odd or even silly to the guest without an understanding of the expected physiological effects and benefits. Earning the guest's confidence and compliance with intelligent answers to his/her questions is an important part of the spa butler service.

Types of Guests

There are at least four categories of spa guests. Identifying them is key to serving them successfully.

"Fluff and Buff" guests are delighted with the ultimate in pampering. They are investing time, energy and money in the expectation they will be treated as kings and queens. They are enjoying a mini vacation from the stresses and strains of everyday life.

"ROI" guests are looking for a return on their investment. They are spa savvy, meaning that they have been to spas before and have preconceived notions about what a great spa experience is and should be. They expect their spa experience to deliver on the health enhancement and therapeutic expectations they have formulated.

"Solution seeker" guests want a spa experience to alleviate pain and discomfort from their ongoing medical conditions, such as multiple sclerosis, osteo-arthritis, etc. and are hoping to find relief and answers that will alleviate some of their suffering.

"Transformer" guests are committed to transforming their own worlds, understanding they play an integral and vital role in optimizing their health and well being. They trust the spa to have highly specialized facilitators who honor the holistic nature of man.

By knowing and understanding each guest's goal and being there for them in their pursuit of that goal, the butler forms a unique relationship with guests and so brings about the ultimate spa hospitality experience.

August 2004

Thin Red Line or Red Ink?
Deterring Terrorism

The likelihood that any single hotel will be the target of a terrorist act is very small indeed, given the number of hotels in the world.

The risks increase with the size of the hotel, its location, it being a trophy building or the destination of guests whose views are antipathetic to those of any of a variety of terrorist groups. Or perhaps the fact that it is an easy, soft target and offers a way of doing what terrorists do best: destroy buildings and lives, undermine the peace of mind and economies of whole nations. So how safe does that make any hotel?

While the hospitality industry is experiencing lower occupancy rates since that pivotal day in September 2001, it is at the same time being forced into spending money on higher insurance premiums and/or greater security measures. Perhaps not vast sums of money in the overall scheme of things, but certainly insurance rates doubling in three years is at odds with the need to reduce expenses. The JW Marriott in Jakarta didn't hesitate to do the right thing, however, instituting more stringent security procedures and so saving the day. Not the lives of some of its security personnel, but certainly of the majority of its guests and the integrity of the building itself, which was structurally intact after the car bomb exploded on that day in August 2003. The October 2004 bombings in Egypt showed what can happen when inadequate security measures are in place.

In August 2004, the hotels on the Strip in Las Vegas (including 18 of the 20 largest hotels in the world) were accused of withholding from the general public the fact that Al Queda low-lifes had been "casing the joint." There was concern reportedly that a public warning might hurt tourism or increase legal liabilities. The casino hotels apparently did increase what was already arguably the tightest security in the industry, but their experience and systems were designed for criminals, not terrorists. One thing is certain, their approach resulted in a PR flap that did little to enhance their image. The fact that these hotels also handed over names and other information on quarter of a million guests to the FBI over the New Year's Eve celebrations 2003/2004 may not have endeared them to those and future guests, either. Dealing with the threat of terrorism isn't easy and was certainly not covered in any great depth during any hospitality training for American hoteliers.

For a look at effective anti-terrorist measures in the hospitality industry, Sea Island provides a better example during the G8 summit in June 2004. A tour-de-force in terms of electronic gadgetry and armed security forces, it was the government not the hotel that drove (and paid for) that security event. Nice if you can get it, but hardly within the budget of any hotel, and certainly the siege mentality was not conducive to the ambiance that generally draws guests to hotels.

So where does this leave hotels? Certainly, terrorists do not make it easy, presenting the prospect of any of a number of ways of creating their effects via an unknown individual at an unknown time. As the homeland security advisor to the governor of Nevada is reported to have said, "We have so little information. We pray a lot." Not to argue with the power of prayer, but a concrete plan would probably sit better with guests, insurers, owners, and employees alike.

Fear is a third-rate motivator employed by weak individuals, so perhaps a better approach to this whole subject of combating terrorism is to view it as a challenge to our intelligence and resourcefulness. Our purpose as an industry is to provide comfort and pleasure to our fellow man and woman. Maybe our goal in providing adequate security, then, should be the retaining of our freedoms and joys, not the fighting of psychotic individuals or the purveying of fear. This may seem like an extraneous piece of philosophy, but any lesser goal on our part lets the terrorists set the rules, makes us play their miserable game.

What's the Problem?

Perhaps the first point to establish is, what is one protecting against? Ill-intended individuals or groups coming onto the grounds and into the premises in any of a variety of ways: by stealth as overnight guests, day guests, guests of guests, convention attendees, vendors and service personnel, employees, ex-employees, on business (whether as reporters, law enforcement, or any number of guises); or by brute force as a swarm of invaders or behind the wheel of a truck or car‹the favored method of the terrorist. And what is one concerned they may do once they have access? The most obvious is use explosives, or weaponry. Then there is the possibility that they may use biological or chemical weapons.

How would these elements be brought into the hotel space? By people on their person, in their luggage or vehicles, or via packages delivered. The next question then is, how does one ascertain that these routes are clear of threat without a) invading privacy and upsetting guests, b) inordinate expense, c) creating a siege mentality and ruining the ambiance, d) delaying guests or tying up employees with added tasks.

The task for security then is to monitor these routes for these harmful elements in a way that is not only effective, but does not interrupt the flow of guests arriving and deliveries being made, and which maintains the ambiance of the hotel. If we were being real smart, we'd find a way to turn the need for security to advantage for guests, possibly even making it fun.

What's the solution?

Let's consider a possible ideal scenario based on existing resources in the market and industry. When guests arrive, their vehicle drives over a simple wireless camera system with infrared capability that beams the license plate and picture of the driver to the security office, while also surveying the undercarriage for bombs attached. The guests disembark at a slight remove from the hotel structure, where bollards have been placed to prevent vehicular access, and are given their favorite beverage served on a tray. They walk through a metal detector at the front entrance (or even part of it) without even noticing it, and through a detector that can sense explosives carried in the plume of hot air that wafts upward naturally from their warm bodies. Their bags are removed from their trunk and the seats of the vehicle and carried up to their room via a scanning machine such as is seen in airports, as well as one that detects the possible presence of biological or chemical weapons or explosives. The valet then inspects the trunk and under the hood before parking the vehicle. Those dealing with the guests are trained to look unobtrusively for tell-tale signs of explosive belts, shifty guests, etc.

Impact on guests? Improved service. Impact on hotels? Slightly larger payroll with more personnel hired to cover valet parking and bellhop, and a better rating for security and service. A bite out of the budget initially for the detection equipment.

What about the employees and ex-employees? Set up parking away from the hotel and institute an ID card that has to be scanned, together with the employee's face, before entry to the grounds/hotel is authorized. These scans are recorded and transmitted in real time wirelessly to the security office.

And tradespeople? Set up a similar procedure that requires their vehicle undercarriage be scanned as covered above at a distance from the hotel, and then a security employee inspects the cargo container (again, this can be done using a camera system with infra red and wireless capability, so unlit areas can be viewed at a command center removed from the truck being inspected). And only then have the driver bring the vehicle to the hotel building, where he or she can be asked to scan his driving license into a machine that snaps a photo of his face and sends both images to a command center. Invaluable for determining that any unexpected or unusual driver is legitimately at the location on behalf of the company he claims to represent.

Looking for Eyes and Ears

When the terrorist alert was raised in Las Vegas, taxi cab drivers were given photographs of wanted terrorists. That was a good idea and capitalizes on the basic truth about all law enforcement: the police cannot possibly maintain the law without the cooperation of the populace. Which means they rely on the general public's eyes and ears to be law enforcement's eyes and ears.

So why not take this one step further? Let guests and employees be kept up to speed on law enforcement needs, as well as public service announcements? Similar to the reality TV shows that highlight America's Most Wanted and Unsolved Mysteries. Imagine then a TV screen embedded in a piece of equipment positioned strategically in a hotel lobby or staff entrance, that shows terrorists and felons, provides Amber Alerts, the latest updates from Homeland Security, and when those are not being broadcast, which shows PSAs (such as hurricane alerts) or ads. Ads, incidentally, which can pay for the equipment. How about if that piece of equipment also provides two-way intelligence? If it took images of people coming and going and relayed these wirelessly to a security office. They could check these against databases, especially where an individual behaved suspiciously (such as hiding his face and walking away rapidly) when he notices the images on the screen.

How about a similar machine that was also a cellphone charger, and which a guest could also stand in front of, call a family member who would log onto a Web site and then be able to see the person calling on his cell phone from the hotel lobby (or convention space)?

This kind of wireless, 2-way intelligence equipment is coming onto the market now (see for instance www.homelandintel.us), driven by the need to use technology to respond to the threat of terrorism at home. This equipment goes beyond the old security cliché of stringing wires to multiple cameras and hoping to catch someone in the act.

The common denominator of these solutions is an intelligent use of technology to ferret out not just terrorists but also criminals. The smarter rationale, however, is one that preempts or discourages anything destructive from occurring by being more overt or obvious. What self-respecting criminal or terrorist would walk into an environment in which his physiognomy was likely to be flashed in a hotel lobby or staff canteen, or snapped in real time and compared within seconds to a data base which he has the misfortune to be featured in? In other words, the real desired product is incident-free days, more than thwarted terrorists. The intelligent approach also solicits the cooperation of guests and employees alike, not because they are frightened, but because they are informed and even pampered a bit.

It takes surprisingly little green in the long term to build a thin red line around a hotel when one goes beyond the idea of snooping cameras, bollards and personnel as the weapons available. It is certainly better than drowning in red ink because guests are sufficiently unimpressed with antiquated or invisible security systems to look for safer ports of call, or because terrorists perceive a soft target in their sights.

September 2004

The Indomitable British Butler

Unabridged text of a speech delivered at the "Restoring the Art" Conference hosted by Starkey International in Denver, Colorado, USA, on March 9-11, 2001

Thank you very much for your vote of confidence. I'll take this applause as an advanced payment and hope that I may do it justice in the next hour. I plan for our time together to err on the side of pleasurable and if I fail in this mission, feel free to walk out. I, for one, would lose too much sleep knowing that anyone here had dislocated his or her jaw executing an overly ambitious yawn.

If I happen to use a word or say something that you cannot decipher, either because I mumbled or someone coughed or my accent was intolerably un-American, please feel free to wave a hand so I can clarify my meaning. It is important that you track with me at all times, otherwise we'll drift apart and you will not be saying anything polite or even printable about me when you leave.

Mrs. Starkey, a wonderful lady, has asked me to talk to you about that strange noun and verb, "butling," British style. She suggested that I read from my book, *The British Butler's Bible*, and while that is terribly flattering, I have a better idea—that you'd be better off getting you money's worth when you purchase the book (which Mary also suggested that I encourage you to do), because then the information would be pristine to you, and not second hand.

And my message, Archduke, ladies and gentlemen, is quite simple. I'll leave it to you to determine what it is, and perhaps you can do me the courtesy of clarifying for me at the end of our time together, what that message might be.

What is a British butler? "Officially," and I quote from *The British Butler's Bible* here, because I couldn't have put it better myself, "according to dictionary consensus, the Butler is "a male servant and head of the household." The Oxford English Dictionary breathes some life into the word with the tidbit that two thousand years ago, "buticula" meant "bottle" to a Roman.

Presumably, after enough bacchanalian orgies, the bottle became synonymous with the person bringing it around to the average reveler; and even though the word evolved from Latin, through French and into its current English form of "Butler," the idea has remained essentially the same: a Butler is a person who caters to the needs and pleasures of the wealthy.

Let us flesh out this definition, however, to arrive at a more complete understanding of the "British butler."

To understand any fact at all, it is necessary to compare it to a datum of comparable magnitude. It would be hard for an aborigine of 17th century Australia, for instance, to understand a car in the absence of a datum of comparable magnitude, such as, let us say, a series of pictographs showing a canoe on wheels that paddles itself much faster than a kangaroo can bound. With this understanding, rather than view this new wonder as some embodiment of an evil spirit, the Aborigine might be more inclined to venerate it in the same way that most Americans do, today.

Similarly, let us draw upon Mrs. Starkey's technology to review a Day in the Life of a butler in the average 12th century castle in England, just after the arrival of William the Conk, as he may have been known by those whom he conquered in 1066. For this window overlooking our past, I am indebted to Joseph and Francis Gies, authors of *Medieval Life in a Medieval Castle*, published by Harper & Row. Personal service, obviously, is not a recent phenomenon, so let's immerse ourselves in the roots and see where doing so takes us.

During the Middle Ages in England, most domestic staff were men, usually themselves of "gentle" birth, working for the nobility as part of their training for court and other activities. As a note, for those who may be wondering, the only women who worked in households were washerwomen, nurses, and "gentlewomen" who waited on the ladies of the castle. The Butler worked under the direction of the steward and was basically responsible for the care and serving of wines. The steward, whom we would now call a Butler Administrator or Household Manager, supervised the domestic affairs of his master's castle, such as the service at the table, directing the staff and managing the finances.

The wine was mostly imported from Bordeaux, which the English ruled at the time. In the absence of any effective technique for stoppering containers, the wine would not keep beyond a year and so had to be drunk young. Vintage, therefore, was not an issue, and the idea of inhaling the bouquet and savoring the taste was still several hundred years away, as Peter of Blois notes in a letter describing the serving of wine one day at Henry II's court:

> *"The wine is turned sour and moldy—thick, greasy, stale, flat and smacking of pitch. I have sometimes seen even great lords served with wine so muddy that a man must needs close his eyes and clench his teeth, wry-mouthed and shuddering, and filtering the stuff rather than drinking."*

This challenge to his professionalism notwithstanding, the butler would receive wine in barrels and decant it into jugs. Some he would spice and sweeten for the final course.

Local brews made from barley, wheat, and/or oats by an alewife, were drunk mainly by the servants and were not the domain of the butler. Part of the reason brewing was left to women was the view held at the time that beer was as much a food as a drink. Perhaps the reason the nobles suffered the wine is because, as the noted authority, Peter of Blois, again describes, "the ale is horrid to the taste and abominable to the sight."

With the most important guests at the high table, the loftiest place reserved for an ecclesiastical dignitary, the second for the ranking layman, a procession of servants would enter after Grace had been said. First came the pantler with the bread and butter, followed by the butler and his assistants with the wine, and beer for those who desired.

Guests were served at dinner with two meats and two lighter dishes. Between courses, the steward would send the servers into the kitchen and see to it that they brought in the meats quietly and without confusion.

Ceremony marked the service at table. There was a correct way to do everything, from the laying of cloths to the cutting of trenchers and carving of meat. A trencher, by the way, is a wooden platter for the serving of food and meat. Part of a squire's training included learning how to serve his lord at meals: the order in which dishes should be presented, for instance, where they should be placed, how many fingers to use in holding the joint for the lord to carve, and how to place trenchers on the table. Not too far a cry from table etiquette today, I think.

The solid parts of soups and stews were eaten with a spoon, the broth sipped. Meat was cut up with the knife and eaten with the fingers. Two persons shared a dish, the lesser helping the more important, the younger the older, the man the woman. The former in each case breaking the bread, cutting the meat, and passing the cup.

Etiquette books admonished diners not to leave the spoon in the dish or put elbows on the table, not to belch, not to drink or eat with their mouths full, not to stuff their mouths or take overly large helpings. Not surprisingly, in light of the finger-eating and dish-sharing, stress was laid on keeping hands and nails scrupulously clean, wiping spoon and knife after use—forks were not used at that time—wiping the mouth before drinking, and not dipping meat in the salt dish. Contrary to legend, Medieval man loved baths and took them regularly in what were called "stews"—large tubs filled with hot water in which one stewed for a while. Hard soaps had just appeared from Spain, luxury articles made of olive oil, soda, lime, and aromatic herbs (hence the modern Castile soap). These replaced the soaps made in the manorial workshops out of mutton fat, wood ash and natural soda, and were greatly appreciated by the butlers of the time.

While butlers could be counted upon, then, not to be too recognizable by their musk, they could be considered hirsute for the very good reason that shaving was difficult, painful, and infrequent. The soap didn't lather and the razors were nothing more than small carving knives, often old and dull.

Haircutting scissors were similar to grass-trimming shears and pulled mightily. As for halitosis, it was another century before even the lord and lady of the manor had access to tooth brushes. The butler had to make do with rubbing his teeth with a green hazel twig and wiping with a woolen cloth.

Does this trip back down the butler's genealogical tree help us appreciate his roots? Possibly not, although I am sure our appreciation, for everything from proper-stopping techniques at vineyards to toothbrushes aplenty on supermarket shelves today, has grown immeasurably.

However, like the dusty vats of malmsey (a sweet wine) that he so lovingly looked after in the cobwebbed cellar, the Butler has matured over the centuries into a richer, rarer and more complex figure in the household.

As the middleclass took to hiring more staff during the industrial revolution —did you know that the lower rung of the middle class was redefined in London to include anyone who could afford only three servants— and as downsizing impacted the large English household in the 20th century, the Steward and his duties were gradually assumed by the butler, who became, as the Oxford dictionary so correctly states today, the head of the servant household. Let us leave England and discover what the American butler was engaged in after the country was granted its independence by dear, mad, King George.

A Mr. Roberts laid down the vital points a butler should know in his *The House Servant's Directory of 1827.*

· The benefit of early rising
· Trimming & cleaning lamps
· Setting up the candles
· Regulations for the pantry
· Regulations for the dinner table
· Setting out the dinner table
· Waiting on dinner
· Extinguishing lamps and shutting up the house
· And lastly,
· Address & behavior to employers

As we can see, the butlers skill-set had extended in America to the candles as well as the pantry. And what is his skill-set today, now that we rarely use candles and few architectural plans include a pantry? I am reminded in this, by the way, of the story of the wealthy English landowner who, upon checking employee records, called a longtime employee into his study.

"Peter," asked the landowner, "how long have you been with us now?"

233

(Devonshire accent) "Arlmowst tweni foive yeer," replied the employee, at which his employer frowned.

"According to these records, you were hired to take care of the stables," the landowner pointed out.

"Thart's c'rrect, Sur," responded the veteran employee.

"But we haven't owned horses for over 20 years," declared the landowner.

"Roit, Sur," replied the old retainer. "Whart werd yer loik mee tu do next?"

I know of no butlers at this time who can boast such a relaxed work schedule, but before we look at Butling as she is did today, let's anticipate the household environment we can look forward to enjoying in the very near future.

As a writer, I have the opportunity of conducting interviews with highly interesting and diverse groups of people, and one particular group I have had the fortune of hobnobbing with is that ethereal, forward-looking minority of beings whom we call, for want of a better moniker, Futurists.

They do not have to go too far out on a limb to draw bizarre-to-our-ears scenarios, because science and technology are advancing at such a rapid pace that we no longer have to wait a lifetime, for the Dick Tracey, two-way audio-visual monitor-on-a-wristwatch to become a reality. We are only a few years away from the growth of computers—not in terms of growth in production or capacity, which we already enjoy, but in terms of computers existing at the cellular level, being grown in Petrie dishes.

So when I tell you that we can look forward to domestic help in the form of R2D2s, you may well say, "Oh, we've been hearing about that since the 1920s." And I won't deny it.

But you may like to know that one Dutch supermarket chain already has robot cleaners in service, machines called Sinas and built by Siemens. Nicknamed Schrobbie, the robots carefully navigate around obstacles and, if an obstacle happens to be a human, will politely ask them to step aside with the words, which I translate into English for the benefit of those present, *(robovoice)* "Excuse me, I'd like to clean here." It's not bad for a robot. Of course, a real maid would know not to disturb guests with her chores—in fact, she would have been let go without references two centuries ago—but this is a restriction that robots no doubt would find most illogical. Now you may laugh, but when Schrobbie isn't scrubbing and vacuuming, he (or she) is distributing mail, conducting inspection rounds, and transporting passengers and goods. If you think change over the last five years has been rapid, better not blink during the next five.

Sony corporation has already built a 10-pound human robot that can kick a soccer ball, walk, wave, and dance. Within a few years, the company expects this robot to perform household tasks. Honda wants to give it voice-recognition capability and the ability to identify faces—with a master plan of assigning them to Honda car showrooms to help salespeople. Obviously, Japanese car salespeople are unlike their American counterparts, as they seem to have difficulty recognizing people and speaking to them, otherwise Honda would not be looking further a-field for its "personnel."

By the way, always being somewhat intrigued by derivations, I looked into this word "robot" and discovered that a Czech dramatist coined it in 1920. He was looking for a name for the artificial creatures in his play. Originally, he proposed the word "labors." His brother suggested "Robota," which means "work" in various Slavic languages. Both provide a clear indication of the destiny man envisions for his robots. Let's hope that, in playing God, we have the foresight to allow them at least one day off a week, or the next thing we know, we'll have Robot unions, go slows and walk outs. Now, why will we see more, not less, robots—apart from the natural proclivity of man to tinker with machines? Not because we will ever run out of those people willing to do the jobs we ourselves eschew. But because we constantly look to control our environment, and robots are imminently more predisposed to obeying orders than humans, who tend to have their own ideas. And that is *exactly* why we will continue to see butlers and other household personnel very much in evidence in households. Because we can think for ourselves and we are alive.

There are, however, some employees who act as if they are robots, needing to be controlled instead of acting under their own direction. They can be exhausting to have around. If even human robots are the bane of households and organizations, then surely the constant inability to ORIGINATE action that is intelligent and out of the norm, will drive employers to consign most of their robots to the back of the golf cart garage, and bring in real people.

Although I do not consider robots the universal panacea that some manufacturers hope for, there is no doubt in my mind that we will be seeing more of them. And used intelligently, they do have their place.

NEC, another company, is building a home robot that can recognize household objects with its two camera eyes and remotely control TV sets and other appliances. By watching points on its owner's face, it can tell whether he or she is happy, sad, frustrated, angry, confused, or apathetic. Something most butlers have a finely honed sense for, as a matter of self-preservation.

NEC's robot even has a built-in video camera for recording video messages. When it sees the intended recipient of the message, it says *(robovoice)* "Hi, I have a message for you" and plays the video. One hopes it will have the intelligence to note that, when the human's face looks angry, it's not the time to play that message from the bank president about the question of the overdrawn account. Or that when the Mrs. is present, the Mr. doesn't want to see that message from his latest secret dalliance.

For those who may not have the time to look after pet messes, vet bills and the daily walk regimen, there is now Robodog from Sony—the electronic pet that will fetch, play, and bark. And more recently, RoboCat was created who, like its cleaning-maid cousin, is also capable of interacting with its owner, needing love and attention and developing his or her own specific feline personality. Just like a real cat, she has emotions, purrs when stroked and sleeps whenever—and wherever—she wants. Microphones let her recognize her own name and react by turning her head and blinking. You'd think that with 58 million dogs and 66 million cats in the US alone, the need for metallic substitutes would be somewhat contrived. However, they do represent the fuzzy and warm end of the robot spectrum. More utilitarian are the robots being created at the Edmonton Research Park in Alberta. Robotics experts there are working on creating teams of cheap, disposable robots to achieve complex tasks without communicating with each other, based on research of, yes, you got it, ant colonies.

It is far cheaper and easier to build a large number of simple robots, apparently, than to build one expensive, complex robot to do the same job. The question is, who wants a colony of metallic ants underfoot in the house, that you can't even plug a name into? Pass the RAID, please.

While robots will appear a handful of years up the line, we are already beginning to see the following.

Automation in the house that includes microwave ovens that read a pre-packaged food's bar code, download recipes from the company's web site and follow instructions for preparing the meal.

A system called Aware Home senses inhabitants and responds to voice commands. Another system uses a small pendant that watches for and responds to gestures that control appliances. Make a drinking motion and the water purifier may start up, for instance. But then again, maybe the fridge door will open and milk and beer will be ejected, too. Humans will no longer have a monopoly on misreading messages.

There used to be a time when bespoke tailors behind Bond Street were the Mecca for the nattier dressed man, when pure Marino wool sweaters were the smarter additions to one's wardrobe. The smart clothing to buy now, it seems, is "intelligent clothing" —meaning clothing that sports small built in computers—trousers with mobile phones, shirts with walkie-talkies. Researchers are working on a keyboard made out of smart fabric that can be sewn into trousers or, for those women working in businesses who still wear them, skirts. To use it, they just sit down and start typing on their lap, making this the first truly laptop computer. The keyboard, by the way, is washable, shockproof, and even ironable. The company is now working on a necktie that functions as a mouse, and I wonder to myself, where are they going to put the monitor? Did you know, by the way, while on the subject of clothes, why men's shirts have the buttons on the right and women's blouses have the buttons on the left? It's not to differentiate the gender of the intended wearer, as commonly supposed.

Buttons were relatively expensive during Queen Victoria's reign and so were generally worn by the wealthy. Ladies who were able to afford buttons were also invariably dressed by servants, most of who were right handed. Do you see the picture? The buttons had to be on the lady's left for right-handed servants. Most gentlemen, on the other hand, while they had valets to lay out their clothes, tended to dress themselves—so their buttons were placed on the right side of the shirt.

The tailors who made shirts for those who could afford buttons, but not servants, copied the style of the wealthy, and so women's buttons have remained stubbornly on the left, even though most women are right handed and no longer need assistance in dressing. Such is the logic of tradition.

Which reminds me, if you will excuse another digression, of another fascinating story, attributed to Professor Tom O'Hare at the University of Texas and written for the delight of engineers. The U.S. standard railway gauge (which is the distance between the rails) is 4 feet, 8.5 inches. This gauge is used because the English built railroads to that gauge and U.S. railroads were built by English expatriates.

Why did the English build railroads to that gauge? Because the first rail lines were built by the same people who built the pre-railroad tramways, and that's the gauge that they used. Why did those wheelwrights use that gauge? Because the people who built the horse-drawn trams used the same tools that they used for building wagons, which used that same wheel spacing. Why did the wagons use that odd wheel spacing? For the practical reason that any other spacing would break an axle on some of the old, long distance roads with well-established wheel ruts. Who built these old, rutted roads? The first long distance roads in Europe were built by Imperial Rome for their legions. The initial ruts were first made by Roman war chariots, which were of uniform military issue.

Thus, we have the answer to the original question. The United States standard railroad gauge of 4 feet, 8.5 inches derives from the original specification for a Roman army war chariot. A specification, by the way, is the technical order that engineers are given to follow in building something.

Let me break briefly from this story to remark that specifications and bureaucracies live forever, it seems, neither of them are popular with crusty engineers. I say this to soften the blow of the good professor's closing remarks:

So, the next time you are handed a specification and wonder what horse's ass came up with it, you may be right on target. Because the Imperial Roman chariots were made to be just wide enough to accommodate the back-ends of two warhorses.

Tradition and precedent can be two-edged swords, as any Butler who has had to wear tails in the great Florida outdoors, during a summer afternoon, can testify.

Returning now to the 21st century, clothes, it seems, have joined the multi-functional bandwagon, being fashioned to alert us when we have forgotten the house keys, to play music that fits our mood, and, lest we forget, to cover our derrieres and other assorted body parts. Maybe my tone smacks of the same indignation British buckle makers must have felt when the shoestring finally put them out of business at the close of the 18th century. But we have gone from quality, natural clothes to permanent press finishes that require no ironing, to the latest advance: a new fabric under development, according to the American Chemical Society, that kills pathogenic and odor-causing bacteria, not to mention a few viruses. So now we need not wash our clothes, either?!

We are a long way from the butlers of the 12th century with their mutton-fat soap and sour wines. But at least they knew they had to work for a living and for a standard of living. What about that other treasured domain of the butler—food? Here, technology is crowding him out again. Stick-on food patches are the 21st century cuisine of choice, romantically named the Transdermal Nutrient Delivery System—I can see it now, "TNDS" stalls right next to the TCBY stalls in airports. The "system," which doesn't even have the marketing sense to call itself a cuisine, transmits the vitamins and nutrients needed to maintain the human body, through the skin. Considering the average person ingests a ton of food and drink each year, that's an awful lot of stick-on patches to stick wherever one sticks them.

Not that first aid is the purview of the butler, but, to round out the picture of the changes ahead, it used to be that when you lost a body part, that was it. Lately, one has been able to sew in a spare from someone else's body. But even this won't be necessary anymore, as the technology is refined for growing body parts from stem cells cloned from one's own cells. Maybe somewhere between this technology and Dolly, that famous English sheep, lies the Fountain of Eternal Youth, the Holy Grail that has galvanized many into ardent action since before the 12th century—my reference being Monty Python, I am sure.

So is there a message amidst all these ramblings? I would hope so. While the British butler represents a great tradition, while he has techniques and technologies for looking after a household in grand style, he will not fare well, and more to the point, nor will his employers, if his forte is the proper techniques for extinguishing candles or reviving sour wine—or even the 20th century equivalents. If he (or she, because women have been butlers in households for several hundred years) considers that there is only one right way to do something, the way that Mr. Smudge, who worked his way up from Third to First Footman to the Queen before he expired in an untimely fashion, used to insist upon, then obviously there's a reality gap. Which brings me to another suggestion that Mrs. Starkey made—that I elaborate upon the pros and cons of the British butler in the American marketplace.

Today's British butler cannot rely upon his old skills. In the immortal words of Vice President Gore, he has to keep reinventing himself—hopefully, less self-consciously than our dearly departed VP.

And I'm tempted to cheat here and give you the gist of the message I want to convey today: that whatever the duties were, are or will be, the British butler will need to move with the expectations and technologies of the time. He will have to adapt to the country he finds himself in. But as long as he realizes that there is one fundamental that will NEVER change, he will always be a success, and his employers invariably satisfied with his performance. This fundamental concerns the tricky art of living for decades on end in someone else's house, when even family and friends stink after three days, as the saying goes. It's quite a trick, when you look closely. I *would* like to look more closely, therefore, not at the tricks of the trade, not at the way an American household Manager wakes up the employer, compared to how a British butler does it. These are peculiarities that can be learned at schools like The Starkey Institute and then refined according to the employer's wishes. I would like, instead, to focus in the time we have remaining, upon the characteristics that make the British butler, one who his worth his salt—which expression, I hasten to add, derives from the medieval practice in wealthier households that could afford salt, of positioning the salt cellar in front of the master.

To his left sat his wife and the other members of the household and to his right sat the guests, placed very carefully in order of wealth and merit. This table etiquette was known as The Order of the Salt, from which we now have the idioms, "worth his salt," "below the salt" and "right hand man."

Attention to detail and a caring to strive for perfection make the British butler the ideal employee for the wealthy, most of who care greatly about their hard-won possessions and enjoying the level of quality that they have attained in their lives. Maybe not the same kind of perfectionism that Leonardo Da Vinci displayed when he painted four completely different versions of Mona Lisa on the same canvas before he was satisfied, but a professionalism closely resembling it. A story I have always liked is the one about the novice at the monastery on Mount Serat in Spain. One of the fundamental requirements of this religious order is that the young men maintain silence.

Opportunities to speak are scheduled once every two years, at which time they are allowed to speak only two words. This particular initiate was invited by his superior to make his first two-word presentation upon completion of his first two years at the monastery.

"Food terrible," he said.

Two years later the invitation was extended once again. The young man used this forum to exclaim, "Bed lumpy." Arriving at his superior's office two years later he proclaimed, "I quit."

The superior looked at the young monk and said, "You know, it doesn't surprise me one bit. All you've done since you arrived is complain, complain, complain."

So while this story may be narrowly focused on the error in complaining, the truth is that over and above keeping his own counsel, the British butler works efficiently to remedy situations, without troubling the employer with the details. He doesn't waste his breath complaining about something that is essentially within his own power to resolve.

We all know that butlers persevere. In fact, the title of this lecture is, "The Indomitable British Butler." An *interesting* choice of word, which I confess I had no part in selecting, "indomitable" means "strong, brave, determined and difficult to defeat, subdue or make frightened."

While I often pose like a body builder in front of the mirror, and strut about like Anthony Robbins, cajoling myself into assume these very qualities, I seem to find the only thing that is indomitable about myself is a Falstaffian belly with ever-expansive ideas of it's newfound role in my life.

"Indomitable" is derived from a Latin word meaning "not to be tamed," and while I have learned a healthy respect for people with "abs of steel," I am not sure that British Butlers as a whole find themselves so endowed.

But I digress again. There is something indomitable about British butlers, and I imagine you'd like to know what it is. Is it the persistence shown by Stevens, the butler in Ishiguro's masterful work, "The Remains of the Day"? Stevens is a character who stands by his employer through good times and bad. Loyal to the point of self-denial, he does not even allow his own father's death to interfere with his duties. Perhaps it is this loyalty that we admire in the doting, old retainers of yore.

My idea of indomitable in relation to butlers is somewhat more insouciant, however, focused on winning with a sparkle in one's eye, not enduring. Take the time Nicolo Paganini was performing with a full orchestra before a packed house in Italy. His technique incredible, his tone beautiful, his fingers flying over the strings, he enthralled the audience. Suddenly, in the midst of an unbelievably complex and fast moving composition, a string on his violin snapped and hung limply from his instrument. Paganini frowned briefly, shook his head, and continued to play, improvising beautifully. Then to everyone's surprise, a second string broke, and shortly thereafter, a third. Instead of leaving the stage, Paganini calmly completed the piece on the one remaining string...

It is the command of all things in the household, a certainty of performance and a determination to carry through with dignity, which marks the British butler as the Indomitable One. As an aside, the strange preoccupation of murder mystery writers with the butler's guilt is perhaps not so far-fetched if one consider that the butler knows more than anyone else about the household, and this knowledge, coupled with impure motives, might well make him the number one suspect. In the same way, the term "knows where all the bodies are buried," was first used in the 1941 film, *Citizen Kane*, when Kane's estranged wife suggests to investigators, in reference to the butler. "He knows where all the bodies are buried." How true. And about all the skeletons in the closet, too. But about all these things, his stiff upper lip is remains permanently sealed. In returning briefly to the concept of dignity, perhaps I can draw from words Ishiguro puts into Stevens' mouth.

"Lesser butlers will abandon their professional being for the private one at the least provocation. For such persons, being a butler is like playing some pantomime role; a small push, a slight stumble, and the facade will drop off to reveal the actor underneath. The great butlers are great by virtue of their ability to inhabit their professional role and inhabit it to the utmost; they will not be shaken out by external events, however surprising, alarming or vexing. They wear their professionalism as a decent gentleman will wear his suit: he will not let ruffians or circumstance tear it off him in the public gaze; he will discard it when, and only when, he wills to do so, and this will invariably be when he is entirely alone. It is, as I say, a matter of 'dignity.'"

In addition to "indomitability" and "professionalism," I'd like to throw some other long words at you, taken from *The British Butler's Bible*, because like this lecture today, I was running out of time earlier this week when preparing this talk and needed something to crib, nowadays done by the simple expedient of cutting and pasting from one document to another. Being a book, the information is delivered with greater intensity, so please excuse the change in style while I rattle off the basic attributes of a butler. You won't need to take notes, as you'll be acquiring a copy of the book later—or so my astrologist assures me.

Trustworthiness is the most basic trait that characterizes a British butler. An employer relies on honesty and reliability when he hands over his house, family, finances, and possessions to a Butler. He doesn't want his possessions disappearing, chores left undone, family sickened from food poisoning or funds being diverted. He does not want to be talked about behind his back or slandered to family and guests, nor to see his name in print via the Butler—so loyalty is another key ingredient, as covered earlier. He does not wish to be upstaged by the Butler, or big emergencies made out of small ones. So the Butler is always in the background, smoothing things over and seeking to make his employer's life as pleasurable as possible. To "butle" successfully, one has to be willing to cause things quietly and let the boss take the credit; or conversely, take the blame in public for a boss's goof, without becoming defensive. One is, in essence, an actor on the stage, playing a part to perfection. As long as one keeps this in mind, the occasional indignities become part of the script and not a life-and-death matter. The employer would like to feel that his Butler really cares for his welfare and that of his family. He wants his Butler to be helpful and willing—a "can-do" type who wants things to work out for the family and who helps them wherever possible.

The Butler has to have some social graces—tactful when confronted with tricky situations so that family and guests are not made to feel uncomfortable. He knows and follows the accepted manners and customs; he keeps track of likes and dislikes of family and guests (*"Favorites"* in the Starkey parlance) and obliges them accordingly; he treats each person individually and with equal dignity, no matter how bizarre they may appear.

In time, he becomes almost as well loved as the rest of the family, but only when he conducts himself as if he is not; because there is an invisible line that he cannot cross. Today, especially, the upstairs and downstairs division (or "back" and "front," as it used to be known in country houses, in contrast to smaller, city dwellings) reflects a familial boundary, more than a societal one. Caring is therefore felt and shown, but always with a certain measure of decorum. Familiarity breeds contempt in the long run, so a British Butler maintains a professional demeanor at all times. It is a matter of actually caring, while maintaining a certain friendly formality in his actions. Being chummy and being impersonal are two extremes, neither of which work for a stranger allowed into the closeness of the nest.

By keeping track of his employer's penchants and moods, he can predict and provide the item or environment that his employer needs before being asked for it. The Butler's attitude is "I am going to do whatever I can to make my employer comfortable and happy." It's a game he plays and the rewards are pleasing to both himself and the employer.

A fundamental distinction is that a good Butler serves, but is not servile. He is there to provide a service that he enjoys delivering. He is willing to accept criticism, and if not justified, to let it ride, or correct it where and when appropriate. But he no longer owes his continued existence to his employer and so can walk tall, if discretely! Whereas he is flexible about the amount of time he works, he is most punctilious about timing, never being late. With regard to other staff in the household, he is also friendly without being too familiar. He is firm about the amount and quality of work done. He cares as well for the staff, that their lives are running well, remembering birthdays and the like.

He is a good organizer, who can manage many people and activities according to a schedule, while keeping up with all the paperwork. As covered earlier, he pays great attention to detail so as to achieve high standards and so essentially communicates an aesthetic message to his employer, the family and any guests. For instance, breakfast could be some greasy overcooked eggs served on a cracked, cold plate by an unshaven, unkempt Butler with a cigarette stub sticking from his lips and a body odor more in place at a zoo. Or it could be a plate of perfectly fried eggs, bacon, mushrooms and grilled tomatoes as the third course in a breakfast that is served on a sunlit balcony by a Butler in morning coat and pinstripes. He offers more hot coffee and the morning's newspapers and all the while, music is playing softly in the background. That's the level of creativity the good British Butler deals in: the making of beautiful moments to put people at their ease and increase their pleasure.

242

At the same time, he has to deal with the raw emotions of upset staff, imperious family members, discourteous guests, indignant bosses, shifty contractors and the best-laid plans falling apart at the last moment—all the while maintaining his composure, his desire to provide the best possible service, and ensuring events turn out satisfactorily. He is much like the proverbial sergeant in the army—the one who organizes the men and actually meets the objectives, sometimes despite the commissioned officers. And at the end of the day, the good Butler still has the energy and humility to ask, "Was there anything I could have improved about my service today?"

There is a bit of the British Butler in everyone—the honesty, the creativity, the caring, the social graces, the phlegmatic; it is rare to find someone with all these qualities, who is able to keep them turned on, day in, day out, despite all the reasons not to. All of which reinforces the value of the British Butler in all his various manifestations and no matter where he finds himself serving.

It is worth pointing out that the Butlers most people see on the silver screen do not usually demonstrate many of the qualities listed above. When Blackadder makes disparaging and scathing remarks to the Prince of Wales' face or behind his back, he may be funny, but he is not being an honest-to-goodness British Butler that any employer would keep for very long—possibly because employers are never quite as naively daffy as they are made out to be in the various media, despite what the following stereotypical story illustrates:

"The wife of a newly-rich Silicon Valley millionaire checked into a hospital for some minor surgery. When the anesthesiologist told her she was going to have a local anesthetic. Her reply was, "Oh, my husband can afford it, order something imported."

To be sure, a British Butler will meet many a situation that challenges his idea of what is sensible. The first Duchess of Marlborough, for example, economized on ink by not dotting her i's or using full stops. Does it need to be said that a sensible Butler will be sensible in dealing with such peccadilloes—that he will refrain from pointing out that the one penny saved each year in ink is uncomfortably offset by the thousands of pounds lost from upset recipients of her letters who no longer want to do business with her, or her husband, because her strange vocabulary and run-on sentences make her sanity somewhat suspect?

So, in closing, I would like to offer an idea for a basic drill to acquire the key characteristics of the British Butler. You don't have to be British, your lip does not have to be any stiffer than normal, and mustaches are optional.

I am referring to the ability to confront or face up to life's situations. A person whose attention is dispersed, thinking of problems or day-today affairs, is not at home, to speak. His (or her) observation of the environment is lacking, because his attention is turned inward, even if to some slight degree. If he cannot observe, he cannot compute properly because he lacks the relevant information on the environment he should be computing upon. And therefore he cannot act appropriately.

Additionally, the ideal condition for a butler to be in, is interest**ed** in the environment and others. If he is being interest**ing**, his attention is on himself, trying to attract attention to himself. I am sure you can see the distinction, one first made by Mr. L. Ron Hubbard.

I think you will find that the mastery of the situation, the unflappable panache of the British butler, is entirely dependent upon Being There as the starting point. The movie of that name gives some idea of the magic that "being there" can awaken.

As we draw to the end of our allotted time together, I would like to spend a few minutes practicing this little drill. Please team up in pairs, and turn your seats to face each other.

Now, just sit comfortably and look at or observe the other person. There is no need to be interest**ing**. You are interest**ed** in the other person. There is no need to smile, entertain or impress the other person, or exhibit any social graces. You are just concerned with being there. It's a simple but powerful truth. Let's try it for a few minutes!

....

Very good. How did you do?

[Historical note: Three of the sets of people who did this exercise out of the hundred people in attendance reached such a level of equanimity with their randomly selected partner that they struck up a close personal relationship subsequently. Not that this is the goal of the drill at all (it was developed by American Educator and Philosopher Mr. L. Ron Hubbard as the first step in communicating effectively—see http://www.scientologyhandbook.org/SH5.HTM), but it shows what can happen when one just sits down and is interested in another person, rather than trying to be interesting to them.]

And so ends this presentation.
If anyone has any questions, I'd be glad to take them. If you have any comments, I prefer to take them with a stiff upper lip rather than on the chin.

Archduke, ladies and gentlemen, it has been my pleasure. Thank you.

A Duty to the Profession

Much media has occurred of late concerning Mr. Paul Burrell and his book, **"A Royal Duty,"** excerpts of which have been run in the sensationalizing *Daily Mirror* tabloid. In addition to using his own observations while serving the Princess, he has drawn upon private letters sent to and from her. Mr. Burrell has stated, "My only intention in writing this book was to defend the princess and stand in her corner." He also stated it was "nothing more than a tribute to her."

From a logical standpoint, this raises some questions:

1. Is anyone actually besmirching Princess Diana's name, as Mr. Burrell claims? Does anyone actually think badly of her, that Mr. Burrell should feel compelled to intercede? My understanding is that she is one of the most popular women in the world. So why is Mr. Burrell tilting his lance at this windmill?

2. How does revealing the details of Princess Diana's private life make people think better of her?

3. Would Princess Diana welcome the effect Mr. Burrell is creating on her sons, who have stated of Mr. Burrell: "... abuse(d) his position in such a cold and overt betrayal. It is not only deeply painful for the two of us but also for everyone else affected and it would mortify our mother if she were alive today. And, if we might say so, we feel we are more able to speak for our mother than Paul."

From other statements made by Mr.Burrell, he published his book because he was angry at the Royal Family for not helping him during his time of need while undergoing trial (for taking items belonging to his former employer). His anger may or may not be justified, but the way he chose to remedy the situation was not the path a true butler would have chosen.

From an ethical standpoint, Mr. Burrell (whom I have shared the stage with on a couple of occasions and found to be a very likeable fellow, so I have no personal axe to grind with him) has unfortunately broken the written and unwritten code of conduct of a butler. If every butler made public the private life of his employer, nobody would ever hire a butler.

Put another way, if Mr. Burrell hired a butler, would he feel aggrieved or satisfied if that butler later wrote a book revealing every intimate detail of his private life? It's the old golden rule at work.

It is for this reason that I feel compelled, in the light of the barrage of media concerning Mr. Burrell's actions, to reaffirm the basic principle and ethic of butling. It is based on trust and confidence. Writing a book may pay in the short term with wealth and fame, but the profession is weakened with each such book, as is the author. Without maintaining our standards, we will cease to have a profession. This may not concern Mr. Burrell at this present time, but it does impact the rest of us, as well as existing and potential employers. I believe it is important, therefore, that whenever we have an opportunity to comment, we put forward the same message as above.

As for Mr. Burrell and his threat to keep on revealing Princess Diana's and the Royal Family's secrets, if he truly feels that he is "the keeper of these (Diana's) secrets," then I invite him to do as he says. I also invite him to make up the damage he has done to our profession in some way that will restore trust and peace of mind among employers.

October 2003

The Job Interview Game

It has been my good fortune to work with various employers and employees of late, and I have some observations to make which may prove salutary to both groups.

When an employer graded a prospective couple as a B-, he was being overly generous, I thought, given that they had talked non-stop, the gentleman in a loud voice, and had complained vociferously about their current employer. This behavior was particularly egregious, as this couple had both been briefed by me to avoid these exact points in their interview, following my observation that they tended in this unacceptable direction.

These two individuals were by no means the only applicants suffering from this lack of awareness concerning employers' needs. A good household and even hospitality employee would do well to bear in mind Sir Winston Churchill's remonstration: "A diplomat is a man who thinks twice before saying nothing." The following is NOT meant to be insulting, and certainly does not apply to all Americans, but there is a subset of the populace that is sufficiently full of their own world and concerns that they feel compelled to talk incessantly about them. The first lesson to learn for them is that there are other people in front of them, and then to observe whether these people are willing and eager to hear everything one is thinking of telling them. Factually, employees are there to listen, not talk, and that is the simplicity of the matter. Listen and respond, or better still, preempt. Otherwise, as some clients have complained to me, "I begin to wonder who is working for whom."

The issue of over-talkative employees brings to mind an observation that a number of people are attempting to enter the household profession without having worked in it before (nothing wrong with this at all), but without realizing that there is a mind-set that goes with working in a household situation, where one is *in* a private household, but not *of* it. It is not the same as working in a cleaning service or an office or the military. These all have their own codes of conduct, and they are not the same as those of the household, even if the mechanical actions (of cleaning or managing others) are the same.

Many Americans in private service and guest services in the hospitality industry have the proper approach, but to those new to (or even experienced in) the field who do not have it down, I would recommend reading this book. And then muzzle your desire to talk up a storm in the presence of, or concerning, your employer. You and they will be the better for it, I assure you.

Lastly, employers, as much as you know that looking after pennies means the pounds (or dollars) will look after themselves, please be aware that you do not increase loyalty or respect in employees by penny pinching on salaries. Here, I am not saying that you should feel bad that you are only paying your Household Manager $90,000. No, I am saying that beating him down from $50,000 p.a. to $47,500 may satisfy your bargaining instincts, but it only tells the employee that Scrooge is alive and well, and that his own services are not valued that much. He or she may well reciprocate by giving you the value of the service as you perceive it.

My question to you is: "What are you going to do with that extra $100,000 you saved over the years when you reach the pearly gates?" Share the wealth a bit more and enjoy the satisfaction of seeing another person (your employee) happy in servicing you. Whether you agree to the notion or not, the fact is that we are each responsible for each other. As the poem goes, "Send not for whom the bell tolls..." Another way of expressing the idea is: "What goes around, comes around."

Your move.

June 2002

Internships—The Missing Link

I understand some butlers and household managers graduating private service schools have difficulty finding positions. I do not believe the economy is on a downswing and that nobody is hiring (more of this in next months column). Even if this were true, it does not give those looking for positions anything they can do. Are they suddenly meant to revert the economy so they can be hired? This makes no more sense than the suggested alternative: to roll over and die; and is about as pleasant as sending resumes into a void.

While there are certainly individual issues that may explain some difficulties in being hired, one that seems pertinent to most is a lack of experience in private service. Prospective employers are reluctant to train on the job, or fearful they may find half way into the first year that their new butler doesn't really think he or she is cut out for this line of work.

How can one overcome this chicken-and-egg Catch- 22?

My suggestion is that all private service schools offer a follow-up apprenticeship. Graduates would receive room and board, a stipend, and most importantly of all, the necessary experience and resume/CV building that will impress future potential employers. In exchange for taking a graduate under his wing, the butler or household manager will have assistance in servicing his or her employer at minimal cost to the employer, and the employer will have extra hands on deck for minimal outlay. The schools could charge a small fee for this, but mainly offer it as a value-added for their graduates, while taking full responsibility for the profession and their own reputation.

I am one of the core instructors at The International Butler Academy in The Netherlands (TIBA). Depending on performance, TIBA offers graduates the possibility of apprenticeships in various countries around the world. The Australian Butler Training School and Starkey International also offer apprenticeships or internships. I would like to see this applied to all deserving graduates in all schools.

The real challenge is to create a network of butlers, household managers and employers willing to participate, but it seems like a win-win for all. Maybe if prospective students and alumni asked for this service, it would come to be!

I suggest that those of you who are currently employed in private service, and who could take a graduate under their wings, contact the school they are affiliated with and work out something to their mutual advantage.

January 2005

Fresh Out of Butler School?

Rare is the week that goes by without word of some upscale hotel offering butler service as a way to improve service and retain or gain that coveted 5-star or diamond status.

That's as it should be. But then consider the story broken recently by the Wall Street Journal of industry veteran Horst Schulze's declaration that he intends to establish a line of hotels with a six-star rating. What does he specify as the criteria for such an august label? Private swimming pools. And personal butlers. Quite right, too.

All this can only be good news for butler graduates looking for work. I acknowledge that the field can be difficult to break into in the private sector until you have experience under your belt and have proven yourself. So don't keep beating your head against a brick wall. Create a position. Go to the nearest four- and five-star hotel near you and tell them they need to hire you right now as head butler if they expect to have the faintest chance of keeping up with their industry trends. Be bold and go where no butler has gone before, because you can pull it off if you yourself are certain of your position.

Have the HR or GM contact your school if you want back-up convincing them.

Once in place, establish and build up the hotel's butler department, train other butlers (using hotel trainers and schools as resources where feasible) and when you receive that perfect offer from a guest to be their private butler, go ahead and groove in your replacement and move on. Or stay with the hotel: many butlers do, for the very good reason that it is a rewarding niche in the profession.

Please let me hear your views on this concept, your successes, and even your failures. Your school will be happy to help connect you up with others who will help, and to assist where possible.

February 2005

Just When You Thought You Knew Everything

Q: I have been reading a science fiction book, *Mission Earth*, and the author, Mr. Hubbard, uses the terms "major-domo," "chamberlain," "seneschal", as well as "butler" and they all seem to be the same thing. What niceties separate these terms? Is any one of them senior to the other? (JD, USA)

A: Well, first of all, it is most surprising to see these terms-of-old applied in a work of science fiction. The answers are quite simple.

"Major domo" is the Spanish/Italian-culture equivalent of the "butler administrator," supervising the running of the estate for an employer (who can include royalty and nobility). Major domo comes from Latin meaning "Chief in the house," a term that arose about 500 years ago. Butler, I think we all know, comes from the Latin for "bottle," referring to the chap who presented the wine to Romans a couple of thousand years ago.

"Seneschal" is the term for the same managerial position 700 years ago, and is no longer in use as a title. It comes from prehistoric German meaning "old" and "servant," a reflection, possibly, on the loyalty of seneschals and/or the fact that only older servants made it to the giddy heights of seneschal.

"Chamberlain" refers to the same position, too, but *only* in the household of a monarch or nobility. Chamberlains predate seneschals by a couple of centuries. The word comes from ancient Greek for "vaulted room," the underlying meaning being "bedchamber attendant." The chamberlain's title is "Lord Chamberlain" in royal households, and they remain the senior most members of a queen's or king's household.

As for which one of these gentlemen is senior to the other, none is, strictly speaking, as they are all masters of their own domain and cover the same basic functions, albeit it on different scales. However, assuming some science fiction were to be applied, with a seneschal rising from his grave and being reincarnated a few hundred years later into our century, and assuming the Lord Chamberlain attended such an event, instead of his many junior staff, then the Lord Chamberlain would definitely be sitting at the head of the table for a formal employee meal, the seneschal to his right, and the major domo or butler to his left, and the American household manager below them—assuming also, that they had compared employers to see which actually outranked the other.

The dinner conversation would no doubt be most intriguing.

As a final note, perhaps we can find encouragement concerning the longevity and demand for our profession, when butlers et al are featured in science fiction stories.

March/April 2005

The Word was Butler

Last month, we discussed other names for "butlers." Of equal interest, perhaps, are the variations of the word "butler" itself. There are many more ways in which it can be used, and if these are brought back into use, it will help anchor the profession more firmly into society.

"Butle," we know of as the verb, but so is the word "butler." For instance, "Every great house should be butlered (served by a butler)." Or "Would you like to butler today?" meaning "take charge of and serve liquor." A variant spelling is "buttle," meaning "to pour a drink" or "do a butler's work."

The fairer sex within our ranks has been known as a "butleress" for the last four centuries (and for the record, the spelling of our title used to be "buteler" or "butelere").

Like the word "stardom," "butlerdom" means "of the estate or class of profession of butler."

We even have a couple of adjectives for our profession: "Butlerian," as in the sentence, "He worked with strict attention to his butlerian duties."

And thanks to Aldous Huxley, we can consider using the word "butlerish" to mean "characteristic of a butler." He wrote in 1923, "He moved with a certain pomp, a butlerish gravity."

"Butler" can be used figuratively, meaning to bring something in the same way as the butler brings the welcome wine. As in the 15th Century example of humor being someone's butler, always serving them with fun.

Along the same line is the phrase, "butler's grace," meaning "a drink." Sample sentence: "Would you care for a butler's grace?"

The butler used to be the high-ranking official in charge of the importation and supply of wine to the royal table. No big surprise there, but how about "butlerage?" That was the duty every importer of twenty tons or more of wine into England, had to pay the King's butler. The duty amount? Two tons of wine!

And talking of perks on the job, the "butler's box" was a box in which card players put a portion of their winnings at Christmas time, to give to the butler. For those who don't know the custom because it is probably dying out even in England,

Boxing Day is called that because the day after Christmas, vendors such as the milkmen and "sanitation engineers" (dustmen) with regular deliveries or pick-ups for households, visit each house with a box, into which homeowners put gratuities for the servicemen's work over the prior year. So butlers, no doubt, worked out a way they could have their own box, and without having to traipse around the neighborhood to fill it up!

The "butlerage" actually had more than one meaning: it was once used to describe the office of the King's butler, and thereafter grew to mean the office of any butler. The physical office in which he sat was called the "butlery."

We refer loosely these days to the butler's office as the "butler's pantry," but it was originally, and still is in many houses, the room where the plate, glass, etc. were kept.

And so we conclude past uses of the word "butler." Maybe we can resurrect some, and certainly, language being a living beast, we can create new ones. The old ones have centered around the concept of wine and its serving. Maybe with the butler's duties being so much more these days, we can create new definitions and have them accepted into the common language. If so, would be better coming from butlers doing good works, rather than infamous activities designed to grab the public spotlight (such as "Doing a butler," which might mean "telling all to the media about the boss for great profit.").

So, does anyone have any suggested new uses of the word "butler?"

May, June/July 2005